# Information Literacy and Lifelong Learning

C0-CCN-722

# CHANDOS
## INFORMATION PROFESSIONAL SERIES

Series Editor: Ruth Rikowski
(email: Rikowskigr@aol.com)

Chandos' new series of books is aimed at the busy information professional. They have been specially commissioned to provide the reader with an authoritative view of current thinking. They are designed to provide easy-to-read and (most importantly) practical coverage of topics that are of interest to librarians and other information professionals. If you would like a full listing of current and forthcoming titles, please visit our website *www.chandospublishing.com*, email *wp@woodheadpublishing.com* or telephone +44 (0) 1223 499140.

**New authors:** we are always pleased to receive ideas for new titles; if you would like to write a book for Chandos, please contact Dr Glyn Jones on *gjones@chandospublishing.com* or telephone +44 (0) 1993 848726.

**Bulk orders:** some organisations buy a number of copies of our books. If you are interested in doing this, we would be pleased to discuss a discount. Please email *wp@woodheadpublishing.com* or telephone +44 (0) 1223 499140.

# Information Literacy and Lifelong Learning

*Policy issues, the workplace, health and public libraries*

JOHN C. CRAWFORD AND CHRISTINE IRVING

with contributions from
Jenny Foreman and Morag Higgison

**CP**

CHANDOS
PUBLISHING

Oxford Cambridge New Delhi

Chandos Publishing
Hexagon House
Avenue 4
Station Lane
Witney
Oxford OX28 4BN
UK
Tel: +44(0) 1993 848726
Email: *info@chandospublishing.com*
*www.chandospublishing.com*
*www.chandospublishingonline.com*

Chandos Publishing is an imprint of Woodhead Publishing Limited

Woodhead Publishing Limited
80 High Street
Sawston
Cambridge CB22 3HJ
UK
Tel: +44(0) 1223 499140
Fax: +44(0) 1223 832819
*www.woodheadpublishing.com*

---

First published in 2013

ISBN: 978-1-84334-682-1 (print)
ISBN: 978-1-78063-348-0 (online)

Chandos Information Professional Series ISSN: 2052-210X (print) and ISSN: 2052-2118 (online)
Library of Congress Control Number: 2013951350

© J.C. Crawford and C. Irving, 2013

British Library Cataloguing-in-Publication Data.
A catalogue record for this book is available from the British Library.

All rights reserved. No part of this publication may be reproduced, stored in or introduced into a retrieval system, or transmitted, in any form, or by any means (electronic, mechanical, photocopying, recording or otherwise) without the prior written permission of the publisher. This publication may not be lent, resold, hired out or otherwise disposed of by way of trade in any form of binding or cover other than that in which it is published without the prior consent of the publisher. Any person who does any unauthorised act in relation to this publication may be liable to criminal prosecution and civil claims for damages.

The publisher makes no representation, express or implied, with regard to the accuracy of the information contained in this publication and cannot accept any legal responsibility or liability for any errors or omissions.

The material contained in this publication constitutes general guidelines only and does not represent to be advice on any particular matter. No reader or purchaser should act on the basis of material contained in this publication without first taking professional advice appropriate to their particular circumstances. All screenshots in this publication are the copyright of the website owner(s), unless indicated otherwise.

Project management by Neil Shuttlewood Associates, Gt Yarmouth, Norfolk, UK
Printed in the UK and USA

# Contents

List of figures and tables                                        xi

List of abbreviations                                             xiii

Acknowledgements                                                 xvii

Preface                                                           xix

About the authors                                                xxiii

About the contributors                                            xxv


**PART 1: OVERVIEW**                                               **1**

1    Background to information policy: a brief historical
     introduction                                                 **1**
     *John Crawford*


2    Information literacy policy within the wider context of
     information policy                                           **11**
     *John Crawford*

     Information policy and the information society                12
     Defining information literacy                                 16
     Information literacy policies                                 25
     Summary of the chapter                                        33


3    Relevant policy documents both from within and beyond
     the LIS profession                                           **35**
     *John Crawford*

     The United States and Australia                               36
     Germany                                                       40

Devolved nations within the United Kingdom: Scotland
and Wales                                                           43

Digital policy documents                                            52

The Chartered Institute of Library and Information
Professionals (CILIP) and information literacy                      54

Summary of the chapter                                              57

**4    Recognising information literacy as an early-years' issue  59**
*Christine Irving*

The importance of information literacy in early years               59

Information literacy and lifelong learning                          60

Early-years' information literacy                                    63

Scottish case study: real and relevant – information
and critical literacy skills for the twenty-first century
learner (early and first level)                                     66

Examples from the rest of the UK and other countries                74

Collaborative partnerships and information literacy
opportunities                                                       83

Summary of the chapter                                              84


**PART 2: SPECIFIC AREAS                                            87**

**5    The challenge of the work environment                        89**
*John Crawford*

The rediscovery of the workplace                                    90

Skills development and the employability agenda                     97

The role of higher education                                        99

Issues of definition                                               101

The workplace and its problems                                     107

Information needs and sources used                                 110

Training issues                                                    112

Examples of good practice                                          113

Summary of the chapter                                             120

6    The Scottish Government Library: a case study        121
     *Jenny Foreman and Morag Higgison*

     Introduction                                         121
     Background                                           122
     Interview-based research results                     123
     *Information Use Survey* results                     124
     Internal achievements                                126
     External achievements                                127
     Future activities and aims (suggestions from the
     original research)                                   128
     SG Library: measuring and evaluating our training for
     LILAC 2010                                           129
     Our evaluation process was divided into the following
     four steps                                           132
     Outcomes of the LILAC research findings              140
     Future developments: what we are planning to do      145
     Conclusion                                           146
     Summary of the chapter                               147
     Appendix A    Scottish Government Library Course
                   Feedback                               149
     Appendix B    Scottish Government Library Course
                   Feedback – 3-week follow-up            149
     Appendix C    Scottish Government Library Services
                   Feedback                               149
     Appendix D    Scottish Government Library Services
                   Questionnaire                          150
     Appendix E    Scottish Government Library Services
                   Questionnaire email (evaluation research)  152

7    Information literacy in health management:
     supporting the public in their quest for health
     information                                          155
     *Christine Irving*

     Introduction                                         155

Health information policy documents and frameworks 156

The need for health literacy skills – research findings 161

Supporting the public's quest for health information 164

Public library activities and initiatives 168

Partnership working 174

Summary of the chapter 175

**8 Employability, informal learning and the role of the public library** 177
*John Crawford*

The nature of information and information literacy in informal learning 177

Users and providers 181

Organisations and structures 185

McNicol and Dalton's cycle of learning in public libraries 188

The role of the public library 189

Public Libraries Information Offer scheme 193

Links with school libraries 194

Funding 196

Physical space 196

Examples of good practice 197

Learning and teaching issues 207

Summary of the chapter 209

**9 Value and impact** 211
*John Crawford*

What is impact? 211

Indicators and guidelines 217

Measuring impact at a national level 220

Methods of data collection 221

Quantitative methods 223

Qualitative methods                                    224

Observation                                            226

Focus groups                                           228

Interviewing                                           230

Resources                                              234

Examples of impact and evaluation                      237

Summary of the chapter                                 244


**PART 3: POLICYMAKING AND ISSUES FOR THE FUTURE      247**

**10    Review and issues for the future              249**
       *John Crawford*

       A review of issues                             249

       What is to be done?                            254


*References*                                           261

*Index*                                                283

# List of figures and tables

## Figures

4.1 W. Beautyman's 'Rich picture that demonstrates the information seeking journey undertaken by the children towards becoming information literate (illustration by Kirsti Beautyman, 2009)'     77

4.2 Beautyman's Model of Cognitive and Affective Influences on Children's Information Seeking Behaviour Including the Theoretical Zone of Optimal Learning     79

## Tables

6.1 The authors' method     135

9.1 Christine Bruce's 'Six frames of information literacy'     219

# List of abbreviations

| | |
|---|---|
| ACRL | Association of College and Research Libraries |
| ALA | American Library Association |
| ASLIB | Association of Special Libraries and Information Bureaux |
| BID | *Bibliothek und Information Deutschland* (Library and Information Germany) |
| BLRDD | British Library Research and Development Department |
| CBI | Confederation of British Industry |
| CfE | Curriculum for Excellence (Scotland) |
| CILIP | The Chartered Institute of Library and Information Professionals |
| CILIPS | Chartered Institute of Library and Information Professionals in Scotland |
| CLD | Community Learning and Development |
| CPD | Continuing Professional Development |
| CQFW | Credit and Qualifications Framework for Wales |
| CV | Curriculum Vitae |
| DSIR | Department of Scientific and Industrial Research |
| ELIS | Everyday Life Information Seeking |
| eRDM | electronic Resource Data Management |
| GSO | Generic Social Outcomes |
| HIL | Health Information Literacy |
| HMIE | Her Majesty's Inspectors of Education |
| HNC | Higher National Certificate |
| IAG | Information, Advice and Guidance |
| ICT | Information and Communications Technology |
| IFLA | International Federation of Library Associations |
| iKnow | information and Knowledge at Work |

| | |
|---|---|
| ILI | Information Literacy Initiative (US) |
| IPR | Intellectual Property Rights |
| KSF | Knowledge and Skills Framework |
| LILAC | Librarians' Information Literacy Annual Conference |
| LIRP | Learning Impact Research Project |
| LIS | Library & Information Services |
| LSP | Local Strategic Partnership |
| MLA | Museums, Libraries and Archives Council |
| NACRO | National Association for the Care and Resettlement of Offenders |
| NEET | Not in Employment, Education or Training |
| NFIL | National Forum on Information Literacy |
| NGO | Non Governmental Organisation |
| NGT | Nominal Group Technique |
| NHS | National Health Service |
| NISP | National Information Society Policy |
| OCN | Open College Networks |
| ODLL | Organisational Development Leadership and Learning |
| OLLI | Osher Lifelong Learning Institute (US) |
| ONC | Ordinary National Certificate |
| OSTI | Office for Scientific and Technical Information |
| PDP | Professional Development Programme |
| PTLLS | Preparing to Teach in the Lifelong Learning Sector |
| PuLLS | Public Libraries in the Learning Society |
| ROUTES | Reaching OUT Extending Skills Project |
| SCL | Society of Chief Librarians |
| SCONUL | Society of College, National and University Libraries |
| SCQF | Scottish Credit and Qualifications Framework |
| SG | Scottish Government |
| SILP | Scottish Information Literacy Project |
| SLIC | Scottish Library and Information Council |
| SME | Small to Medium Sized Enterprise |
| TLRP | Teaching and Learning Research Programme |

| UNESCO | United Nations Educational, Scientific and Cultural Organization |
| WALT | What I Am Learning Today |
| WILF | What I am Looking For |

# Acknowledgements

In preparing this text we would like to acknowledge the valuable comments, advice and guidance from the following: the two Tonis – Toni Bunch, retired and Dr Toni Weller, Visiting Research Fellow in History, De Montfort University, Leicester for comments on Chapters 1 and 2; Patricia O'Brien, retired, for translating portions of *Medien- und Informationskompetenz – immer mit Bibliotheken und Informationseinrichtungen!*; Christine Clark, Project Officer, South East Wales Libraries Partnership for information about the Welsh Information Literacy Project; Jacqueline May, of CILIP's policy team for information about CILIP's information literacy activities; teachers and members of the Curriculum for Excellence (CfE) Team who worked on the case study reported in Chapter 4 and everyone who worked collaboratively in supplying information which contributed to the chapter; Wendy Beautyman for sharing information from her PhD dissertation research; Scottish Government Library staff Jenny Foreman and Morag Higgison would like to thank their colleagues who helped with their research for Chapter 6; Eilean Craig for providing an update on the NHS Education Scotland Information Literacy Framework and to all those who responded to a request for information about health information literacy activities in public libraries for Chapter 7; Jason Tutin, Area Development Librarian – Learning, Leeds Library and Information Service; Anne Archer, Library and Information Officer, Information and Digital Team, Adult and Cultural Services, City Library, Newcastle upon Tyne;

Rachel Dryburgh, Assistant Librarian, School Library Service, Midlothian Council for contributions to Chapter 8; Ruth Sharpe, Community, Learning & Information Librarian, and Cathy Petersen, Cultural and Community Services Department, Derbyshire County Council; Sean McNamara, Learning Services Librarian at Inverclyde Libraries for information about information literacy training programmes there for their contributions to Chapter 9. This book is, to a great extent, the outcome of lessons learned from the work of the Scottish Information Literacy Project, 2004–2010, and we would like to take this opportunity to thank all those who contributed to the work of the Project, whether from within the information sector or elsewhere. We learned a lot from all those who collaborated with us and they may see something of what they contributed in this book.

*J.C. and C.I.*

# Preface

This book arose out of the work of the now-concluded Scottish Information Literacy Project which functioned between 2004 and 2010. It was brought about by a much smaller but significant earlier project, the Drumchapel Project, which examined the ICT and information-seeking skills of school pupils in a deprived area of Glasgow. Although the Project was intended to be a fairly general study, its findings focused strongly on the need to develop information literacy skills among schoolchildren which could then be carried over into higher education or directly applied in the workplace. It was originally envisaged that the Scottish Information Literacy Project would last only a year and would have the sole objective of producing an information literacy framework linking secondary and tertiary education in Scotland. It soon became clear that such a project would take much longer than anticipated, that it was necessary to work with a range of partners both within and outside the information world and that considering only formal education, at secondary and post school levels, was simply not enough. It was necessary to consider early years and primary education, the post-education and work environment, lifelong and informal learning, employability and skills development and health literacy. There has been much debate about what information literacy actually is and that is discussed at length in the book. However, it became clear to us as the Project progressed that information literacy involved not only considering conventional information literacy sources but also social policy issues, relating to the relief of inequality and disadvantage, skills development for a post-industrial society, critical thinking and lifelong learning, an activity which information literacy informs and supports. There are also the issues of digital literacy, school and higher education curricula, early-years' learning, health issues, the dynamics of the workplace, learning and teaching skills and strategies with an increasing emphasis on teaching and learning in informal situations. Information literacy has often been compared to a chameleon which changes colour to blend in with its background and this seems a very apt metaphor. Work in information literacy has been much concerned with higher education and, in particular, the generation of learning products to be used with undergraduates. This was strongly reflected in the literature, much of which was devoted to higher education. Our work increasingly came to focus on information literacy outside the academy and we undertook studies of the workplace and informal learning among other topics. We also got to know many of the people working outside the academy and studied the work of important commentators like Annemaree Lloyd. We acquired a large number of collaborators and partners, some of whom we were interested to find were not librarians but who shared some of our concerns and objectives. By the time the Project closed in 2010 we had built up expertise in information literacy and policy development in noneducational environments and our work had attracted attention not only in the UK but also in the United States, Finland, Australia and latterly Wales and the Republic of Ireland. Our experience of presenting a petition to the Scottish Parliament made us aware of both the need for high-level advocacy and the difficulties involved in influencing key decision makers. Although we did not anticipate it when we set out on our journey we effectively became engaged in national information literacy policymaking.

The conclusion of the Project left us with a good deal of expertise, an understanding of the issues and many contacts both in the UK and abroad. It seemed an obvious step to write a book which would build on our own knowledge and experiences and would review the work of expert participants from a range of countries. The result is this book which, hopefully, will lead to more work in this area and perhaps shift the focus of research and development away from higher education and into studying and supporting the information needs of ordinary people in their work and daily lives. That is the message of such documents as the *Prague Declaration* and the *Alexandria Proclamation* which are discussed in the book. Chapters 1–3 are authored by John Crawford, Chapter 4 by Christine Irving, Chapter 5 by John Crawford, Chapter 6 by Jenny Foreman and Morag Higgison, Chapter 7 by Christine Irving and Chapters 8–10 by John Crawford. It is important to progress work in the areas outlined above at a strategic and policy level, and it is hoped that this book will support these agendas.

*J.C. and C.I.*

# About the authors

**Dr John Crawford** retired in December 2009 after a career mainly spent in academic libraries, although he initially worked in public and school libraries. He was the founder and director of the Scottish Information Literacy Project which began in 2004 and concluded in the spring of 2010. He now leads its successor project, an online community of practice – Information Skills for a 21st Century Scotland (*http://www.therightinformation.org/*).

He was a Trustee of the Chartered Institute of Library and Information Professionals (CILIP) from 2010 to 2012 and served on its Council. He has authored over 85 articles in professional and academic journals on information literacy, the evaluation of library and information services and library and information history. He has written two books and contributed chapters to others. He has guest-edited two special issues of the American academic journal *Library Trends* on the theme of 'information literacy outside the academy' – *Library Trends*, 60(3–4), 2011–2012 – and more recently has guest-edited a special issue of *Library and Information Research* on the theme of 'information literacy and lifelong learning'. He is a member of both the Standing and Programme Committees of the European Conference on Information Literacy (ECIL) and serves on the Scottish Parliament's Cross Party Group on Digital Participation. He has presented extensively at conferences, both in the UK and abroad, including keynote presentations. Since retirement his main interest has been in the development of information literacy policy and practice outside higher education. He is also a trustee of Leadhills Heritage Trust.

**Christine Irving** is a freelance information professional and Research Fellow in the Centre for Social Informatics at Edinburgh Napier University where she is involved in Library and Information Science research projects. Prior to that she was the Scottish Information Literacy Project Researcher/Project Officer and worked on the development of the National Information Literacy Framework (Scotland). She now plays a key role in the online community of practice – Information Skills for a 21st Century Scotland. Her knowledge and expertise has been called upon in the role of expert advisor for several organisations/projects including the NHS Education Scotland Information Literacy Framework, CILIP's Learning Round Table on Information Literacy and the Arcadia Project: The Cambridge Curriculum for Information Literacy. She has authored and co-authored several journal articles, conference papers and book chapters. In 2008 she was a keynote speaker at the Library and Information Literacy Annual Conference (LILAC). Previous projects she was involved in include a cross-sectoral project that developed online IL interactive material for lifelong learners/post-16-year-olds. In 2004 she co-authored an Information Handling Skills national qualification at Intermediate 2 for the Scottish Qualifications Authority and the accompanying assessments – a world first.

# About the contributors

**Jenny Foreman** is a librarian with the Scottish Government Library and is particularly interested in all aspects of information literacy, social media and developing training for civil servants.

**Morag Higgison** is a Chartered Librarian with the Scottish Government Library – working with training in the areas of social media and collaborative tools, Internet searching and keeping up to date. She also assists with enquiries and literature searching.

# Part 1
## Overview

# Background to information policy: a brief historical introduction

*John Crawford*

**Abstract:** This chapter introduces the text of the book as a whole by focusing on a range of historical issues which inform the text. These factors are found to be not merely of historical significance but to inform the contemporary debate as well. These include the nature of information and what it is, the uncertain role of government, the frequently poor relationship between information and governments and the move from information searching being seen as a specialist skill to an activity for all. Information literacy in a historical context has yet to be considered.

**Key words:** information policy, information literacy, information history, library history, library policy.

The aim of this chapter is to undertake a brief historical overview of information issues with the aim of discovering whether a historical perspective can illuminate contemporary problems.

Information history (the history of information) is still a relatively young discipline but has attracted the interest of a number of scholars operating from different perspectives. A key question, not just for researchers in this area, but also for those concerned with information literacy, is the matter of definitions and what information history means to different stakeholders. Information history does not seek to define what information is and does not seem to identify a need to do so. Indeed, information history is viewed as a very varied activity and is considered to include topics as diverse as Roman Imperial foreign relations in late antiquity, Japan in the early modern period, political information in early modern Venice and the use of information during the California Gold Rush of 1849–51. Much attention however has centred round the consequences of socioeconomic and technological change since the late eighteenth century such as the developments in transport, communication, printing and literacy (Weller 2010).

Historical studies in information literacy seem to be unknown. An example of what might be undertaken could be the use of information by landowners and farmers to develop capitalistic agriculture in the eighteenth century. Overview evidence for this does exist in agricultural history sources although it has not been studied in detail. No studies of this generic type appear to have been undertaken by information historians at the time of writing (2013).

However, there seems to be general agreement that between 1700 and 1850, information, however defined, came of age. In the eighteenth century the encyclopaedia encapsulating knowledge appeared. Literary salons developed all over Europe where a wide range of topics were discussed. Accurate maps were produced reflecting a new culture of measurement. Scholarly societies and their publications appeared. (In fact, the Royal Society's *Philosophical Transactions* had been appearing regularly since 1665.) In the nineteenth century the telegraph and telephone were developed and mechanical printing led to an expansion of the publishing industry. State-sponsored or funded 'memory institutions', museums, libraries and art galleries began to appear. In the first half of the twentieth century, these were supplemented by film, radio and television. Books, magazines, newspapers, records, tapes and photographs became the staple for the production and transmission of information. The emerging modern nation state became both a provider of information and an agent of surveillance, using such data-gathering and planning strategies as regular population censuses. The late nineteenth century was characterised by the growth of manual information systems and office technology. The need for the management of information was recognised by the development of new techniques like punched cards and microphotography which were mainly found in offices and specialised information services (Black et al. 2007: 11–29).

The so-called 'informationisation' of the late nineteenth century was further enhanced in the twentieth century by the active involvement of library and information services. In this process economic renewal and innovation were key themes. As early as 1901, L. Stanley Jast, the pioneering public librarian, argued for technical collections in public libraries and subsequently opened an information bureau in Croydon to supplement the traditional reference service. He identified two stakeholder groups, the industrial community for whom technical libraries should be provided and the business community for whom commercial libraries should be offered. Some of the large provincial public libraries, at this time, contained collections relevant to local economic activity – for example, mining in Wigan, textile manufacturing in Manchester, woollens in Rochdale and watch making in Clerkenwell, in London. However, it was the consequences of the First World War that generated major activity. It soon became apparent that Germany's technical superiority gave it a military advantage. It was therefore necessary for Britain to develop its scientific and technical infrastructure and information services to support it. Technical and commercial libraries appeared in Birmingham in 1915, in Glasgow,

Northampton and Richmond upon Thames in 1916, in Lincoln, Coventry and Liverpool in 1917 and in Bradford, Leeds and Darlington in 1918, towns for the most part with a strong industrial base. More followed after the war in other industrial towns (Black 2007) of which the most remarkable for its efficient organisation was Sheffield. By 1924 there were 70 industrial collections in the UK. A promotional leaflet still survives from Leeds Commercial and Technical Library from 1920 which includes a drawing of a tradesman in overalls and cloth cap showing the practical nature of the service and at whom it was targeted (Black et al. 2009: 39).

While these initiatives originated within the profession, government intervention now became a major factor. In 1915 the British Government created the Department of Scientific and Industrial Research (DSIR) which promoted research associations: sectoral groupings of industrial firms which quickly adopted an information role. In 1919 the Ministry of Reconstruction decided that, in future, technical and commercial information services should be located within research associations and not in public libraries although the initiatives listed above show that this decision was widely ignored (Muddiman 2007: 55–78). It is a rare example of direct government intervention in information activity.

However, other factors were at work. After the First World War professional discourse became focused on the agendas and interests of the general public. 'Cultural democratisation' through the promotion of quality reading became the principal 'Library' agenda and this became the main focus of activity for the Library Association. It was an agenda well suited to public libraries which dominated the management of the Library Association for much of the twentieth century. Library and information work came to be viewed as different activities which was to lead to a schism between librarianship and information science and to become particularly marked after the Second World War. The emergence of special libraries and information bureaux, as they were called at the time, was recognised in 1924 by the creation of the Association of Special Libraries and Information Bureaux (ASLIB), a voluntary organisation of corporate members whose primary concern was the organisation and documentation of scientific and technical information thus forming a strong link between information and science and technology which was to last for many decades. Such a strategy gave semiofficial status to information organisations while keeping the state at arm's length. After the Second World War there was a major debate within scientific circles as to whether scientific and technical publishing should be nationalised and centralised under a proposed British Publishing authority. However, the plan was abandoned as the British scientific establishment was anxious to remain independent of the state. This debate effectively ended the argument about state control of information. However, it did have one important consequence. The debate had been begun by J. D. Bernal, crystallographer and Marxist, who had unsuccessfully championed the centralisation of scientific and technical publishing. He also believed that documentation and communication were social rather than technological phenomena and that information science should recognise its social role (Muddiman 2003). The idea that the usage of information is essentially a phenomenon of social interaction is a recurring theme throughout this book.

By the 1960s no coherent set of people had emerged to take control of the qualitative development of information work and continuing dissatisfaction with this pluralist situation was signalled by the formation of a new information organisation, the Institute of Information Scientists. Founded in 1958, its members had a strong interest in developing and exploiting new methods of information retrieval such as

Boolean operators and the relationship between relevance and retrieval. These have become the common coin of information skills training within information literacy. It was a time when information retrieval dominated the professional agenda. Between 1965 and 1985 information retrieval dominated the coverage of 40 library and information science journals. Although, as the veteran analyst of scientific communication and documentation, Professor Jack Meadows, has pointed out, a definition of information science acceptable to everyone always proved difficult to find throughout the second half of the twentieth century. In the 1970s what was then known as automated information retrieval became a major research interest and this link between computers and information searching, although highly beneficial to the end user in the long run, has also been a source of confusion because it introduces an inextricable link between information searching and ICT (information and communications technology) infrastructure. The 1980s saw the first studies of information seeking in which the end user of information retrieval tools became a subject of intensive study, something which in the 1990s led to the development of increasingly user-friendly database interfaces, applied initially to CD-ROM based information databases but soon to online databases made available over the Internet thus completing a process by which information retrieval had moved from being a specialist activity to an activity available to everyone whether they had the skills or not. The growing volume of information on the freely available Internet, accessed by a competing range of search engines, although greatly increasing the volume of information available to the ordinary citizen, raised important questions about the quality of information available and how it should be objectively evaluated. The research agenda too had moved away from a focus on science towards information research. In the mid-1960s the Department of Scientific and

Industrial Research was split up and one of the new bodies emerging from it was the Office for Scientific and Technical Information (OSTI). Although ostensibly concerned with science OSTI funded research into information retrieval and in the 1970s OSTI was, in turn, absorbed into the newly formed British Library and its name was changed to the British Library Research and Development Department (BLRDD) acknowledging an explicit shift to information research covering all subject areas. The decline of specialist approaches to information searching and retrieval was further signalled by the disappearance of the Institute of Information Scientists in 2002 as a separate entity when it amalgamated with the Library Association to form the Chartered Institute of Library and Information Professionals (CILIP) from which it was hoped a more unified professional ideology would develop (Meadows 2008).

From this brief historical overview five main points seem to emerge:

1. There is little agreement about what information actually is and people's views are influenced by education, experience, personal agendas and issues of technology.

2. The role of government is poorly defined and government engagement with information issues is intermittent and frequently vestigial.

3. The relationship between governments and information organisations is often weak and frequently nonexistent. Information organisations themselves may not cooperate harmoniously.

4. Information retrieval or information searching, however defined, has travelled from being a specialist issue/skill,

based round science and technology, to being a skill for everyone and covering all subjects.

5. Information literacy in a historical context is invisible.

The relevance of these points to the contemporary situation will be explored in future chapters.

# Information literacy policy within the wider context of information policy

*John Crawford*

**Abstract:** This chapter discusses the nature of information, the characteristics of the information society and the formation of information policy. Definitions of information literacy are reviewed and the history of the development of the concept since the 1970s is considered. The influence of such major documents as the final report of the Presidential Committee on Information Literacy (ALA 1989), the Prague Declaration (UNESCO 2003) and the Alexandria Proclamation (Garner 2005) is analysed. The chapter concludes with a discussion on information literacy policies, the factors affecting them, what they should contain and how they should be promoted.

**Key words:** information policy, information society, information literacy, library science, library policy.

This chapter reviews policy issues in information literacy and its place within the wider area of information policymaking. Information literacy and the information society and the policies which inform the latter are not only inextricably linked but the very concept of information literacy flows from the demands of an information-based society. Its impact on individuals is to create a requirement for functioning effectively within it and some of the associated capabilities are encapsulated within the context of information literacy (Town 2003: 83–4). These capabilities are associated with developments which have been gathering force since the 1960s: the pervasive development of technologies for information production, circulation and access (ICT infrastructure), the repositioning of the workforce in the service sector and the growth of intellectual activity at the expense of manual labour. Factors having a major impact on the information environment include the mass access to information through the Internet, the need for lifelong learning, the increasing proportion of available information with an uncontrolled production life cycle, the proliferation of information services and tools and the prevalence of intellectual over manual activities (Basili 2011: 397).

## Information policy and the information society

The term 'information society' defines a society in which the creation, distribution and treatment of information have become the most significant economic and cultural activities. The information society is often contrasted with societies which are primarily industrial or agrarian. An information society also covers many related sectors which include industrial and economic policy, technology policy, telecommunications policy and a huge sector: social issues and policies that comprise e-government, education, e-health, media policy and cultural issues within which much of the material of information literacy lies.

What information is has attracted various definitions and interpretations. It is often related to such concepts as meaning, knowledge, communication, truth and representation and mental stimulus (UNESCO 2009: 123–4).

Elizabeth Orna, looking at it from an organisational perspective has noted:

'One of the ironies of the "information revolution" is that so few of those involved can give any definition of what information is" (Orna 1999: 18).

She offers her own definition:

'*Information* is what human beings *transform* knowledge into when they want to communicate it to other people. It is knowledge made visible or audible, in written or printed words, or in speech.

From the point of view of the *user*, information is what we seek and pay attention to in our outside world when we need to add to or enrich our knowledge in order to act upon it. So we can usefully think of it as the *food of knowledge* because we need information and communication to nourish and maintain our knowledge and keep it in good shape for what we have to do in the world. Without the food of information, knowledge becomes enfeebled.

The transformation of information into knowledge, and knowledge into information, forms the basis for all human learning and communication . . .' [italics are author's] (Orna 1999: 8–9)

The idea of information as a form of enrichment is helpful as is the emphasis on communication. There are other definitions available, many of which focus on the idea of reducing uncertainty, although this presupposes that information must be useful and reduces uncertainty which is not necessarily the case. Information can also be viewed as having two distinct elements: an act or process and a communication or message

(Walker 2010: 37–8). It seems however that the appearance of a concise generally accepted definition is unlikely.

A general definition of national information policy was offered by Charles Oppenheim in 1994 when he described national information policy as 'a series of decisions taken by a national government, which are designed to encourage a better information infrastructure' (Orna 2008). It does not say that these decisions should be structured, systematic and centrally lead.

While UNESCO does not attempt to define National Information Society Policy (NISP) it identifies three goals:

- *To democratise access*: to place within the reach of all persons the means to access and use information and communication technologies, guaranteeing the enjoyment of citizen rights, fostering education, local development, eradication of poverty, gender equity, digital inclusion, universal access, public transparency and efficiency, and participatory governance.

- *To develop capacities*: to create, support and promote strategies, tools and methodologies to generate capacities and skills to utilize information and information and communication technologies for all sectors and societal groups, at all levels of formal and informal education . . .

- *To achieve an adequate legal and regulatory framework*: to create the necessary norms and regulations to guarantee the right to information . . .

A society which provides information for all might include information-literate communities where people in all walks of life exercise information literacy skills to achieve personal, social, occupational and educational goals, where all people have access to information services in any form, access to public and school libraries staffed by qualified professionals, access to computers and the Internet in public libraries and a society in which ICT and media literacy skills are widely diffused (UNESCO 2009: 7, 11–12).

Information policies, in practice, tend to be applied more haphazardly. A key theme in the emergence of modern information policy is whether the general public should have access to the information it wants or to the information the government wants it to have. Here is a key divergence between Great Britain and the United States. In the US, freedom of information legislation was passed in 1966 but the UK Freedom of Information Act was not passed until 2005. By 1970 most of the elements that make up contemporary ideas of information policy had emerged: what governments tell their own population and those of other countries for their own policy purposes, protection of personal data and freedom of information, collection of statistical data for policymaking and the use of ICT to manage and analyse information. While some countries have explicit information polices, others do not. There are two broad models of national information policy: *laissez faire* in which the state leaves most responsibility to the market and *dirigiste* which places more emphasis on the role of the state. Unlike East Asia and parts of Europe the UK relies on informal and piecemeal 'muddling-through' policymaking which makes it impossible to identify one single document which describes what British national information policy actually is. Governments find it hard to get to grips with information policy because they find it difficult to define information, which arises from the fact that it is dynamic and innovative and has social and economic implications, all of which makes information hard to handle, a problem not limited to governments. In the UK no single cabinet minister is responsible for developing the information society.

While ICT has, throughout the world, been recognised as a benign technology offering rewards to all social classes, in practice, the implementation of ICT tends to exacerbate the difference between the information rich and the information poor. Access to ICT can also directly cut costs to those who can access it by giving access to comparison websites, reduced cost online booking, etc. Furthermore the potential of ICT for handling and manipulating information has exerted an irresistible attraction on the thinking of governments about information policy which have often relegated actual information to a minor role. This situation is compounded by the fact that there is little input from information professionals into government policymaking (Orna 2008).

## Defining information literacy

Even a brief overview shows the lack of certainty in information policy definition and activity, although there is at least a role for information literacy within it and one which offers both opportunities and challenges to information literacy activity in nonformal and nonacademic environments. This appears to take place in three connected stages. First, a nation perceives a need for competitive reasons to be a player in the global knowledge economy. This, in turn, suggests a need for the upskilling of its population to work effectively in this sort of economy, resulting in a national 'learning agenda'. The 'learning agenda' also tends to become explicitly associated with the skills of citizens, the development of these skills within educational programmes and their subsequent application in the workplace. Third, the growth of digital media and communications results in widespread information overload, leading to the need for both individuals and corporations to have effective information and knowledge management. This sequence tends to run from national concern to process analysis to products for developing information literacy (Town 2003: 86). In practice, process analysis and product development receive the most attention with most of the product development (learning and teaching materials) taking place in the education sector, primarily in higher education and much less in the lifelong learning and workplace sectors.

The term 'information literacy' was coined in 1974 by Paul Zurkowski and its origins were not specifically located in higher education. Zurkowski used the phrase to describe the 'techniques and skills' known by the information literate 'for utilizing the wide range of information tools as well as primary sources in molding information solutions to their problems'. Zurkowski himself was founding president of the US Information Industries Association, a trade and industry association which represented the USA's leading print publishers. One advocacy strategy he employed was to insist that because information products and services, aided and abetted by the exploding ICT technologies, were beginning to multiply it was necessary for informed citizens and policymakers to become more 'literate' in their use of these information services and products. However, Zurkowski himself admitted that there was little understanding of what the term meant until about ten years after he had coined it (Horton 2011). Other writers at the time expanded the concept to include an instrument of political emancipation and a requirement for competiveness in organisations (Pinto et al. 2010). The 1980s were a transition decade characterised by the rapid development of ICT technologies and, in particular, the appearance of the first personal computers. A key early and enduring document is the American Library Association's *Presidential Committee on Information Literacy: Final Report* (ALA 1989). The committee outlined six principal recommendations:

1. to 'reconsider the ways we have organized information institutionally, structured information access, and defined information's role in our lives at home in the community, and in the work place';

2. to promote 'public awareness of the problems created by information illiteracy';

3. to develop a national research agenda related to information and its use;

4. to ensure the existence of 'a climate conducive to students becoming information literate';

5. to include information literacy concerns in teacher education; and

6. to promote public awareness of the relationship between information literacy and the more general goals of 'literacy, productivity, and democracy'.

This wide-ranging statement shows that a clear role was identified for information literacy in the workplace, lifelong learning and as a civil and civic right. However, the 1990s were a period when librarians became increasingly dissatisfied with traditional user education and began to search for a more meaningful and appropriate term for an age of increasingly self-directed learning and the term 'information literacy' began to replace user education. It was also a period when information literacy became principally located in education and especially in higher education where the librarian became both its main advocate and also its proprietor. The new century has seen the internationalisation of the concept with increasing support from UNESCO which has resulted in two major international policy statements, the Prague Declaration (UNESCO 2003) and the Alexandria

Proclamation (Garner 2005). These are major advocacy tools. The Prague Declaration outlined the following principles:

- The creation of an Information Society is key to social, cultural and economic development of nations and communities, institutions and individuals in the twenty-first century and beyond.

- Information Literacy encompasses knowledge of one's information concerns and needs, and the ability to identify, locate, evaluate, organize and effectively create, use and communicate information to address issues or problems at hand; it is a prerequisite for participating effectively in the Information Society, and is part of the basic human right of lifelong learning.

- Information Literacy, in conjunction with access to essential information and effective use of information and communication technologies, plays a leading role in reducing the inequities within and among countries and peoples, and in promoting tolerance and mutual understanding through information use in multicultural and multilingual contexts.

- Governments should develop strong interdisciplinary programs to promote Information Literacy nationwide as a necessary step in closing the digital divide through the creation of an information literate citizenry, an effective civil society and a competitive workforce.

- Information Literacy is a concern to all sectors of society and should be tailored by each to its specific needs and context.

- Information Literacy should be an integral part of Education for All, which can contribute critically to the achievement of the United Nations Millennium Development Goals, and respect for the Universal Declaration of Human Rights.

These principles link information literacy to wider human rights issues, specifically link it to the information society, define it and link it to civil rights, the closure of the digital divide, reduction of inequality and improvement in workplace performance. It also suggests that information literacy is not a fixed concept but 'should be tailored by each to its specific needs and context', an important point, the implications of which are discussed throughout this book.

The Alexandria Proclamation (Garner 2005) reiterates some of these points. Information literacy:

- comprises the competencies to recognise information needs and to locate, evaluate, apply and create information within cultural and social contexts;

- is crucial to the competitive advantage of individuals, enterprises (especially small and medium enterprises), regions and nations;

- provides the key to effective access, use and creation of content to support economic development, education, health and human services, and all other aspects of contemporary societies, and thereby provides the vital foundation for fulfilling the goals of the Millennium Declaration and the World Summit on the Information Society; and

- extends beyond current technologies to encompass learning, critical thinking and interpretative skills across professional boundaries and empowers individuals and communities.

It links information literacy strongly with critical thinking and goes on to urge links with lifelong learning.

Australia also sees information literacy in this light contributing to: 'learning for life; the creation of new knowledge; acquisition of skills; personal, vocational, corporate and organisational empowerment; social inclusion; participative citizenship; and innovation and enterprise (ALIA, 2006). Information literacy and lifelong learning are related concepts: they are both largely self-motivated and self-directed and do not need the mediation of an outsider, individual or corporate (assuming, of course, that the individual has the necessary knowledge and skills); they are both self-empowering and benefit everyone irrespective of social or economic status; and they are both 'self-actuating' or self-enlightening processes especially if practised over a lifetime (Horton 2008: 3-4).

Information literacy is therefore about personal and civil rights, participative citizenship, lifelong learning, using technology wisely, reduction of the digital divide, skills and economic development, education and critical thinking and maintenance of a healthy lifestyle.

How information literacy should be defined has been the subject of much scholarly debate (Bawden 2001). Paul Zurkowski described information-literate people as: 'People trained in the application of information resources to their work ...' emphasizing the importance of the workplace, but in 1979 the US Information Industries Association widened the definition of an information-literate person as someone who 'knows the techniques and skills for using information tools in molding solutions to problems' and Corbette Doyle (1994), succinctly defined it as 'the ability to access, evaluate and use information from a variety of sources', a definition which in various forms has survived ever since. However, by the early 1990s two factors had emerged which are crucial to this study: there was little agreement within the information profession about what information literacy actually is and there was little understanding of the concept outside the profession. There was also criticism of the idea as being too 'library centred' and that information should include films, television, posters, conversations, etc. The coming of widespread use of the Internet in the 1990s greatly strengthened this view. In 1989 the American Library Association offered a new definition:

> 'To be information literate an individual must recognize when information is needed and have the ability to locate, evaluate and use effectively the information needed ... . Ultimately information literate people are those who have learned how to learn. They know how to learn because they know how information is organized, how to find information, and how to use information in such a way that others can learn from them'.

Despite attempts to broaden the definition of information literacy and make it less 'library centred' it became increasingly linked with formal education and was taken up enthusiastically by academic librarians who saw it as a natural progression from traditional bibliographic instruction and who, in the United States, had seen a considerable expansion in student demand for training in information skills at the expense of reference services. However, it is not clear to what extent this was a genuine policy change or simply a rebranding exercise. Information literacy in higher education came also to be linked with the idea of a hierarchy or 'laddering' of skills by which various levels of information skill were linked to successive levels of undergraduate and postgraduate learning, a good example of which is the SCONUL Seven Pillars of Information Literacy (SCONUL 2011). This has led to dominance of the concept by academic and to a lesser extent by school librarians which has reinforced the 'library-centred' model of information literacy as a skill imparted by and dominated by librarians and one which has an element of academic assessment. This has led to a focus on individual student performance and the development of self-sufficiency through independent learning. However, the debate is now widening thanks to a limited but growing interest in workplace and wider community studies, although these for the most part are attempts to translate librarians' perceptions in relation to the 'operalisation' of a list of skills and standards derived from the education sector. There is little reflection on whether information skills appropriate to the education sector are valued by workers and their employers. It also appears to be accepted that information literacy focuses on individual information use rather than information use as a collective activity. In reality, workers use other workers' embodied knowledge and experience as a source of evaluated information. Research suggests that the role of the community is central to information literacy practice and that information literacy is not a skill but a practice which takes place through a range of social activities. Information literacy is therefore to be understood as a collaborative and communal activity. To complicate matters further the language used by the information sector does not mean much outside it, which means that, when the term 'information literacy' leaves its domain, it loses its power (Lloyd 2011: 279–83). Within the profession itself sectoral approaches tend to be dissimilar and specific to the needs of the sector. In the health sector information literacy tends to be evidence based but in special libraries a more corporate approach may apply. Academics tend to be concerned with learning outcomes and pedagogy while public librarians are more concerned with social inclusion. A study of the use of the term in the published literature showed that 50 per cent of the documents analysed derived from the subject areas of information, education and computing. Business and management were insignificant areas (Pinto et al. 2010: 14). For those concerned with information literacy in relation to lifelong learning issues the previous emphasis on education, problems with definitions and authority outside the information world represent major challenges.

The definition adopted for this study is proposed by the Chartered Institute of Library and Information Professionals (CILIP 2004) which could be 'understandable by all information-using communities in the UK':

'Information literacy is knowing when and why you need information, where to find it, and how to evaluate, use and communicate it in an ethical manner.

This definition implies several skills. We believe that the skills (or competencies) that are required to be information literate require an understanding of:

o A need for information

o The resources available

o How to find information

o The need to evaluate results

o How to work with or exploit results

o Ethics and responsibility of use

o How to communicate or share your findings

o How to manage your findings.'

The present writers have used this definition in a variety of contexts including workplace and employability studies in which interviewees were presented with this definition. It was found that they understand it immediately and then began to reinterpret it in the contexts of their own education, qualifications, work experience, personal and professional contacts and life experiences. Information literacy has sometimes been compared to a chameleon which changes colour according to the circumstances in which it finds itself and this is a useful metaphor for a concept which changes with the needs of the situation.

The problem with definitions is not just a theoretical issue. It confuses the debate about policymaking and advocacy for it. The policy process itself is complex. It includes groups of people from a variety of sectors including government agencies, legislatures, research, journalism and the general public. The process itself can take at least ten years (Weiner 2011a: 298). A policymaking issue should be unambiguous and this poses a problem while information literacy is still relatively unclear both as a concept and a practice (Haras and Brasley 2011).

## Information literacy policies

Concise definitions of what an information literacy policy actually is seem difficult to come by but it could involve three stages: gathering of information, identification of root causes and analysis of their connections and the making of policy decisions. There are also questions:

- Should information policy documents include those which are partly or largely concerned with ICT or educational issues or should they be strictly limited to information literacy (Basili 2011)?

- Should policies have a level of state recognition and, if so, at what level?

- Is endorsement by a professional body sufficient?

- Should they be simply prescriptive skills based documents or should they encourage independent critical thinking and problem solving skills? Who should be responsible for information literacy?

(Whitworth 2011: 318)

25

Clearly they must take account of the numerous policy documents and definitions which have appeared over the years and link objectives and outcomes to them. According to Basili (2011) in most countries information literacy has not entered the policy agenda and it is still necessary to promote policy awareness about the information literacy issue. She identifies a total of 54 policy initiatives, although most of them do not focus specifically on information literacy. Although she finds that most policy measures are initiated by Ministries of Education the idea of information literacy appears mostly in ICT policy documents. Some of the policies are in fact higher education course materials. Whitworth (2011) offers an analysis of the six policy documents which are available in English and are in some sense at least national documents. Three of the states or parts of states are small: Finland, Hong Kong and Scotland (two other smaller states, Norway and Taiwan, were not included) which raises the question of whether information literacy policies are easier to implement in small states. There are perhaps two factors which favour this view. In small countries educational policies are not just about education. They can help to define the values of the state and identify what factors differentiate it from other larger countries nearby. This is certainly the case in Scotland. The other factor is simply size. It is easier to form networks of interested partners and meet and influence decision makers, politicians, civil servants and staff of nongovernmental organizations (NGOs) who share some of the values of the information literacy activist. Whilst separate declarations have been published for Scotland and Wales, there are no declarations for England at the time of writing. A common denominator is that both Scotland and Wales engaged with their legislative bodies (the Scottish Parliament and the Welsh Assembly) to produce the declarations. As England has no parliament of its own there is no national conduit through which a specifically English information literacy policy could be developed.

Mono versus multilingualism and levels of economic development are other factors. South Africa does have an information literacy policy but is hampered by economic constraints and a multilingual society. Finland's policy is one of the few to have full state recognition. However, the policy is only concerned with higher education, does not mention social impact and information literacy is not seen as a holistic concept. The *Australian and New Zealand Information Literacy Framework* is the product of a professional body and the emphasis is in higher education. The Hong Kong policy is, like the Finnish example, state sponsored. It is the most comprehensive of all the documents examined and the only one to pay real attention to the affective dimension – that is, the idea of pleasure being a motivator of information searching, a filter for information and a support for informational interaction. What is missing is the impact of information literacy on democracy and active citizenship. Most information literacy policy documents reflect the thinking of Western liberal democracies and this cannot be taken for granted. The Scottish document is the product of collaboration between universities, further education colleges, schools and NGOs. It originated as a framework linking schools and higher education, but was subsequently expanded to include the workplace, employability, skills development and lifelong learning. Unlike other documents it is very much an evolving work in progress, having begun life as a printed document which evolved into a web-based product incorporating exemplars of good practice and has now become a community of practice, hosted by the Scottish Library and Information Council (SLIC 2012). In South Africa there is little evidence of professional bodies taking the lead and despite some 15 years or more of activity at institutional level this had led to little coherent policymaking beyond passing references to information literacy in recent bills and the professional body has made no easily accessible public statement. Both Whitworth and Basili examine the situation in some detail and offer evaluative criteria, but from the evidence available five elementary criteria emerge which are not generally being met:

1. Information literacy policy documents should be about information literacy and not something else.

2. They should have some form of government endorsement and support.

3. They should be genuinely cross sectoral covering all education levels from early years to PhD level, the workplace, health, lifelong learning, employability and skills development and citizenship and civil rights.

4. They should be at least informed and preferably led by the professional bodies of the countries concerned.

5. They should be collaborative with input from all organisations in the countries concerned such as skills development bodies, employers' organizations, trades unions, teaching and learning organisations and relevant NGOs.

Some sort of standardized template for information literacy policies seems desirable. In the meantime some basic questions might be:

- What is an information literacy policy?

- What are information literacy policies for?

- What is the role of an information literacy policy within the wider world of information policymaking?

- How can information literacy be defined to distinguish it from ICT infrastructural issues?

- Who should make information literacy policy?

- How can the information professional exert influence outside the information sector?

- What sort of agendas should information literacy policymaking identify/collaborate with – for example, educational and social policy, lifelong learning and health awareness?

- Is information literacy recognised in policy agendas worldwide?

- Can information literacy exploit digital inclusion agendas?

- What kind of state is receptive to information literacy policies?

- Have information literacy policies been systematically tested and evaluated?

Policymaking for information literacy is best seen as an evolving, collaborative work in progress rather than an exercise in completeness. When Paul Zurkowski originated the concept in 1974 his aim was to achieve universal information literacy in the United States by 1984. This should act as a warning to us all. Policymaking is not about generating a product but a process. Evidence derived from the cited authorities and the authors' work on the Scottish Information Literacy Project suggests that the following points are useful in what should be an ongoing process:

*Advocacy and policymaking*

- Advocacy strategies are essential to policymaking but this raises the issue of at what level should making the case be made. Horton recommends aiming for the top, and the best example of this is probably Barack Obama's presidential proclamation of Information Literacy Awareness Month in the United States. Such coups are difficult to achieve and require a lot of planning and lobbying. In small states access to decisions makers is easier but it is also important to tackle the issue at a practitioner level and encourage partners and supporters to make the case in their own organisations.

- The process of advocacy, collaboration and networking is slow and time consuming so plan for the long term. As Horton says (2011: 272), it might take years or even decades.

- Develop strategies and advocacy from existing national and international social and educational policies or, as Horton (2011: 273) puts it: 'Link information literacy to important and long-standing, intractable national or institutional or organizational goals and reforms'. These might, for example, be health education policies with links to information literacy.

- Policymaking must address intellectual property rights (IPR) issues and these must include 'popular' as well as more traditional issues deriving from the academic experience such as downloading of music and videos and issues to do with the sale of illegal copies to the public

- Include Internet safety in the policy agenda. It is both an important issue in itself and is a matter of public concern.

*Working relationships*

- Partnerships and networking is crucial using both personal and professional contacts.

- Work cross sectorally and not just with librarians and information specialists.

- Develop a community of practice. This may be web based but could also involve face to face meetings. It should not be restricted to the library and information science profession.

- Identify organisations to work with – skills development agencies and other organisations involved in workplace training, organisations concerned with promoting digital inclusion, curriculum development bodies in education, teachers and university lecturers' organisations, professional organisations which have an education and training role, job centres and careers advisors, community learning and development organisations, telecommunications regulators such as Ofcom in the UK, chambers of commerce, employers' organizations and trades union representative bodies. All these can have an interest in information literacy outcomes.

- Offer support to practitioners. Support at policy levels informs the development of good practice at institutional levels which can be fed back to further policy development, thus creating a virtuous circle. This is particularly helpful to small organisations or solo operators like school librarians.

- Have meetings and involve people. Encourage reporting on activities by activists. This gives activists an opportunity to present their ideas and receive comments and constructive criticism. Outcomes can then be fed into policymaking.

- Develop a common vocabulary with which all stakeholders and partners can engage. Avoid 'librarian' speak.

*Research and development*

- Much of the information literacy agenda has a utilitarian content, such as education (specifically education for employment), but there is a need to balance the utilitarian educational agenda against what has been called the affective dimension, personal social development and self-fulfilment, outcomes which are difficult to measure but are for the people involved the most important of all.

- The development of learning material content should be an outcome of policy thinking but must be cross sectoral and should not simply be higher education material 'bolted' on to another context such as workplace information literacy skills development. The role of project partners is essential in developing materials and exemplars of good practice.

- Do your homework in the widest sense. Be aware of relevant research and engage in market-orientated action research, preferably with other partners and including those outwith the information sector. Exemplars of good practice and case studies can add value as local in-house initiatives can inform wider practice.

- Funding: policymaking (especially if viewed as long term) is expensive and requires dedicated staff. Developing strategy strands which are likely to attract funding from governments and NGOs are worth pursuing.

- Encourage writing and reporting so that others both within the country and abroad can be aware of your work and learn from it and comment on it.

- Evaluate activity preferably with partners.

- Link relevant information literacy skills levels to the school curriculum. Literacy curriculum outcomes are the most obvious but other areas are also relevant.

- Recognise and work with innovative learning and teaching agendas which recognise independent learning as they are likely to be sympathetic to information literacy.

# Summary of the chapter

An analysis of the contemporary situation shows that historic issues still persist, although progress has been made in discussion and analysis of information policy issues. Information literacy has found an identifiable role within the information society but it remains difficult to define and therefore difficult to translate into policy terms. There is a lack of clarity about what information literacy policies actually are. They are frequently subsumed within ICT policies, often lack authoritative state support, lack comprehensiveness and are not cross sectoral. Policymaking is not about producing a finite product but a continuing process of dialogue and development and the lessons to be learned from the process. Two other largely unaddressed factors arise: the emergence of evaluative criteria to analyse information literacy policymaking and the desirability of some sort of standardized template for information literacy policies. The second factor however is difficult to deal with because of the wide variation worldwide in school curricula and social and welfare policies.

# 3

# Relevant policy documents both from within and beyond the LIS profession

*John Crawford*

**Abstract:** This chapter continues the policy theme of Chapter 2 by considering examples of information literacy policy and advocacy activity drawn from the United States, Australia and the United Kingdom. Most but not all originate within the information profession. Examples include the work of the National Forum on Information literacy in the United States, a German advocacy document prepared for a parliamentary Committee of Enquiry, the work of the former Scottish Information Literacy Project and the activities of the Welsh Information Literacy Project. The role and relevance of 'digital' policy documents is reviewed, together with the work of the Chartered Institute of Library and Information Professionals in Great Britain. The need for a rigorous evidence base is identified.

**Key words:** digital policies, information literacy, information literacy projects, information literacy policies, professional organisations.

Chapter 2 looked at information policy and information literacy policy documents in fairly general terms. This chapter looks at specific examples of policy and other relevant documents, some produced within the profession while others are not but are relevant to information literacy. The emphasis is on documents focusing on a wide agenda.

## The United States and Australia

As indicated in Chapter 2 the American Library Association's *Presidential Committee on Information Literacy: Final Report* (ALA 1989) is a key document. This wide-ranging statement shows that a clear role was identified for information literacy in the workplace, lifelong learning and as a civil and civic right and that, as a concept, it extended well beyond the education sector. It has led in different directions. In 2004 the (American) Association of College and Research Libraries published standards setting out the defining characteristics of an 'information literate individual' which are intended primarily for higher education (Puttick 2011: 100). However, in 2001 the ALA produced an early example of an advocacy pack: *A Library Advocate's Guide to Building Information Literate Communities*. The ALA in 2001 explicitly recognised the work of the 1989 Presidential Committee and built on it to address a wide range of target audiences. Key messages for audiences and what it is hoped they will do are listed. As well as librarians this includes the business community, community leaders, decision makers, both legislators and public officials, the education community at all levels, employees of all types, and library users and potential users. A key message, for example, for the business community is:

'Good decisions depend on good information. Information literacy is vital for a competitive workforce.'

And for decision makers:

'Americans of all ages must develop information literacy skills if they are to prosper in the global information economy. Libraries and librarians are critical to this effort.'

There is a list of sample questions and answers and some 'stories', brief paragraphs, as well as long case studies giving practical examples of information literacy achievement. There is a succinct section 'Delivering the message' which provides practical tips for librarians in case making and advocacy. Collaboration and partnership are recurring themes in policymaking and there is a section 'Building partnerships' which gives ten tips for success in partnership building of which the most important is perhaps the fourth:

'Respect that partner groups have different constituencies and agendas. It is important to keep an open mind, stay flexible and be willing to negotiate.'

Practical examples of successful partnerships are given. Sample documentation is also included: a news release, a sample letter to the editor of daily newspapers, a draft of an opinion-forming article (also for newspapers) and a sample speech explaining what information literacy is, why it is important and what the ordinary citizen can do to progress the information literacy agenda. There are some useful facts, 'Quotable quotes' and lists of information literacy competence standards. The document concludes with a list of resources in a variety of formats and relevant organisations.

Three features of the document stand out: it assumes a leadership and policymaking role for librarians, it is cross sectoral with a strong appeal to lifelong learning. It is also written in nonspecialist language and is easy to understand. However, the evidence base relies on the brief case studies and there is little other hard evidence to support the statements made.

The Australian Library and Information Association (ALIA 2003) has produced its own version: *A Library Advocate's Guide to Building Information Literate Communities* which in layout and general content follows the American model although there is detailed variation and adaption to meet local needs, most obviously in practical examples, 'Fast facts', information resources and relevant organisations and contacts. The main local variations however are the inclusion of the Australian 'Information and ICT Literacy Matrix of Student Learning', the Council of Australian University Librarians' 'Information Literacy Standards' and the 'ALIA Statement on Information Literacy for All Australians'. It has the same advantages and disadvantages as the parent document although it has more to say about education but, as no impact assessment has been undertaken, it is difficult to assess its influence.

A direct organisational outcome of the Presidential Committee on Information Literacy is the National Forum on Information Literacy, established by the Presidential Committee in 1989, a volunteer network of organisations committed to raising public awareness on the importance of information literacy to individuals, to diverse communities, to the economy, and to engaged citizenship participation. The Forum represents over 90 national and international organisations, all dedicated to 'mainstreaming the philosophy of information literacy across national and international landscapes, throughout every educational, domestic, and workplace venue'. Although originally founded as a national organisation the National Forum on Information Literacy has made significant strides internationally in promoting the importance of integrating information literacy concepts and skills throughout all educational, governmental and workforce development programmes. The National Forum co-sponsored with UNESCO and the International Federation of Library Associations (IFLA) several 'experts meetings', resulting in the Prague Declaration of 2003 and the Alexandria

Proclamation of 2005 each underscoring the importance of information literacy as a basic fundamental human right and lifelong learning skill. In 2006 the National Forum co-sponsored the first National Summit on Information Literacy which brought together over 100 representatives from education, business and government to address America's information literacy deficits as a nation currently competing in a global marketplace. A major outcome of the Summit was the establishment of a national ICT Literacy Policy Council to provide leadership in creating national standards for ICT literacy in the United States. The Forum recognises that achieving information literacy has been much easier for the socially and economically advantaged. For those who are poor, non-White, older, disabled, living in rural areas or otherwise disadvantaged, it has been much harder to overcome the digital divide. A number of the Forum's members address the specific challenges for those disadvantaged – for example, the Children's Partnership advocates for the nearly 70 million children and youth in the United States, many of whom are disadvantaged. The Children's Partnership currently runs three programmes, two of which specifically address the needs of those with low incomes: the Online Content for Low-Income and Underserved Americans Initiative, and the California Initiative Program. Although the Forum works primarily with educational, business, and nonprofit organisations it is very much a body with a strong social conscience and a commitment to aligning information literacy with lifelong learning (NFIL 2012).

More recently, the Forum has launched a campaign to persuade all 50 state and territory governors to issue gubernatorial information literacy proclamations following on President Obama's presidential proclamation of 2009 establishing October as National Information Literacy Awareness Month. In October 2011, Governor Deval Patrick of Massachusetts issued a proclamation describing the importance of information literacy to the citizens of the Commonwealth and, following on this success, a number of information literacy advocates are pursuing proclamations in their states (Jackman 2012).

## Germany

Germany has produced an information literacy advocacy document. In February 2011 Bibliothek & Information Deutschland produced a brochure of recommendations, to contribute to the thinking of a German parliamentary Committee of Enquiry: *Medien- und Informationskompetenz – immer mit Bibliotheken und Informationseinrichtungen! Empfehlungen von Bibliothek & Information Deutschland (BID) für die Enquete-Kommission "Internet und digitale Gesellschaft" des Deutschen Bundestages [Media and Information Literacy: From Library and Information Services! Recommendations from Bibliothek & Information Deutschland to the Parliamentary Committee of Inquiry into the Internet and Digital Society]* (BID 2011). The document advocates the value and key role of libraries, pointing out the extent to which libraries are already supporting information literacy, digital literacy and e-learning. It makes recommendations at federal, state and district levels, for formal and adult education, and it gives examples of good practice.

It points out that, as with most other countries, media and information skills have been most successfully developed in higher education but staffing shortages in university libraries means that there is limited time for information literacy instruction which is needed to support the skills required in new degree courses. The creation of a central organisation for all types of library, therefore, is urgently needed, to take on the appropriate development work and see it through into practice. Such an organisation would have as its remit:

'The bringing together of all relevant information about media and information skills in a nationally promoted information portal with the task of assessment and recommendation. Certification or development and application of a seal of approval for media and information skills from the Federal Ministry for Education and Research would be required.'

Successful examples of implementation would include:

- Initiation of new local, regional, national and even international activities in the area of media and information skills, and an expansion of the cooperation of existing initiatives.

- Initiation of research into the relevance of media and information skills in their subject-based, methodological and teaching/educational dimension.

- Development of methods of evaluation for research into the long-term use of information and media skills for career as well as degree course success, in cooperation with education and psychology research bodies.

In order that the aforementioned aims be achieved by 2020, BID recommends the implementation of further sector-specific measures.

*In schools and training*

- Introduction of standards for media and information skills, formulated by international library and information organisations, for schools and for work training in Germany.

■ Every school should have by 2020 a school library/media centre.

■ Definition and implementation of the teaching of media and information skills as a key skill in state education plans, and in educational standards for schools and subject areas, so that the professional acquisition, assessment and use of information contribute to the swift achieving of a school certificate, and enables lifelong learning.

*In higher education*

■ Ongoing development of standards of media and information skills at a national level, differentiated according to subject and level.

■ Expansion of the course curricula of librarians and information scientists to include methods of information and media skills, with regard to methods of evaluation.

*In adult education*

■ Reinforcing the partnership of public libraries, further education, and other local education and leisure class providers, as well as national initiatives for the dissemination of media and information skills.

A leadership role for librarians is identified as the document recommends:

'Dissemination of media and information skills must become the political remit and specialised task of librarians and establishments within the information infrastructure, as is described in the already adopted library laws of some states (Thuringen, Sachsen-Anhalt, Hessen).'

As a bold statement with a direct appeal to politicians it has few parallels with other similar documents and seeks to build on pre-existing legislation within individual states within the Federal Republic.

# Devolved nations within the United Kingdom: Scotland and Wales

## The Scottish Information Literacy Project 2004–10

The Scottish Information Literacy Project is worthy of note for several reasons (Irving 2011). It was the first national information literacy project within the British Isles and its aims and objectives travelled from an initial focus on secondary and tertiary education to a much wider agenda embracing primary education, lifelong learning, employability, skills development, the workplace, health and adult literacies. The Project grew out of a previous project, the Drumchapel Project which researched the ICT skills of school pupils in a deprived area of Glasgow. This showed that school pupils were not acquiring basic information literacy skills which they could then develop further at university, or use in the workplace or for leisure purposes. This suggested the need for an information literacy strategy which would link schools with further and higher education. A parallel study showed that Glasgow Caledonian University alumni recognised that information-seeking skills learned at university could be applied to the workplace. The original concept, formulated in October 2004, was for a one-year innovative national pilot to develop an information literacy framework with secondary and tertiary partners which would link secondary and tertiary education and produce secondary school leavers in Scotland with a skill set which post school education could recognise and develop or which could be applied to the world of work. However, such an aim takes many years to achieve and when the Project ended in the spring of 2010 much still remained to be achieved especially in lifelong learning, health literacy and the workplace.

To develop a framework of information literacy skills, pre-existing models at both national and international levels were used wherever possible and every effort was made to avoid replicating work already done. These models included the UK-wide Society of College, National and University Libraries' (SCONUL) Seven Pillars Model. Within Scotland the Edinburgh School Library Services ExPLORE model, aimed at younger school pupils, was used as it was recognised that the framework should be linked to the Scottish school curriculum. The curriculum, however, was about to change and the emerging curriculum (A Curriculum for Excellence) (CfE) was being developed while the framework was being prepared. Later this was to give the project an opportunity to work with the Literacies Curriculum Development Team to ensure that information literacy outcomes were included within the literacies part of the revised curriculum. As the curriculum was to change fundamentally it was decided to map information literacy skills against the Scottish Credit and Qualifications Framework (SCQF), which supports a continuous learning framework understood by other learning providers and is nationally recognised in education, the workplace and lifelong learning. Adopting the SCQF Framework lent authority to the planned information literacy framework. This was a key decision and one which was to be adopted by the Welsh Information Literacy Project described below. By using the SCQF Framework and pre-existing models and definitions wherever possible the Project could demonstrate a continuous learning process and 'pegged' each information skill level to an appropriate learning level as specified by the SCQF Framework.

Although the Framework was principally linked with formal education it also contains sections on definitions, information literacy and lifelong learning, information literacy education and how the Framework could be used. The outcome of the process, a 68-page document suitable for supporting implementation of the Framework and advocacy both to the education world and the wider community was completed and evaluated in 2007–8. This showed that the printed Framework needed to be transformed into a more flexible tool that enabled case studies and exemplars of good practice to be added. Additionally, more work was needed to integrate information literacy into the Curriculum for Excellence's Literacy across Learning Outcomes, the Framework needed to be linked to the Scottish Government's skills agenda and the lifelong learning section needed to be expanded as a result of the research and development work conducted in the workplace and adult literacy areas. Outcomes from evaluation included a study of the use of information in the workplace which increased the number of the Project's workplace partners, introduced it to adult literacy networks and drew attention to the role of public libraries in developing information literacy–training programmes. The Framework was duly transferred to a weblog using Web 2.0 technology and was enriched with exemplars of good practice drawn from several sectors. This was a departure from other national frameworks developed in Australia, New Zealand and America. This led to 13 separate case studies being placed on the website. The evaluation exercise showed that use of the Framework included being employed as part of an information literacy skills audit, to develop information literacy in schools, to structure research skills workshops and to inform an Institution's information literacy framework.

Although the Project's initial aim was to link secondary and tertiary education it soon became apparent that to be 'effective, an information literacy policy must be firmly pegged to the information, lifelong learning, inclusion and digital policies of the state', a point which has subsequently been taken up by the Welsh Information Literacy Project. The Project needed to engage in the wider world outside academia. This led to contacts with a wide range of organisations outside the information world some of which were more successful than others including Ofcom Scotland, the Confederation of Business and Industry (CBI) in Scotland which represents employers, the Scottish Trades Union Congress which represents employees, the Glasgow Chamber of Commerce which represents local business and industry and Skills Development Scotland, the Scottish Government's skills development agency. This last agency proved to be the most successful contact as its staff recognised the importance of information literacy both as a skill for their staff, for career selection and for jobseekers. Some work was also done with adult literacy tutors and community learning and development staff to investigate the potential for developing information literacy as an employability and workplace skill in conjunction with public libraries – an area which has considerable developmental potential. The Project also provided expert input to the CILIP Task and Finish Group on information literacy with the Project director being invited to join the Task and Finish Group.

As with many information literacy initiatives and policies its direct impact on government was limited and it was most influential at nongovernmental organisation (NGO) level and with direct education providers. It also set standards which have subsequently been followed in other areas. Although firmly based in Scotland and reflecting Scottish educational and socially inclusive values it aimed to be recognised both UK wide and internationally. It received visitors from the United States, Finland and Australia and built up contacts with initiatives in other parts of the world, including the National Forum on Information Literacy in the United States. It directly inspired the Welsh Information Literacy Project and received respectful attention in the Republic of Ireland. Some of the many lessons learned from the Project are also known elsewhere but four stand out:

- Develop strategies and advocacy from existing policies including, education, skills development, employability and social inclusion policies. Do not restrict yourself to information policies.

- Form partnerships and collaborate with a wide range of agencies, especially NGOs. Do not work only with fellow information professionals.

- Offer support to practitioners. They can benefit from your support which they value and you can use the findings from their work to inform policy development.

- Advocate and lobby tirelessly, especially outside the information world.

Although the Project concluded in 2010 it was reborn in 2012 as an online, cross-sectoral, information literacy community of practice entitled *Information Skills for a 21st Century Scotland* (SLIC 2012) which is open to everyone who is interested in information literacy and associated skills and competencies, both within and outside the information profession, primarily in Scotland but also elsewhere. Its aims are:

- Developing core information literacy skills in further education.

- Assessing the impact of information literacy training.

- Advocacy for information literacy.

- Instructing teachers in information literacy.

- Information literacy as an employability skill.

- Information literacy toolkits for young people.

- Teaching information literacy skills in public libraries.

- Links between schools and public libraries.

- Use of electronic information literacy resources in public libraries.

- Online training packages in higher education.

- Workplace information literacy skills.

- Social media.

- Training materials for teachers.

The community of practice encourages reporting and discussion of new ideas and practices. It is hosted by the Scottish Library and Information Council (SLIC). The Framework will be developed and updated by incorporating new research, adding case studies, sharing good practice and reporting on relevant news, conferences and events. Although still in its early stages facilitators representing a range of library sectors have been recruited and have identified several areas of interest to be taken forward including work relating to young people and also in the further and higher education sectors (SLIC 2012).

## The Welsh Information Literacy Project

The Welsh Information Literacy Project was initiated at the Gregynog conference in Powys in November/December 2009 where one of the speakers was the Director of the Scottish Information Literacy Project. As the Project document notes 'This project builds upon the work that was done in the National Information Literacy Framework Scotland' (WILP 2010). As well as being inspired by the Scottish Information Literacy Project the Welsh Project was able to build on two projects in the lifelong learning/public sector which had important information literacy implications. The first of these, the ROUTES (Reaching Out Extending Skills) Project, had four local authority partners and ran from November 2002 to October 2004. It aimed to show how ICT-based access to lifelong learning could improve people's quality of life and support social inclusion, establish a network for exchanging experiences and identify critical success factors for sustainability. The second project, the Gateways to Learning Initiative (Gateways) was a two-year, £2 million project which aimed to widen participation in lifelong learning and make it more accessible, particularly to people in disadvantaged communities or circumstances. The Project's activities included offering both accredited and nonaccredited information literacy training. Although these projects gave the participants valuable experience of information literacy training delivered by public libraries, the finite nature of the projects naturally led to discontinuity in development and neither project covered the whole of Wales.

During its first phase the Welsh Information Literacy Project highlighted the 'political drivers' in Wales which information literacy directly supports. The agenda for the Welsh Government was set out in the *One Wales* document which outlines its vision of a prosperous, sustainable and better educated Wales. The document states:

'We will equip people with the skills they need, at all levels, to enable them to make the best possible contribution to the economy and their communities and to fulfil their individual potential.' (WAG 2007)

The document also envisages Wales as 'a society in which learning throughout life is the norm, where the people of Wales are actively engaged in acquiring new knowledge and skills and skills from childhood to old age'. For the Project this was a convenient 'peg' on which to hang information literacy (WILP 2010). Digital inclusion, which is discussed below, is supported by the Project from a social inclusion perspective. Individuals who are digitally included are better able to find work and purchase goods and services at lower prices. The Project rightly identifies a key role for public libraries in social inclusion. Public libraries are trusted in their local communities, and people in vulnerable groups are often happier developing digital skills in this environment. This develops the skills and confidence required for digital inclusion. The Project is unusual in recognising e-safety as an information literacy priority which is seen in the general context of information literacy as an evaluative strategy. It is both a priority for schools in safeguarding the welfare of children and for older adults who fear online hoaxes and frauds.

As with all such projects education policy is a key driver, and curriculum development in Wales recognises the importance of cross-curricular studies in supporting attainment across subject boundaries. The *Skills Framework for 3 to 19-Year-Olds* (WAG 2008), as is usually the case, does not explicitly recognise information literacy but it supports six key skills which can correlate to information literacy: communication, application of numbers, ICT, improving own learning and performance, working with others and problem solving. The Project highlighted that the learning outcomes for ICT, in particular, were in fact information literacy by another name, with many focused on information rather than technology (WILP 2011b: 8) Although independent learning is essential to the skills curriculum in practice, it is still insufficiently developed in Wales, a gap which information literacy could fill if school libraries are better integrated with the learning experience in Welsh schools.

The *Information Literacy Framework for Wales* (WILP 2011b) takes inspiration from the Scottish Framework model. It draws on pre-existing work such as the SCONUL Seven Pillars and is structured as a sequential continuum matching information literacy skill levels against the Credit and Qualifications Framework for Wales (CQFW). The 'laddered' Framework extends from Entry Level 1 to Level 8 Doctoral.

The Welsh Information Literacy Project liaised closely with the National Institute of Adult and Continuing Education and *Dysgu Cymru* (Learning Wales) during the creation of the Framework to ensure that the terminology used for the levels is appropriate to the CQFW. As a result of this partnership, the project was able to work with *Agored Cymru* (Open Wales), a CQFW awarding organisation, to create seven units of learning to accredit lifelong learning in information literacy. These units range from Entry Level 1 through to Level 4 – Certificate of Higher Education, HNC (Higher National Certificate) or first-year undergraduate level. They can be delivered by librarians or adult and community learning trainers and are designed to recognise the learning achieved in information literacy.

To support organisations in using the units, the *Information Literacy Handbook* (WILP 2011a) was put together by the Credit and Qualifications Framework for Wales, *Agored Cymru*, the National Institute of Adult and Continuing Education, *Dysgu Cymru* and WILP itself. It includes seven units of learning from Entry Level 1 to Level 4 (Certificate of Higher Education, HNC) and has been produced in conjunction with the Credit and Qualifications Framework for Wales. The *Handbook* contains guidance for trainers, details the learning units and offers assessment materials and sources of further information. As a form of learning and training material intended for use outside conventional education it sets an important new precedent.

Further information about the units, along with case studies explaining how they are being used, are available at *http:// library.wales.org/en/information-literacy/cqfw-units*

## Digital policy documents

While many relevant policy documents originate inside the profession, the growth of the digital environment is producing documents that are useful to information literacy but make little reference to the information profession. Since they address digital issues they inform digital information literacy which differs from the more general term, information literacy, only in the sense that it is restricted to the use of information in the digital environment. A good example is the UK government's *Digital Britain* (DCMS 2009) policy document which outlines the United Kingdom Government's strategic vision for ensuring that Britain not only has a leading role in the global digital economy but also addresses the issues of digital participation, copyright and Internet safety. It contains much of the rhetoric familiar in information policy and information literacy policy documents:

'The digital society offers us, as citizens, increased access to information, participation and influence, not least in the democratic process ...

The necessary education, skills and media literacy programmes to allow everyone in society to benefit from the digital revolution will be a central part of the Digital Britain work and key to our success. We must ensure that being digital is within the grasp of everyone.'

Among five objectives it outlines for a Digital Britain an important one is:

'Fairness and access for all: universal availability coupled with the skills and digital literacy to enable near-universal participation in the digital economy and digital society.'

It tackles the education and skills agenda these points raise by identifying three broad categories of skill:

- digital life skills – needed by all

- digital work skills – needed by most

- digital economy skills – needed by some.

The pervasive nature of digital skills is also recognised:

'The simple message at the core of this interim report is that we cannot afford to treat education and training for digital technologies as just another 'vertical' subject area. It underpins everything we do in the 21st Century.'

The report also recommends starting digital skills education and training at a very young age, something discussed in Chapter 4, and also the need for teachers themselves to be appropriately trained. This is a major issue from the information literacy point of view as school pupils are unlikely to be appropriately trained in information literacy if teachers themselves lack these skills. Internet safety, largely based on the Byron report, is also discussed (Byron, 2008). Unlike most information literacy policy documents the report has something to say about copyright issues, noting a need for '... education and information activity to educate consumers in fair and appropriate uses of copyrighted material as well as enforcement and prevention work', a timely reminder that intellectual property rights (IPR) issues have now moved far from the rarefied world of higher education to include matters of concern to the general public, like the production and sale of pirated CDs and DVDs and illegal downloading of copyrighted material from the Internet.

## The Chartered Institute of Library and Information Professionals (CILIP) and information literacy

CILIP is a relative newcomer to information literacy policy.

The *Report of the Digital Britain Media Literacy Working Group* (Ofcom 2009), itself supplementing the *Digital Britain* report (DCMS 2009), was an important document for CILIP. It describes three interdependent components of digital engagement:

(i) *Opportunity* – requires that no community of citizens is prevented from access. This is referred to as the digital inclusion agenda.

(ii) *Capability* – requires that citizens acquire and develop the digital skills needed for employment and beyond. This is digital life skills.

(iii) *Engagement* – the top of the media literacy pyramid, the use, understanding and ability to create digital media. This is digital media literacy.

This model comes with the acknowledgement that, for people in everyday life, these strands have no boundaries but represent different stages on an individual's digital journey.

When looked at in this way information literacy becomes more fluid and might not be able to be accommodated by any current library-driven framework or standard – for example, the new emphasis being given to what has been called 'social information literacy'. This broader definition promotes twenty-first century skills extending the definition of information literacy to reflect people's broader range of life information behaviour – for example, skills people might develop include staying in touch with their families, sharing, storing and organising photographs online or doing family history research.

Discussions around information literacy and its possible central role for CILIP were reinforced by the results of a large consultation exercise CILIP had with its members between April and June 2010 about the future of the organisation. The final report confirmed the view that information literacy was a growing aspect of its membership's working lives. If CILIP wished to be responsive to the needs of its members it needed an information literacy strategy.

In 2009 a Learning Round Table was convened to look at how CILIP should be advocating the principles set out in its Learning Statement which at that time was the 'home' of most of CILIP's pronouncements on information literacy. It was agreed that one of the areas in which CILIP needed to increase its work was in understanding the nature of information literacy and its importance not only to the learning agenda but also to what was then usually referred to as the information society, professionalism (promotion of information literacy as a key skill of library and information staff) and public health.

A turning point came in 2009 when the CILIP Policy Forum resolved that information literacy should be viewed as a policy priority area in itself, rather than specific (like information literacy in health or higher education). It was clear that if CILIP was to make a difference it had to be accepted as a stakeholder and key participant in information literacy across a range of issues. In digital policy documents, libraries are only cursorily mentioned – if at all – and the role of public libraries as a key training agency receives little attention. Information organisations in the United Kingdom seem to have little impact on digital policymaking.

An information literacy Task and Finish Group was set up to establish a strategy. It was seen as crucial that this group was representative of all sectors, and this was achieved. The Task and Finish Group drew up a draft information literacy strategy and this has been widely accepted by interested parties within the CILIP community.

In essence, CILIP's information literacy strategy seeks to promote fair and equitable access to quality information necessary to support people in making life choices. This will only be achieved if CILIP helps to develop an awareness of the value and importance of information literacy within government and all economic sectors – private, charitable and public.

In 2012 CILIP endorsed the Alexandria Proclamation on Information Literacy. This Proclamation was chosen due to its aspirational vision and its concern at the outset with social inclusion and lifelong learning. In affirming this vision CILIP set out a work programme for the following two years.

The key objectives of this work programme are:

- for CILIP to be seen as a key stakeholder and participant in information literacy across a range of issues;

- for CILIP to develop a suite of associated policies regarding information literacy;

- to integrate information literacy into key areas of CILIP activity.

To achieve these objectives CILIP has worked on a number of areas.

It hosted an Information Literacy Executive Briefing where some of CILIP's key stakeholders were invited to speak about their current projects and priorities. Throughout 2012 and continuing in 2013 CILIP has made timely press statements on information literacy issues, particularly in areas where CILIP has not previously been considered by external organisations as having an interest. CILIP has also commented on research circulated by its key stakeholders, in particular those concerned with digital inclusion issues.

CILIP has begun work on policy statements on e-safety and digital inclusion and has made sure that information literacy has been integrated into CILIP's new Body of Professional Knowledge and Skills. Relevant changes to CILIP's Code of Professional Conduct have also been made to reflect the importance of information literacy.

An Information Literacy and Your Work Survey was sent out to over 4000 of CILIP's members working in the UK in 2012 with the results anticipated in 2013. Future work could see CILIP providing some online information literacy learning modules for its members (May 2013).

## Summary of the chapter

It is clear that leadership from within the information profession both by professional bodies and groups of information professionals is crucial. Information professionals can propose definitions and broad policy outlines which others can recognise and follow, but it is equally the case that partnership with noninformation agencies which value information and understand the benefits it can bring is essential to making the case beyond the information profession. These include all agencies that have any involvement in skills development in virtually any form whether it be chambers of commerce, trades unions or adult literacy activists.

National information literacy programmes are a good way forward but they must be clearly linked to the social and educational policies of the state in which they are based and this link must be clear to political and community leaders. The social policies of most modern states are socially inclusive and it is important that information literacy is seen to have a role in the reduction of inequality and the reduction of social and educational disadvantage. Involvement in digital inclusion initiatives is both a useful activity in itself and can bring prestige to libraries and public libraries, in particular, which are well placed to take the lead.

National programmes are a good way of promoting an agenda which may take years to achieve, but the downside is that they cost money and are difficult to sustain in the long term. As the Welsh Project and digital literacy documents show, information literacy must embrace Internet safety issues and a 'popular' rather than scholarly IPR agenda.

Lastly, the issue of impact evaluation is much neglected. Projects or policy documents are often insufficiently tested in terms of practical measurable outcomes. This issue will be considered further in Chapter 9.

# 4

# Recognising information literacy as an early-years' issue

*Christine Irving*

**Abstract:** This chapter looks at an understudied area of information literacy and looks at why information literacy is important in a child's early years and its link to lifelong learning. It highlights the role of parents and suggests useful collaborative partnerships. It includes a Scottish case study of what early-years' information literacy looks like and exemplars of information and critical literacy activities for four, five and six-year-olds incorporated into active/independent learning in nursery and the early years of primary school. Examples from the rest of the UK and other countries are briefly looked at.

**Key words:** information literacy, early years, critical literacy, collaborative partnerships, parents, education and information professionals.

## The importance of information literacy in early years

Whilst traditionally much of the information literacy literature has been located in higher education there is a growing interest in information literacy and young people (Shenton and Hay-Gibson 2011; Rowlands et al. 2008; CIBER 2008) and in schools. Work being carried out in schools, particularly secondary schools, includes the growing number of transition initiatives with secondary school librarians working with primary school pupils on transition projects preparing them for their first year in secondary school (Irving 2009, 2010a). Little, however, is heard of work relating to the earlier years in nursery and primary schools. A nursery is a pre-school education institution which is part of early childhood education; in other countries like the US, Canada, and some parts of Australia the term 'kindergarten' is used.

Through its work on 'the link between secondary and tertiary education' (Crawford and Irving 2007) the Scottish Information Literacy Project (SILP) arrived at the conclusion that it was too late to teach/develop information literacy skills in higher education students. It needed to start much earlier in primary schools and continue throughout education into the world of work – in other words, it needed to be part of lifelong learning (Irving and Crawford 2006).

This view is supported by CILIP's (Chartered Institute of Library and Information Professionals) Information Literacy Group in their introduction to information literacy. 'In an era of lifelong learning, this effectively means that information literacy has relevance for all ages from *primary school* [author's emphasis] to senior citizens' (CILIP 2009). The need for information literacy training at a young age is a view also supported by the CIBER report and *Digital Britain* report (CIBER 2008, DCMS and BERR 2009).

## Information literacy and lifelong learning

Information literacy has been linked to the lifelong-learning agenda by many information literacy advocates including the *Prague Declaration: Towards an Information Literate Society* which states that:

> 'Information Literacy encompasses knowledge of one's information concerns and needs, and the ability to identify, locate, evaluate, organize and effectively create, use and communicate information to address issues or problems at hand; it is a prerequisite for participating effectively in the Information Society, and is part of the basic human right of lifelong learning' (UNESCO 2003).

Whilst lifelong learning would suggest cradle to the grave for all learning whether formal, informal or nonformal, the term is commonly used in relation to learning that takes place in post-16 education and adult education (Brookes 2006), particularly in relation to employability skills undertaken on a formal basis within educational institutions and learning centres. It is understandable therefore that the focus of lifelong learning is on employment as learning and education have traditionally been in preparation for the world of work. Brookes (2006: 39), however, points out that 'as the 21st century continues education should become a process through which people acquire the capacity to meet the challenges of living and working in an increasingly diverse world.' In other words we need to learn how to learn and be equipped with generic skills such as problem solving, critical thinking and evaluation so that we can deal with any new situation that arises.

We learn how to learn from a very early age/the minute we are born into the world. In the early years the learning comes from parents, siblings, other relatives and childminders plus professionals responsible for health and general well-being. It moves from informal to more formal environments within the education system from nursery to primary school. The importance of a child's early years' education is highlighted within the Scottish Government's skills strategy.

'Young people's education, from the early years of a child's life through their compulsory education, coincides with a period of rapid development and lays the foundations of skills for life and work. What they learn and how they learn have a major bearing on wider outcomes including employability and participation in society in later life.

Key elements in supporting positive development in the early years include:

o helping parents and carers to provide a nurturing and stimulating home environment;

o providing children with high quality pre-school and school education;

o helping parents with literacy and numeracy to enhance their ability to support their children's learning;

o achieving effective early interventions to improve outcomes for all children but particularly those who face particular disadvantage or a high risk of poor outcomes later in life; and

o supporting effective transitions between the stages of learning, including the transition from nursery to primary school.'

(Scottish Government 2007a: 14)

According to Education Scotland (n.d.) 'research informs us that during our earliest years and even pre-birth, a large part of the pattern for our future adult life is set; therefore we acknowledge that positive early years experiences give children the best start in life.'

One could therefore argue that a parent's level of information literacy could have an influence on a child's information literacy if it is incorporated as part of the child's early-years' learning. Christopher Walker's PhD 'The information world of parents', which focused on the everyday life information seeking of parents of young children in primary schools in Leeds, England (Walker 2009a, b; 2010, 2012), reports that his 'findings support the notion that a parent's own skills and education seem to have a direct effect on his/her information literacy (Childers & Post, 1975; Moore & Moschis, 1978: Niederdeppe, 2008)' (Walker 2012: 561). A parent helping her 'son search the Internet for local history for his school project' (Walker 2012: 552) is an example of such an effect.

## Early-years' information literacy

As highlighted earlier, little is heard of work relating to the earlier years in nursery and primary schools. In Scotland, school library services have been working with primary schools in efforts to link information literacy skills to the Scottish School Curriculum for some time; however, little has been written about them. The National Information Literacy Framework Scotland (NILFS 2009a) highlights case studies/ exemplars (NILFS 2009b) in this area including the City of Edinburgh *Information Literacy Model – ExPLORE* (NILFS 2009c), *North Ayrshire Information Literacy Toolkit – Primary Schools* (NILFS 2009d) and Aberdeenshire Library and Information Services SKIL website – *Aberdeenshire Schools Toolkit for Information Literacy* (NILFS 2009e). These were all based on the previous 5–14 Curriculum guidelines and are being relooked at in light of the current curriculum, the Curriculum for Excellence.

The link to the school curriculum is an important point and the Scottish Information Literacy Project (SILP) recognised this and advocated for official recognition for information literacy within education and influencing

Scottish Government policymaking. The project used the Scottish Parliament's petition system to address this issue strategically rather than approach individual agencies piecemeal. The petition 'called on the Scottish Parliament to urge the Scottish Executive [now the Scottish Government] to ensure that national school curriculum recognizes the importance of information literacy as a key lifelong learning skill' (Scottish Parliament 2005a, b).

The petition attracted a high number of signatures and the petitioners were granted the opportunity to deliver it in person making a short presentation and answering questions from the Petitions Committee. After listening to the evidence the committee decided to seek comments from a range of educational NGOs (nongovernment organisations). Based upon the responses the petition was closed with one MSP (Member of Scottish Parliament) committee member stating that:

'All the responses seem to support the petitioner. The responses from the Scottish Executive, Her Majesty's Inspectorate of Education, the Educational Institute of Scotland and the Scottish Qualifications Authority in particular clearly support "A Curriculum for Excellence" as the way forward. The petitioner has therefore been pushing at an open door and no further action on the petition is needed.' (Scottish Parliament 2006)

The favourable responses were useful for further advocacy work and the mention of the curriculum as 'the way forward' supported the project's ongoing advocacy work with the Curriculum Review Team in their work to create a 'A Curriculum for Excellence' (CfE) for Scotland.

One of the early information literacy success stories of the new curriculum was the recognition of information literacy by the Curriculum for Excellence Literacy Team and the development of a resource by one of the Team's Literacy Development Officers, Louise Ballantyne, a Primary 7 teacher on secondment to the Literacy Team. It was aimed at the upper primary/early secondary stages (11 to 12/13-year-olds) and reflected the purposes and principles of the Curriculum for Excellence as well as linking with specific literacy for all (Education Scotland 2009a) and literacy and English (Education Scotland 2009b) experiences and outcomes. The resource was informed by the draft National Information Literacy Framework (NILFS 2007) and activities/ input from West Lothian school librarians. It was presented at the Scottish Learning Festival in 2008 as *Real and Relevant – Information Literacy Skills for the 21st Century Learner* (Ballantyne 2008).

As a result of this work and a developing relationship with the Curriculum for Excellence Literacy Team the opportunity to work with the Literacy Team on extending the above resource (in draft at that time) to other levels of the new curriculum were explored along with the recognition of the need for CPD (continuing professional development) in this challenging area for teachers. The resulting outcome was funding to create a quality CPD Information Literacy toolkit/ resource pack whose target audience would be early-years' teachers and professionals of children in Primary 1 and 2 (five and six-year-olds). Innovative work being carried out in nurseries was incorporated during the life of the project.

This work makes a useful case study of what early-years' information literacy can look like and provides exemplars of information and critical literacy activities for four, five and six-year-olds incorporated into active/independent learning in nursery and the early years of primary school.

# Scottish case study: real and relevant – information and critical literacy skills for the twenty-first century learner (early and first level)

The Early Years (Primary 1–2) CPD Information Literacy toolkit/resource pack aim was to provide:

- background information about information literacy

- learning and teaching approaches

- supporting resources and case studies/exemplars of good practice.

The project firstly identified the information and critical literacy experiences and outcomes in the early and first level stages (Irving 2010b). Boxes 4.1 and 4.2 give examples of literacy across learning outcomes.

---

**Box 4.1   Information and critical literacy – early level: pre-school years & P1**

I listen or watch for useful or interesting information and I use this to make choices or learn new things. *LIT 0-04a*

I use signs, books or other texts to find useful or interesting information and I use this to plan, make choices or learn new things. *LIT 0-14a*

As I play and learn, I enjoy exploring interesting materials for writing and different ways of recording my experiences and feelings, ideas and information. *LIT 0-21b*

To help me understand stories and other texts, I ask questions and link what I am learning with what I already know. *LIT 0-07a/ LIT 0-16a/ENG 0-17a*

I enjoy exploring and choosing stories and other texts to watch, read or listen to, and can share my likes and dislikes. *LIT 0-19a*

---

---

**Box 4.2   Information and critical literacy – first level: P2 to end of P4**

As I listen or watch, I can identify and discuss the purpose, key words and main ideas of the text, and use this information for a specific purpose. *LIT 1-04a*

As I listen or watch, I am learning to make notes under given headings and use these to understand what I have listened to or watched and create new texts. *LIT 1-05a*

I can select ideas and relevant information, organise these in a logical sequence and use words which will be interesting and/or useful for others. *LIT 1-06a*

To help me develop an informed view, I am learning to recognise the difference between fact and opinion. *LIT 1-08a*

Using what I know about the features of different types of texts, I can find, select, sort and use information for a specific purpose. *LIT 1-14a*

To show my understanding across different areas of learning, I can identify and consider the purpose and main ideas of a text. *LIT 1-16a*

---

It is important to note that information encompasses a wide range of formats. The Curriculum for Excellence provides a useful all-encompassing definition

*'a text is the medium through which ideas, experiences, opinions and information can be communicated.*

Reading and responding to literature and other texts play a central role in the development of learners' knowledge and understanding. Texts not only include those presented in traditional written or print form, but also orally, electronically or on film. Texts can be in continuous form, including traditional formal prose, or non-continuous, for example charts and graphs. The literacy framework reflects the increased use of multimodal texts, social networking, digital communication and the other forms of electronic communication encountered by children and young people in their daily lives. It recognises that the skills which children and young people need to learn to read these texts differ from the skills they need for reading continuous prose.' (Education Scotland 2009c: 4).

Exemplars of information and critical literacy activities in early and first level classrooms were then sourced producing some interesting results – see Boxes 4.3, 4.4, 4.5 and 4.6.

---

### Box 4.3   Nursery

*Questioning – Kilmacolm Nursery's innovative Blooming Blooms approach*

*www.therightinformation.org/framework-blog-home/2012/6/1/ questioning-kilmacolms-innovative-blooming-blooms- approach.html*

*www.therightinformation.org/temp-exemp-kilmacolm*

Children (four-year-olds) and parents are introduced to the benefits of questioning. Questions were based on Bloom's Taxonomy linked to familiar fairytales such as *Jack and the Beanstalk, Goldilocks and the Three Bears*, etc. and produced in conjunction with a group of parents. The books and questions are used both in the nursery and at home.

---

## Box 4.4   Junior/Primary 1 (5-year-olds)

*Information literacy in Junior (Primary) 1 –*
St Margaret's School, Edinburgh

*www.therightinformation.org/silp-blog/2009/12/17/information-
literacy-in-primary-1.html*

### Finding and using information: early level

I listen or watch for useful or interesting information and I use this to make choices to learn new things. *LIT 0.04a*

1. children (five-year-olds) had to listen for a specific piece of information from a story being read to them, remember it and use it later

2. select books in groups to find information about a particular night animal that the group had chosen (i.e., a fox, badger, bat).

## Box 4.5   Critical literacy @ Lasswade Primary School

*www.therightinformation.org/temp-exemp-lasswade*

*www.therightinformation.org/framework-blog-home/2012/6/1/
critical-literacy-lasswade-primary-school.html*

The school formed a working group to plan and implement critical literacy. For early years this includes looking at pictures for clues and forming opinions of characters in stories. For example Primary 1 are using *Goldilocks and the Three Bears* to look at the text from different points of view – What would you do? Using role play and looking at moral issues. What would they (the children) have done in her (Goldilocks) shoes: Goldilocks went into a house that she didn't know – would you? She sat in chairs which broke, etc.

---

**Box 4.6   Junior/Primary 2 (six-year-olds)**

*Information literacy in Junior (Primary) 2 –*
St Margaret's School, Edinburgh

*www.therightinformation.org/framework-blog-home/2012/6/1/
information-literacy-in-junior-primary-2.html*

*Research and evaluation* – by investigating the range of foods available I can discuss how they contribute to a healthy diet. *HWB 1-30a*

*Evaluation exercise* – working in pairs the children had to carry out an 'evaluation of their piccalilli monster' discussing and using an evaluation form that had three questions on it – what they liked best about the project, the part of the body they liked best and why and if they could change their monster would they and why?

*Research activity* – facts about our topic – working in pairs the children research a topic (fruit, vegetables, bread, dairy products) finding interesting facts about their topic using a selection of books from the school library that the teacher had picked and displayed in her classroom.

---

Some interesting observations arose out of the project.

The teachers welcomed another professional's knowledge and understanding of the skills involved in these activities as well as sharing useful tips and techniques such as creating effective search strategies.

The copying of text in a Junior 2 class by a six-year-old child as part of her information gathering for the research activity (Box 4.6) raised the question: 'Is this where copying starts?' In learning to write we copy text unless instructed not to or shown a way to make notes (included in the Curriculum for Excellence). One teacher's solution to avoid copying text from books is:

1. children pose question

2. highlight bullet points

3. close books

4. use bullet points and put information into their own words.

In information literacy terms this is part of forming your research question and identifying key words and a search strategy. The important point is it involves critical thinking and learning strategies/techniques and whatever information you are looking for and whatever age or stage in life you are at school, college, university or work.

Active learning is a wonderful thing to see but it is labour intensive and it is not realistic for a single teacher (educator) to be able to interact all the time with all the individual pupils or pairs in their class. The exercises/learning worked best when there was an interaction between the children and the teacher or on one or two occasions with the researcher (the chapter author Christine Irving) interacting with the children questioning and encouraging their thinking.

Observations of children using computers in nursery and Primary 1 highlighted that, whilst children looked engaged with on-screen activities, on closer inspection many but not all were just pressing buttons. They did not seem to be aware of what they were supposed to be doing. Whilst this may be circumstantial, it raises the question of the benefits of young children interacting with computers without input from teachers, nursery nurses and other early-years' practitioners.

Getting the school/teachers involved in the Critical Literacy initiative (Box 4.5) is the result of a local authority (Midlothian) one-day training for their staff (Primary and Secondary school teachers and librarians – although it is not known whether any librarians actually attended) as part of their CPD. The one-day training was developed and facilitated by the University of Edinburgh. CPD training for information literacy would be a great step forward as would be information literacy included as part of teacher training. Tentative steps have been taken in both these areas by information literacy activities within Scotland including the Real and Relevant projects, specifically the Early Years CPD Toolkit (Irving 2010b).

Discussions with universities regarding teacher training is a recurring issue which hopefully will bear fruit one day.

An important resource that teachers may not have used or thought of are local authority Education Resource Services or Library and Information Services such as Early Years and Young People's Librarian, Primary School Librarian, or Information Literacy Officer:

'The nature of school library resource centre provision varies across Scotland, depending on the local authority; however, libraries are part of a wider resource-sharing, information and support network. In addition to book collections and libraries in educational establishments, there are 554 community libraries and 81 mobile libraries, some of which make visits direct to primary schools.' (SLIC 2009: 2).

As stated above librarians and libraries are not just about books, they also offer/provide other services, professional advice, and some have educational tools and artefacts. In Scotland they are involved in Curriculum for Excellence activities (Irving 2010a); and their contribution is highlighted within the *Principles and Practice: Literacy across Learning* paper:

'It is expected that the literacy experiences and outcomes and this accompanying paper [principles and practice], will be read by a range of practitioners, including those who work in school library resource centres, who make an enormous contribution to the literacy skills of children and young people.' (Education Scotland 2009c: 2).

They support, engage and work with:

- teachers on a wide range of curriculum and information literacy activities, subject specific or class wide; cross curricular and or on school-wide projects; transition projects – developing transition links between primary and secondary schools;

- school activities through school committees such as literacy teams, training and in-service opportunities, promoting a whole-school approach and developing transition links between secondary and primary schools.

They use their professional chartered skills and competencies to the benefit of teachers, pupils and schools.

The above work begs the question: 'Is this work unique to Scotland or is it happening elsewhere?' Before we look at work that is taking place elsewhere it is worth noting that there are several factors that need to be taken into consideration. The first is a country's education system and curriculum as this plays a major role in what happens in schools.

Most countries have their own education systems and curriculum or they are based on another country which used to have ruling power over them (e.g., Britain and Hong Kong).

With regard to the UK education system (this does not apply to Scotland as Scotland has its own education system) Beautyman (2012a: 47) notes that the:

'UK Government acknowledges that children need to be able to use information and the Curriculum website states the importance that "Children have the skills to learn effectively. They can plan, research and critically evaluate, using reasoned arguments to support conclusions" (The National Curriculum Primary Handbook 2010: 15) [DfEE and QCA 2010] ... yet nowhere within the National Curriculum Primary Handbook are the terms "information literacy" or critical thinking" used. Instead the emphasis for developing information literacy skills appears to have become entwined with the need for children to be proficient users of technology.'

She then compares it with America, highlighting that whilst the

'structure of educational legislation may be similar between the UK and America, there is one key difference between the two. The American Government acknowledge the importance of developing information literacy and critical thinking skills and explicitly state that the need to acquire and use advanced technology, incorporated into the curricula of the school, to develop and enhance the information literacy, information retrieval, and critical thinking skills of students.' (Beautyman (2012a)

# Examples from the rest of the UK and other countries

## UK examples

Whilst there may be some wonderful innovative information literacy work being carried out in schools around the UK one seldom gets to hear about them as, unfortunately, there is relatively little literature describing actual examples of information literacy in schools and a dearth of literature on early years (primary schools and nursery).

In 2009 a request on LIS-INFOLITERACY@JISCMAIL. AC.UK for information literacy projects in primary schools received only one response, and that was from John Crawford (Boekhorst 2009) about the work of the Scottish Information Literacy project (including the case study covered within this chapter). In 2011 a review of the literature of the evolution of information skills and information literacy and associated research in UK schools over the past 30 years was carried out (Streatfield et al. 2011). Included in the review was a small study of library-based information literacy work in primary schools in England, conducted by Streatfield to find out more about whether and how primary schools use their libraries when seeking to develop the information skills of children. The review reported that:

'UK primary schools have seldom been able to afford to employ a dedicated school librarian (although a few have entered into sharing arrangements, usually brokered by schools library services, which involve a professionally qualified librarian sharing time across several schools). Partly as a result of this dearth of specialist librarians there has been relatively little attention paid to systematic IL development in primary schools.' (Streatfield et al. 2011: 9)

Despite the above inhibitors there are other influences such as self-efficacy – a belief in yourself and that your actions will make a difference (Bandura 2010) linked to motivation and opportunity (the opportunity can either arise or be created) plus collaborative working (which we will come back to later in the chapter) that lead people on to do some amazing work which contributes to our knowledge and understanding.

Below are a couple of examples of such work.

## The road to information literacy: primary school children and their information-seeking behaviour

Beautyman (2012a, b) for her doctoral research study investigated the way in which Key Stage 2 children (7 to 11-year-olds) are taught to look for information. The study examined how children in a state-run primary school in North East England were taught to develop information-seeking strategies that would allow them to become lifelong literate users of information.

During the autumn term, the children were observed studying history (the Tudors). The spring term was geography (investigating the Island of St Lucia) and in the summer term the children studied the Aztecs.

To demonstrate 'the process that the children went through on their journey towards information literacy' Beautyman created what she calls a rich picture which 'acts to explain the influences that helped shape the journey' that happened over the academic school year (see Figure 4.1). The journey starts with the teacher defining the information need, using WALT (what I am learning today) and WILF (what I am looking for) to prepare the children for the information they will be looking for. At the end of the lesson the teacher again uses WALT and WILF 'in order to both consolidate what they have learned in the lesson and also to raise any questions they might have about what they have learned' (Beautyman 2012a: 104).

Beautyman explains that as the children progress through the academic year, they were

'introduced to information seeking strategies and shown how different resources could be utilised in order to gather information. The younger children were taught how to gather information from different resources at a basic level, whereas the older children were expected to adopt a higher level of information seeking behaviour, building on skills that they

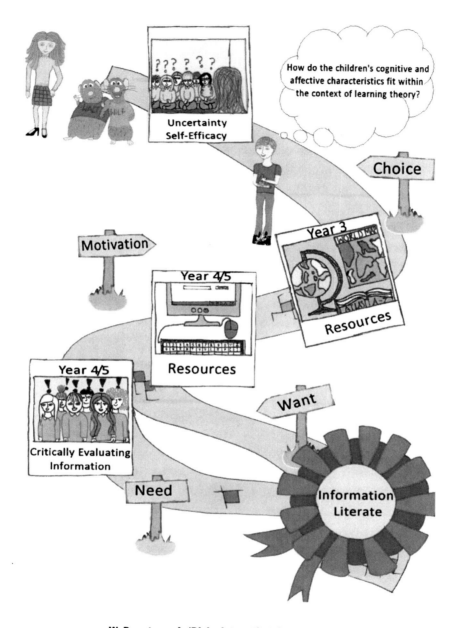

**Figure 4.1** W. Beautyman's 'Rich picture that demonstrates the information seeking journey undertaken by the children towards becoming information literate (illustration by Kirsti Beautyman, 2009).'

would have learned when they were in year 3. This helped to establish the level of teaching of information strategies to the children . . . The year 4/5 children were also taught how to critically evaluate information as well as how to store and retrieve information. The final step on the journey is depicted as being that of information literacy, as the children progressed through the previously identified stages, they were gathering skills and strategies that they could develop and build upon.' (Beautyman 2012a: 104–5).

Emerging from the study are accelerators and inhibitors: uncertainty and self-efficacy; motivation; choice; need and want. These are included in the rich picture, as they were seen to influence the information-seeking behaviour of the children. Whilst the rich picture is shown as a linear progression in reality, as with most information literacy models or frameworks, it was not a linear progression.

As part of the research, Beautyman looked at learning theory and styles and went on to develop 'A Model of Cognitive and Affective Influences on Children's Information Seeking Behaviour Including the Theoretical Zone of Optimal Learning' (see Figure 4.2). She explains it as 'a model of the cognitive and affective influences to information seeking behaviour demonstrated by the children' and that 'it is at the point where the child begins to tentatively search for information that they enter the zone of optimal learning.' Moreover, by 'investigating the model, it will be possible to demonstrate how uncertainty, self-efficacy, motivation, choice, need and want all play a part in not only the children's information seeking behaviour but also their cognitive development of information.' (Beautyman 2012a: 208)

Beautyman highlights that the UK Governments 'appear to attach very little importance to information literacy skills at primary school level' (Beautyman 2012a: 235) and that 'it is

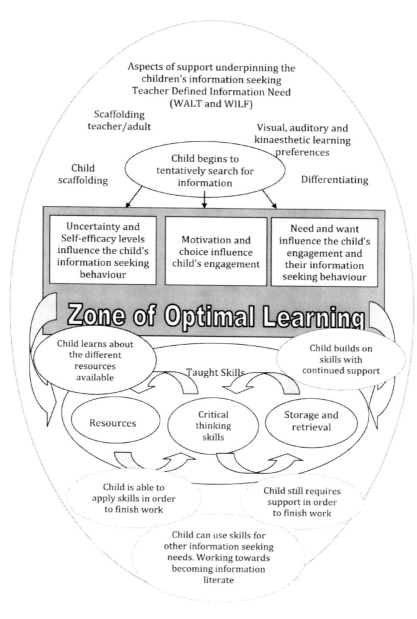

Figure 4.2 **Beautyman's Model of Cognitive and Affective Influences on Children's Information Seeking Behaviour Including the Theoretical Zone of Optimal Learning**

not possible to locate this term [information literacy] on any curriculum website' (Beautyman 2012a: 47). The research study highlights 'some areas of strength and weaknesses in the teaching of information seeking strategies to Key Stage 2 children' (Beautyman 2012a: 235). Four guidelines for promoting information-seeking strategies are offered:

1. As far as is possible, children should be encouraged to define their own information need.

2. Information-seeking skills and strategies should be embedded within topics

3. Children need to be taught to develop their critical thinking skills

4. Understanding should be demonstrated contextually.

(Beautyman 2012a: 235, 2012b)

As she says, 'providing children with information seeking skills both on a physical and intellectual level seems to be a huge mountain to climb but by taking it step-by-step, it is not only possible but necessary if the education system is to produce critical lifelong learners.' (Beautyman 2012a: 237)

## Education outreach project in Wrexham

In Wales the National Library of Wales' Education Service is delivering a programme. As part of the project, one secondary school and nine primary schools in Wrexham gained first-hand experience of the kinds of resources available at the National Library of Wales and 'how to access, search for and acquire this information, and how to evaluate, use and refer to it. Working with over 500 school pupils in Key Stages 2 and 3 (Key Stage 2 is ages seven to eleven and Key Stage 3 is ages eleven to fourteen), the project delivered 18 two-hour workshops covering topics such as research activities, presenting information, interpreting sources, placing items within timelines, and communicating results to peers' (Library Wales 2009).

## Examples from other countries

A review of recently published information literacy activities in schools around the world predominately produced articles relating to secondary schools rather than primary schools, a situation similar to the UK. The reported secondary school activities were based in Pakistan (Batool and Mahmood 2012), Singapore (Chang et al. 2012) and Malaysia (Tan et al. 2012). Primary school activities were based in Sweden (Lundh and Alexandersson 2012) and Hong Kong (Chu 2012). A brief outline of each of the primary school articles/activities is outlined below.

### Collecting and compiling: the activity of seeking pictures in primary school

In Sweden, Lundh and Alexandersson's study aimed to gain further understanding of the activity of children seeking pictures in primary schools. Video recordings from an ethnographic study of primary school children working with problem-centred assignments were analysed and revealed

'how the activity of seeking pictures is shaped by the assumption that pictures are different from facts and information; pictures are seen primarily as having decorative functions. The activity is also characterised by playful, yet efficient cooperation between the children; they make the activity meaningful by transforming it into a play and game activity where pictures become important as physical objects, but not as a semiotic means of learning.

The study is limited to the activity of seeking pictures in a specific primary school; however, it shows how modes other than textual modes can be included in the study of information activities.' (Lundh and Alexandersson 2012)

They highlight that 'research on information seeking and information literacies rarely focus on multimodal aspects of information activities or the seeking of pictures outside special collections, despite the increased significance of visual material in the contemporary media landscape' (Lundh and Alexandersson 2012).

## Assessing Information Literacy: A Case Study of Primary 5 Students in Hong Kong

In Hong Kong, Chu (2012: 1) reports on an 'exploratory investigation of the information-literacy levels of Primary 5 students in Hong Kong (aged about eight years old). Factors such as gender and reading ability were also examined. Primary 5 students from four local schools completed a fourteen-item information-literacy assessment.' In Hong Kong the government has 'recognized the growing importance of IL [information literacy]. A framework for IL education at primary and secondary levels has been drawn up and circulated as the *Information Literacy Framework for Hong Kong Students: Building the Capacity of Learning to Learn in the Information Age*' (Chu 2012: 2). The education structure in Hong Kong was 'established during colonial rule, and mirrors that of the United Kingdom. Students attend three optional years of Kindergarten (usually starting at age three), six years of primary school (grades P.1–P.6) (HKHE 2013). The study results imply 'an association between student's IL and reading-comprehension ability' and two variables which 'may have a reinforcing effect on each other. Better language ability can help students extract and process information more effectively, and higher IL levels allow students to access better sources' (Chu 2012: 15). On the gender front, the study showed that female students generally scored higher on the assessment than the males. It is a small but interesting study providing additional insight into this little-studied area of information literacy.

Although the above activities are taking place in countries not traditionally reported as engaging in information literacy activities, this reflects the 'growing awareness of the importance of IL education, recent research has been conducted in many other countries, representing a global IL perspective and awareness' (Johnson et al. 2010 cited in Chu 2012: 4).

Perhaps the seeds of international declarations such as the *Prague Declaration* (UNESCO 2003) and the *Alexandria Colloquium* (Garner 2005), the work of IL activists including UNESCO and the International Federation of Library Associations and Institutions (IFLA) is producing fruit.

In the UK the School Library Association is playing a role in the development of publications and documents. Publications such as *Cultivating Curiosity Information Literacy Skills and the Primary School Library* (Dubber 2008a) and *A Primary School Information Skills Toolkit* (Dubber 2008b). Documents such as the 'School Library Manifesto, a framework document that laid the foundations for defining the role of school libraries in IL education' which suggested that 'when librarians and teachers work together, students achieve higher levels of literacy, reading, learning, problem-solving and information and communication technology skills.' (Chu 2012: 4)

# Collaborative partnerships and information literacy opportunities

You can achieve so much more working collaboratively and a network of contacts can often help individuals to gain access to people within organisations who are otherwise difficult to identify or reach. Partners can also help identify issues and provide a body of evidence (Irving 2012: 51). The Scottish case study outlined in this chapter could not have been achieved without networking and working collaboratively with the CfE Literacy Team and the teachers in each of the schools. The same will have applied to the other activities mentioned in this chapter.

Information literacy opportunities and activities are usually not labelled as information literacy nor involve librarians, but could offer librarians collaborative partnership opportunities. They therefore have to be sought out or created in collaboration with other professionals within education, other LIS (Library Information Services) professionals working in other sectors and then shared.

It is interesting to see how work in this area has evolved from early information literacy activists in schools – for example, research carried out by Williams and Wavell (2007) into 'Secondary school teachers' conceptions of student information literacy' which is still cited today. Moreover, Herring's (n.d.) *PLUS Model* is still used today and his 1996 book *Teaching Information Skills in Schools* (Herring 1996) has recently been translated into Japanese (Herring 2012).

## Summary of the chapter

Experience and reports are showing that leaving information literacy until university is too late. With declarations and proclamations linking information literacy to lifelong learning it enables opportunities for information literacy to be introduced at the start of the learning process in the early years of a child's education development. Children's earlyyears are key to their development and start with parents, siblings, family and professionals engaged in their health and development. The case study and examples of what is happening in the UK and other countries show that more information literacy research and development work in children's early-years' education is slowly becoming visible, these include information literacy skills, competencies, activities and standards at primary and secondary school level education and even in the nursery.

We are also seeing information literacy work emerging in countries other than the UK, America, Australia and New Zealand, which is encouraging, possibly as a result of work by organisations like UNESCO and IFLA working on an international basis and bodies like School Library Associations working on a national basis but having an international influence.

Work in this area has shown that there are opportunities to work with teachers and the education profession. They do not however come labelled as information literacy and we need to seek them out in the world of education and early-years' education as they are part of the learning and teaching activities that are happening in schools and nurseries. They are strongly linked to learning and teaching and require all those engaged in this area to be aware of education legislation, the curriculum, how information to a child is multimodal and far richer than the written word associated with traditional information literacy. For early years, information comes in the shape of pictures, what they see, listen to and hear. Once children learn to read then, as we have seen, there is a link to their information literacy ability.

Key to work in this area is influencing education legislation and curriculums and more collaborative partnership working with other professionals in education. Finally, work in this area needs to be shared more often, reported at conferences and written about so that knowledge and understanding in this area increases and develops.

# Part 2
# Specific areas

# 5

# The challenge of
# the work environment

*John Crawford*

**Abstract:** This chapter discusses a relatively underreported area, information literacy activity in the workplace with a strong social and collaborative element, compared with the higher education environment with its reliance on standardised print and online resources. After reviewing the literature of workplace learning the chapter discusses skills development and employability in relation to information literacy and the role of higher education. How information literacy should be redefined for the workplace environment is analysed and the problems of information usage in the workplace are considered. Examples of training materials are discussed but there is a dearth of such sources.

**Key words:** information literacy, workplace learning, training, skills development, employability, workplace information literacy.

This chapter reviews information usage in the workplace. This is an underreported area, compared with the numerous studies which are available on information literacy teaching and research in higher education, and much of the research which has been undertaken has been done by academics who comment on each others' work thus introducing an element of circularity into the process. The voice of the workplace information user is little heard. It raises both theoretical and practical questions about what information literacy means in the workplace as opposed to traditional higher education interpretations.

Generally, in this sector there have been two approaches to workplace information literacy research. The first approach parallels the education sector's understanding of information literacy as a skills-based literacy where information literacy is seen in terms of the individual achieving competence and appropriate behaviours in the development and execution of information skills. The second more recent approach adopts a sociological perspective which aims to theorise information literacy in a broader setting by exploring how the setting and its participants influence the development of information literacy practices and the outcomes which are produced (Lloyd 2010: 72).

As a key commentator on workplace information literacy studies Annemaree Lloyd has noted:

'Information literacy is trapped between a rock and a hard place. The rock being the current conceptions of information literacy that represent information literacy as a skill or competency that is confined to information access and use, and, associated with tools such as text or technology. The hard place refers to attempts to translate this conception from the formal learning regimes of education and academic libraries to other sectors where it is less structured or systematized but is just as important (i.e. workplaces).' (Lloyd 2011: 279)

## The rediscovery of the workplace

Interest in learning in the workplace dates from the mid-1980s to early 1990s when the idea that the 'academy' was the only

place where learning could take place began to be challenged. In this process reflective practice (defined below) is crucial.
According to Boud et al. (1985 :19)

'Reflection is an important human activity in which people recapture their experience, think about it, mull it over and evaluate it. It is this working with experience that is important in learning.'

This idea has been developed by Lave and Wenger (2002) who emphasise the social dimension of learning which goes beyond the formal curriculum. They argue that, in a community of practice, the curriculum is the daily round of tasks that has to be undertaken to sustain the community. Learning is embedded in the community and the possibility of knowledge transfer either inwards or outwards is marginalised. This highly situated view of learning in the workplace has led to the observation that communities can be cradles or cages.

Eraut et al. (2002), in investigating examples of formal learning, found them highly situated and dependent on social relationships within the workplace. Although the authors admitted that people do learn from formal sources they also learn from other people, their peers and holders of specialist knowledge. However, Eraut's examples point to the pace of change in patterns of employment, and therefore question the meaning of communities of practice over short time spans. Eraut also notes that individuals may be members of a number of communities of practice at one time. This means that knowledge, acquired in one context, can be resituated in a new context and then integrated with new knowledge acquired in this new situation. This challenges the concept of absolute situatedness as resituation suggests that learners identify general principles in one context which can be used in another.

Eraut (2000: 113–36) also argues against regarding knowledge as solely individual in nature. He argues that, in some situations, individual knowledge is necessary but not sufficient, and workers are not able to perform on their own. Second, knowledge is shaped by context, is embedded in a situation which comprises a location, a set of activities and a set of social relations in which these activities are placed. In summary, Eraut argues against the 'simplistic' concept of situated learning which ignores the influence of different learning histories that learners bring with them and fails to recognise the different types of learning that take place in different situations. Eraut suggests that we need to look at the situation itself and the contributions of the learning careers of individual participants.

Here we have two opposed views. Eraut proposes a model composed of a combination of the individual's prior knowledge and experience and the social dimension of a situation in which the process is embedded. Lave and Wenger, however, take a static view of the community of practice.

A third view is proposed by Guile and Young (2002) who question the traditional assumption that learning at work is radically different from learning in the classroom. Due to the knowledge-intensive nature of work and numerous changes in commerce and industry, employers require their workers to acquire more and more formal types of knowledge. They emphasise the importance of transferability and skills between organisational contexts. People must learn to develop an ability to 'think beyond the immediate situation they find themselves in'.

Siebert et al. (2009) considered, via a qualitative study, their work-based learning programme in a university in the light of current pedagogic theory. They found that 'prepositional knowledge', provided by the University, allows students to challenge professional practice, and that work-based learners learn both from their community of practice in the workplace and their communities of practice as work-based learning students.

Clearly, for the information literacy specialist there are major challenges here. Lave and Wenger and Eraut all see learning in the workplace as a form of social interaction, although Eraut at least is prepared to accept a wider range of influences than Lave and Wenger. The views of Guile and Young and Siebert et al. who see workplace learning as being more similar to traditional learning are more reassuring.

What role do the pedagogic theorists attribute to information? Gerber (1998) identifies no fewer than 11 ways to learn in the workplace:

1. 'by making mistakes and learning not to repeat the mistake

2. through self-education on and off the job*

3. through practising one's personal values

4. by applying theory and practising skills*

5. through solving problems*

6. through interacting with others

7. through open lateral planning

8. by being an advocate for colleagues

9. through offering leadership to others

10. through formal training*

11. through practising quality assurance*'

Ways 2, 4, 5, 10 and perhaps 11 (marked by *) seem to have some link to information literacy but the emphasis is very much on activity.

Felstead et al. (2005) in a survey exercise reaffirmed the view that workplace learning is a form of social interaction. The survey results showed the relatively high importance of social relationships and mutual support in helping individuals to improve performance compared with the relatively low importance attached to qualifications and attendance on courses. Learning was found to be something which arises naturally out of the demands and challenges of everyday work experience. It is not 'something that requires time out from being engaged in productive activity.' Felstead uses two metaphors: learning as acquisition (i.e., qualifications and training) which is still in the ascendancy; the second is learning by participation (i.e., social learning). The latter has three components: the crucial role of action on learning, the impermanence of learning outcomes in the absence of regular practice and the fact that learning is borne out of the interaction with the world in which we reside. In designing their methodology Felstead et al. noted that less formal methods of instruction tend to be underreported (e.g., reading a book or manual). They also noted that respondents took a narrow view of the meaning of training and that 'teaching yourself' (books, manuals, etc.) is an important, if underestimated, mode of training. The data were collected in two components: learning as acquisition ('filling the human mind with materials') and the more socially interactive process of learning as participation with information use located more in the former. Use of the Internet was viewed as no help at all by almost half the sample while over half found that simply doing the job helped them learn most about how to improve. However, while only 10.6 per cent of respondents saw the Internet as a 'great deal of help' in improving job performance, 21.4 per cent thought that reading 'books, manuals and work related magazines' was 'a great deal of help'.

There was a definite hierarchy of responses, with those at managerial, professional and 'associated technical' levels attaching the highest importance to learning by acquisition including the Internet, books, etc. Operative and 'elementary' levels of staff valued work-centred learning more highly than outside activities. It would seem that higher levels of staff will find information literacy, as it is traditionally interpreted, more appealing. The appeal to the professional is also noteworthy.

Eraut (2007: 6–19) recognises within his framework of activities, Learning Trajectories (stage 1) and places 'Using knowledge resources' including paper based and electronic within the subcategory Academic Knowledge and Skills, categorising it away from communal activities.

A Teaching and Learning Research Programme (TLRP) report (Brown 2009) takes the issue a little further. There are references to 'problem solving', 'getting information', 'locating key resource people', 'accessing relevant knowledge and experience', 'using knowledge resources' and 'using knowledge resources (human, paper based, electronic)'. This seems to be as near as the report gets to information literacy. Terminology suggestive of knowledge management, 'use of knowledge previously created by others' and 'use of tools and knowledge embedded in the work environment' also appear but again it is not specifically referred to.

Irving (2006, 2007a, b) in an interview-based pilot study found that, although generally employers are not explicitly looking for information literacy skills and competencies by name, they are assuming that employees will come with these skills – particularly for professional positions – and that people generally think they have the skills and competencies they need for their information-related activities.

Given that these skills and competencies are considered to be important in the workplace, an individual's prior learning or lack of learning of information literacy skills and competencies is of paramount importance both to the individual and their employer. It is important therefore to dispel the assumptions that everyone has these skills and competencies at a level that they need, that they are explicitly and uniformly taught within education or are learned in conjunction with ICT or by osmosis.

It is also worth noting that the pedagogic philosophy seems a little strange to the information specialist. There is little if any discussion about the purpose and function of knowledge generated in the workplace. It is viewed, if at all, as a sort of abstract 'good' rather like knowledge generated in academia. Knowledge is generated in the workplace to support the work of the organisation. It may well be intended to support competition, not cooperation. The idea of competition is well understood by workplace employees. Crawford (2006a) found that information literacy was viewed by workplace respondents as a tool to facilitate competition between staff and support them in the battle for promotion. It was not viewed as a cooperative tool. The pedagogic model also seems to be fixated on the large organisation with staff development and training programmes and appraisal procedures. It ignores the small to medium-sized enterprise (SME) and the nature of the learning that goes on there which is relatively little understood. There is also no link with the Adult Literacies agenda which is closely related to workplace training. This is discussed in Chapter 8.

Workplace learning theorists therefore have something to contribute. They see workplace learning as a form of social interaction but disagree as to whether workplace learning is exclusively workplace situated or not. As we shall see, information literacy research informs both points of view. They recognise the importance of the level at which staff function and the importance of academic and professional qualifications but they are less concerned about the practical consequences of the development of workplace knowledge which must be a key concern for the information literacy specialist. They are also mainly preoccupied with the large organisation.

# Skills development and the employability agenda

## *Employability defined*

In *Skills for Scotland: A Lifelong Skills Strategy* the Scottish Government (2007a), as part of a generally applicable statement, defined 'employability' as 'the combination of factors and processes which enable people to progress towards or get into employment, to stay in employment and move on in the workplace' and employability skills as 'a term that refers to skills, behaviours, attitudes and personal attributes that are necessary for an individual to seek, gain and sustain employment and function effectively in the workplace and are transferable to a variety of contexts. Employability skills prepare individuals for work rather than for a specific occupation.'

Policy documents on skills development have been appearing since about 2005. The British Government's report, *Skills, Getting on in Business, Getting on at Work* (DfES/DWP 2005: vol. 1.1), emphasised the need for a skilled workforce and, although only ICT skills are specifically mentioned, there is a clear need for information literacy skills to be promoted within this context. The report notes:

'Skills are fundamental to achieving our ambitions, as individuals, for our families and for our communities. They help businesses create wealth, and they help people realise their potential. So they serve the twin goals of social justice and economic success.'

The situation does not seem to have changed much over the years. The *Skills for Life* document (DIUS 2009: 14) notes that 'ICT has a major role to play in helping to deliver our ambition to become a world leader in skills ... it provides a route into learning for people to improve their literacy and numeracy skills ...' but there is no mention of information literacy. Here information literacy has yet to be specifically referred to and is rolled up with ICT skills, a problem extensively discussed in Chapter 2. The terms 'digital literacy' and 'media literacy' are however creeping in. They are referred to in two reports previously discussed in Chapter 3. The *Digital Britain* interim report (DCMS 2009: 63–4) states that digital life skills are needed by all – 'education and training for digital technologies ... underpins everything we do in the 21st Century'; 'digital work skills are needed by most and digital economy skills are needed by some'. The *Report of the Digital Britain Media Literacy Working Group* (Ofcom 2009: 29) goes further describing it as an entitlement 'In order to participate fully in a Digital Britain, people should have the opportunity to develop and improve their digital skills, confidences, competencies and knowledge' and it specifically recommends that digital engagement should be aligned with 'workforce employment and promotion strategies' and organisations should be encouraged to address the media literacy needs of employees. The terms 'digital literacy' and 'media literacy' here seem almost interchangeable.

# The role of higher education

Universities are becoming increasingly interested in furthering the employability skills of their graduates and establishing links with businesses. Some universities have recognised the needs of the knowledge economy and 'employers placing a greater emphasis on information handling skills, as a key competitive advantage' (Milne 2004: 10) and embedding information literacy across universities' learning outcomes. Jackson (2010), however, asks an important question of universities: 'How well do we equip students for life in the information-rich world of employment? In celebrating our successes in making significant contributions to learning through information skills programmes, are we missing the point – are the information skills we teach appropriate to the workplace?' According to the research findings of Head (2012) the answer would seem to be 'no'. She interviewed 23 US employers and conducted focus groups with 33 recent graduates from four US colleges and universities. The new graduates in their first jobs found the transition from college to the workplace daunting. They had to meet unrelenting deadlines but were challenged by vaguely defined workplace research tasks and received little feedback on their performance. The basic online search skills new college graduates bring with them to their first post are attractive enough for them to be offered a job. Yet, employers found that, once in the workplace, these educated young workers seemed tethered to their computers. They failed to incorporate more fundamental, low-tech research methods that are as essential as ever in the contemporary workplace. While employers were pleased that newly hired employees had online searching skills that exceeded their expectations, they were disappointed to find that new employees were prone to deliver the quickest answer they could find using a search engine, entering a few keywords, and scanning the first couple of pages of results. Many employers were surprised that the majority of new employees rarely used any of the more traditional forms of research, such as making telephone calls or thumbing through an annual report or similar paper source. Although many new employees successfully applied techniques learned at university for evaluating the quality of content, close reading of texts, and synthesising large quantities of content usually available online, they found that they had to develop adaptive strategies for solving information problems in the workplace, often on a trial-and-error basis. Most of these strategies involved cultivating relationships with a trusted co-worker who could help them to find quick answers, save time, and learn work processes.

Emerging research within the workplace suggests a variable picture. A study by Crawford (2006a) of students and alumni at Glasgow Caledonian University showed that students considered information literacy to have a clear relationship to work activity. This included searching for jobs on recruitment websites, planning CVs and using it as an additional factor to impress prospective employers. Alumni also made these points too but also saw information literacy as a tool to support their work, something which gave them a chance to exercise initiative and even have an advantage over their colleagues. It was also viewed as a promotion skill. Some even said they could not do their work without it while others saw it as a shared skill or learning experience with colleagues. Alumni reported varying attitudes among employers with some being sympathetic to the information literacy agenda and willing to support it while others were not, an interesting finding in itself.

This study has been replicated by Travis (2011) at California State University at Long Beach, who found that a majority of the students questioned thought that their research skills played a role in getting their current job although 36 per cent did not. She also found that 48 per cent felt that their information literacy skills were a factor in getting a job and 77 per cent felt that 'finding information is an essential part of my work.' This shows that the usefulness of information literacy skills in the workplace is acknowledged as much by graduates as by business. Studies have shown, much to the chagrin of academic librarians, that students turn to friends for help rather than librarians and, as we shall see, this pattern is replicated in the workplace. An important and disturbing finding is the low ranking of librarians, online tutorials and library instruction sessions in contributing to the growth of information literacy skills.

The perception of the value of information literacy varies from subject to subject and is not a uniform phenomenon. In a comparative study of academics in English and marketing disciplines at British universities Webber et al. (2005) found that conceptions of and commitment to information literacy are heavily influenced by subject, with those working in marketing being more inclined to appreciate the value of information than English scholars. Whereas Crawford et al. (2004), in a study of undergraduates at a Scottish university, found that subject was the main determinant in the usage of electronic information services, with health and paramedical databases being most heavily used, followed by business studies, computer science and engineering. As we shall see, the importance of subject carries over into the workplace.

## Issues of definition

There are few better descriptions of information literacy skills development in an educational setting than that provided by Lloyd (2011: 280):

'The skills prescribed in searching for information, accessing and using it are formalized by particular rules, regulations and curriculums that are underpinned by an instrumental rationality. This allows the acquisition of knowledge to be measured against formalized sets of criteria. In this setting, primacy is awarded to knowledge that is canonical, objective, and explicit and there is a focus on individual performance and the development of self-sufficiency through independent learning.'

It could also be said that it is a setting in which librarians award themselves the role of judge and arbiter. It is all very different in the workplace. Here tasks and problems tend to be messy, complex and open ended. They may be difficult to analyse. They may employ different approaches to information seeking and use that go beyond the mastery of information-seeking skills to knowing ways of thinking and seeing. In the workplace tasks are context specific, not generic. The focus is less on identifying information needs because problems are very specific and may be assigned to an employee to resolve (Weiner 2011b). As workplace learning theorists have discovered, workplace information literacy activity is a collaborative experience. Rather than skills based, individual activity in workplace information literacy is a collaborative and social activity. To quote Annemaree Lloyd again:

' ... I have reconceptualized information literacy as a practice that facilitates a "way of knowing" about the sources of information that will inform performance and participation. These information sources are not confined to textual sources but also physical and social sources that constitute an information landscape, producing an information experience that has "embodied and social dimensions in addition to the cognitive". Consequently, I understand information literacy as being holistic.' (Lloyd 2010: 89)

In the workplace the view of what constitutes information is different from education with its reliance on standardised print and online sources – books, journals, technical manuals, passworded bibliographic databases and Internet sources. There is less reliance on secondary and codified sources. Lloyd (2009) in her study of Australian firefighters found practitioners to be a critical source of information. She considers that information literacy should be extended to include bodily experiences like touch and smell. For her information literacy should be viewed as 'the catalyst for learning about work and professional practice.' In a study of workplace information usage in Glasgow (Crawford and Irving 2009) the principal source of information used by employees was other staff. This is an entirely reasonable point of view. People can be evaluated as a source of information just like any other. Colleagues with appropriate qualifications, training, experience and who have the respect of their peers can reasonably be viewed as a reliable information source. It was also found that human relationships are key to development of information literacy in the workplace. The choice of Internet sites to view was also influenced by how colleagues view one another. Websites were accepted as reliable on the recommendation of staff respected by colleagues. Among other sources of information pressed into service were advisory leaflets produced by governments and information posted on notice boards. It is not surprising that, in such a world, the role of the librarian as an authority figure is much diminished.

Another key difference from education is the concept of 'laddered skills' as exemplified in the frameworks discussed in Chapter 3 where a hierarchy of skill levels is established which is then linked or 'pegged' to educational and social policy documents, depending on the perceived needs of the situation. As indicated above the workplace situation is 'messy' and there are identifiable factors (Lloyd 2010: 75–6):

- information seeking is not always necessary

- information seeking is by trial and error

- getting information is not equal to getting the answer

- information seeking is not linear

- information seeking is not a one-man job

- information relevance criteria change.

However, there are some 'pegs' on which to hang skill levels. Senior staff engage in different information literacy activities from other staff. They use more primary sources such as internally generated information than secondary sources; the latter are more important in academic work. For senior staff networking is also a productive way of gathering information (Weiner 2011b). There is something of a hierarchy in the workplace with staff in senior and management positions with degrees and similar qualifications having a more sophisticated grasp of what information literacy is and how to use information. This is particularly marked in the public sector where specific qualification levels are attributed to particular levels of work and where there is a culture of continual professional development and relevant skills training (Crawford and Irving 2009). The downside of this is that staff with low-level skills in manual or semiskilled posts can be viewed as a sort of information literacy proletariat. Cooke and Greenwood (2008) found that job function is the most critical factor in determining whether employees will have reasonable workplace access to ICT. While manual staff are keen to learn, the attitude of line managers is crucial if skill levels are to progress beyond basic IT competency. The danger of a digital divide was one of the authors' main conclusions.

While workplace information literacy is clearly a different beast from its educational equivalent it does have something in common with another workplace ideology, knowledge management. Knowledge management is concerned with an individual's knowledge, much of which is tacit knowledge residing in people's heads: 'Knowledge management comprises a range of strategies and practices used in an organization to identify, create, represent, distribute, and enable adoption of insights and experiences. Such insights and experiences comprise knowledge, either embodied in individuals or embedded in organizational processes or practice. Knowledge management efforts typically focus on organizational objectives such as improved performance, competitive advantage, innovation, the sharing of lessons learned, integration and continuous improvement of the organization (Wikipedia 2012). Ferguson (2009) notes that, while the sites of information may be broader in a workplace context than they are in a higher educational institution, the focus remains on individual learning. Although it should be noted that the lessons from workplace information literacy studies show that, whilst the learning itself is individual, information literacy workplace activity is generally collaborative. With knowledge management the focus is on the organisation's capacity to learn, not the individual's. However, as indicated above, traditional concepts of information literacy cannot be sustained in the work environment. Whilst information literacy and knowledge management have separate roots, they increasingly have issues in common. As Lloyd (2009) highlights, information literacy 'pursues the same goals as knowledge management . . . which is to develop and nurture the knowledge sharing practices and information literate workforce that are necessary if organisations are to be adaptive, innovative and robust.' There are four significant areas of similarity between knowledge management and information literacy (Abell and Skelton 2005):

1.  'Both are inextricably linked in the minds of many people with learning – lifelong learning in the case of the individual, the learning organisation in the case of the organisation.

2.  The arguments for developing information literacy and knowledge management capability within the workplace/ organisation are indisputable. Very few senior managers deny the benefits of managing and using the organisation's knowledge effectively ... Both knowledge management and information literacy underpin the way the organisations work and develop. But such acceptance has not necessarily brought action.

3.  Both are difficult concepts to "sell" in terms of business values and outcomes. Both can be perceived as "nice to have" or "common sense" rather than a key organisational capability.

4.  Both have had a problem with their label. Except for those in the know, the terms do not immediately conjure up a clear picture of what they mean.'

Information literacy and knowledge management share problems of definition and recognition but they have complementary roles in the workplace and are complementary organisational ideologies. However, they are most applicable in the larger organisation.

# The workplace and its problems

The importance of information in the workplace is not in doubt. An early twenty-first century American study showed that employees spend an average of 9.5 hours per week 'obtaining, reviewing, and analysing information' (Oman 2001) but is this time spent wisely? An estimated 6.4 hours per employee are spent looking for information on the Internet each week in the UK; 37 per cent of searches prove unsuccessful. In financial terms, an estimated £3.7 billion is spent on time wasted by SMEs looking for information that cannot be found (De Saulles 2007). While the views of major employers are sympathetic, they not unnaturally link information literacy with information technologies and networking rather than focusing specifically on information literacy. Attitudes, however, continue to vary. A 2008 survey, commissioned by Microsoft, of 500 top UK decision makers found that by 2017 ICT and information literacy will be viewed as second only to team working and interpersonal skills as the most important success factor for business. Indeed, around a quarter of those surveyed ranked it as the number one skill set for future success (Microsoft Research 2008: 11). On the other hand, a survey of nearly 1000 chief executives in 1996 in the UK showed that, while 60 per cent claimed that their company had an information policy, only 20 per cent were aware of the company having an information budget, half had no formal information provision and the majority did not know who was responsible for the information resource. In 2005 the situation seemed little better. A survey of 119 information management and IT professionals showed that 44 per cent of respondents did not have a document and information management strategy (Orna, 2008: 555–6).

What many organizations lack is an infrastructure that helps provide the required complementary information literacy skills (Oman 2001). How is this to be done and how can a case be made?

Should the initiative for information policy be led by senior management or should top management entrust subordinate groups with responsibility for new developments. One of the world's leading environmental consulting services, Environmental Resources Management, led by senior managers, has embarked on a knowledge-sharing programme to support the organisation's business growth. This resulted in information literacy training being embedded in the organisation's intranet (Cheuk 2008). Many organizations in practice have an information policy which is implicit, rather than explicit, and has no formal management recognition. Each organisation has an implicit policy but it is usually founded on its staff, internal sources such as intranets and eRDM (electronic resource data management) systems, the Internet and a small range of printed sources and contacts both within and outside the organization (Crawford and Irving 2009).

To make progress, several steps are necessary (Oman 2001). First of all, an appraisal of the organisation's ICT which carries information to staff is required. A skills audit is also necessary. Different categories of employees will have different skill levels and needs. A newly employed member of staff straight from university may have learned information literacy skills there but may not know as much about the information requirements of the organisation as an experienced member of staff whose formal information-seeking skills, however, may be poor. It is important to understand what information literacy means to particular organisations and to use the language of the organisation to express it so the message will be understood. Information literacy should not be introduced to an organisation in isolation. Information literacy plans should be linked to employee development and standard competencies expected of all employees. Human resources colleagues can help to gain acceptance and support employee-training initiatives such as advanced Internet searching which is an essential skill all employees should have and show how to combat information overload. It is also important to 'sell' information literacy as a practical rather than theoretical concept. Improved searching skills save the time of the organisation and therefore money and this is a good point to make. Skills training, however, must be aligned with corporate programmes. As indicated above some topics/subject areas are more sympathetic to information use than others. Staff engaged in market research or research methods are likely to be interested.

There is a divide between the large organisation and the SME (small to medium-sized enterprise). The large organisation may have a library or someone charged with information responsibilities. It may have an eRDM system or intranet which staff can refer to. There will be members of staff with academic and/or professional qualifications who will be to some extent information aware, at least at their own operational level. Large organisations have training and CPD programmes into which information skills training programmes can be introduced. No such assumption can be made about the SME. Ahlgren (2007), in a study of a manufacturing SME, found that the emphasis was on technique acquisition and that workplace learning focused on short-term training for immediate work-related payback. Long-term skill acquisition was not considered important, an environment unconducive to the development of information literacy training. Information skills development and utilisation in the SME is a major issue. The focus is on the ability to use computers and standard software applications but not on how to structure, find, evaluate and use the information accessed via a computer. SME employees use the Internet as their primary source of information for business-related matters and spend an hour a day on average looking for information on the Internet. Given that advanced Internet training is an essential skill for all SME employees it is unfortunate that it has attracted little research interest (De Saulles 2007: 75).

## Information needs and sources used

De Saulles (2007) found that information seekers tend to be confident about their information-seeking skills and can use search engines such as Google at a basic level but are not aware how to refine searches or where to find information that Google does not point to, such as paid-for company information sources. Keenan and McDonald (2009), in an extremely practical study based on a training programme, found that workplace attendees on an information literacy training course were unaware of advanced Internet searching; Boolean operators were seen as interchangeable and the concept was difficult to explain; people overestimate their searching skills and underestimate the skills of information professionals. Crawford and Irving (2009) found that people are the principal source of information used in the workplace and that the traditional 'library' view of information as deriving from electronic and printed sources only is invalid in the workplace and must include people as sources of information. Advanced Internet searching was not understood but advanced Internet training (the use of a search engine's advanced search facility and/or Boolean terms) can greatly extend employees' information horizons. Most people interviewed in the study used only a limited range of sources which, apart from colleagues, consisted of an intranet or eRDM, a limited range of Internet sources and a few printed sources. eRDM systems and intranets themselves were a limiting rather than an extending factor, as people tend to rely on them rather than using a wider range of searching tools. Indexing of items added to eRDM systems also tends to be extremely poor as staff assigning the indexing terms of items scanned know nothing about indexing and use terms which are vague or too general. Cheuk (2008: 138) lists some points which reinforce the above findings:

- 'The use of outdated information because it is convenient to do so

- Not aware of existing resources within the organisation which can address a business issue

- Do not know how to use the tools and make the best use of information services to access the information required

- Assume Google is the best search engine to look for information

- Unable to manage personal email boxes resulting in email overload

- Do not want to share information for fear that information shared will be misused or abused by others.'

Lloyd's (2009) study of ambulance officers emphasises the social aspects of data collection and use. They use storytelling as a means of passing on information and use practitioners and other allied health professionals to provide critical sources of information. She found that experienced practitioners rarely mentioned codified sources of information during discussions. When questioned about textual sources, experienced practitioners did not identify them as a central source of information. Novice ambulance officers reported restricting their search for text-based information to print information that had been sanctioned by ambulance educators, and most of the novices suggested that the intensity of the training period left them feeling unable to process the information they had received. There was little evidence among them of using information in critical thinking about information or the sources used. This was because the training experienced was a very pressured one, focusing on a limited range of experiences. There is more than a hint of Lave and Wenger's 'cage' here. Viewed through the conventional information literacy lens the overall picture is one of low skill levels and a need for training. However, it is also the case that sophisticated social, interactive and collaborative processes are going on, which the information literacy specialist cannot ignore.

## Training issues

Clearly, there are training issues to be addressed which raises the question of who should deliver them. Chambers of Commerce and employers' organisations such as the Confederation of British Industry (CBI) are possibilities, but in practice show little interest in offering information literacy training. Part of the problem is that employers themselves are unsure about their employees' training and learning needs. The Robert Gordon University Business School obtained European Union funding to develop training programmes for SMEs in the Aberdeen area but found that local businesses were unsure of their training needs (SILP 2009). Trade unions are another possibility and trade union learning representatives are very willing to engage with the information literacy training agenda but are hampered by lack of funds at a time when trade unions have other more pressing priorities.

Courses must be highly focused on the target audience and tailored to meet their needs. Generic courses which do not directly engage with learner needs are unlikely to be successful. A course which contains convincing examples of how information has benefited a company's performance is more likely to impress SMEs than one which does not. Parallel work in the schools sector shows the benefit of using case studies/exemplars of good practice (Irving 2009).

There is a considerable dearth of suitable training materials, so building up 'stocks' should be a priority. Most information literacy training materials have been produced by and for higher education and are unsuitable for the workplace and employability training environments as they tend to focus on more formal sources and the needs of the higher education sector (Graham 2011: 121–50).

## Examples of good practice

There is relatively little literature describing actual examples of good practice. Keenan and McDonald (2009) have described an information literacy course they ran for an Australian company earlier in the decade. It consisted of:

'*Overview*

History of the Internet and World Wide Web
How the Internet works

*Accessing and navigating the Internet*

Web browsers
Internet Explorer layout
URLs and accessing a website
Adding Favourites

*Preparing your search*

Analysing the question
Identifying search terms
Identifying synonyms and truncation
Connecting search terms
Searching tips and hints

*Using search engines*

What are search engines
Searching with Google
Advanced search on Google
Searching on Vivisimo and Dogpile
Advanced searching on these and other examples.'

Searching on passworded databases was also included. This is a useful format and addresses some of the issues discussed above such as advanced Internet searching.

The learning objectives of the course for attendees to focus on were:

- 'Consider what they are really looking for – how do you know they have found "it" when you don't know what you are looking for?

- Be focused and disciplined with their time

- Get an understanding of the breadth of the information resources available to them and how to use them

- Understand the difference between Internet based/non refereed sources of information and Internet based refereed sources of information.'

The course was highly customised to meet the practical needs of attendees, again a recurring theme in other work. A particularly useful feature is a checklist of questions which attendees found extremely helpful:

- 'What is the question?
- What is the level of information?
- What type of information and amount?
- When do I need the information by?
- Where have I already looked?'

The course worked because it was highly personalised and customised, people could see the results of searching on different search engines and they had access to information professionals who could discuss other resources and search strategies. Although the course was successful within the organisation, attempts to sell it to other organisations including Government departments were not successful for reasons mainly to do with hardware issues.

Cheuk (2008) also discusses a company programme for an organisation with over 3000 staff in 40 countries. This is an intranet-based resource called Minerva which defines information literacy in the workplace as allowing employees to experience information literacy in seven ways or 'faces' (informed by Christine Bruce's *Seven Faces of Information Literacy* – Bruce, 1997) which can be compared with Keenan and McDonald (2009). While it is a more sophisticated model there are points in common:

- 'Face 1: using information/knowledge management systems, ICT tools, emails
- Face 2: knowing the existence of and ability to use specific sources (e.g. experts, databases, intranet, journal subscriptions, website)

**115**

- Face 3: awareness of a process to find and use information (e.g. to understand customers' needs, to evaluate a business problem)

- Face 4: organising and controlling information so it can be retrievable (e.g. design database structure, design intranet sites, manage folders in the local file server, manage personal email boxes)

- Face 5: learning or gaining new knowledge through interacting with information

- Face 6: gaining new insights and thinking about an issue in a new or different perspective

- Face 7: using information wisely for the benefit of the organisation and society.'

These dimensions are in turn linked to the organisation's programme of cultural change. It is interesting that people are identified as an information source and that academic models lie at the back of this. To roll out the programme 50 knowledge champions were recruited and 3000 staff received 60 minutes of training. The involvement and support of senior managers has been a key theme.

North Bristol NHS Trust has developed an information literacy training programme for staff which is consciously embedded into NHS staff development (Hadley and Hacker 2007). The target audience was qualified nurses, support staff and those without recent formal learning experience. The programme is explicitly linked to the NHS Knowledge and Skills Framework (KSF) and Development Review Process which define and describe the knowledge and skills which NHS staff need to apply in their work to deliver quality services. Relevant KSF indicators include 'effectively uses appropriate methods and sources for obtaining and recording the data/information' and 'correctly identifies the need for additional knowledge and information resources to support work'. Initially, the course was devised and managed by a librarian with a teaching background and ran for five days, one day a week over five consecutive weeks. After the first two courses it was clear that the course needed to be more learner centred and recognise the different learning paces and levels of student experience. This led to a two-stage course, the first stage being on grammar and writing skills, while the second stage dealt with information literacy skills. Workbooks were developed to give the students a resource for future reference and self-directed learning. Between February 2005 and January 2006 the course attracted 63 learners, mostly nurses. Evaluation of the course showed that it either needed to be longer or the students needed more encouragement to undertake self-directed learning. This led to a blended approach including e-learning and provision of self-study materials, via distance learning to meet the needs of the individual earner.

More recently, the Open University has been piloting generic learning materials called iKnow (Information and Knowledge at Work), offering bite-sized learning materials which can be done 'in just a few minutes at your desk or on the move' to help 'save time in finding, using and organizing information at work' (Open University 2010). The design of training materials was preceded by a planning workshop in which the now familiar themes of what information means in a workplace context and what information sources are both surfaced. The most popular competencies selected by workshop participants were, perhaps not surprisingly:

- 'Finding information

- Know your sources

- Evaluating information

- Information handling

- Organising information

- Keeping up to date.'

These were duly converted into 'bite sized' learning materials, the titles of which included:

- 'Planning your search

- Finding sources of business information

- What is good information?

- Don't believe everything you read: why evaluation is important

- Using the 5 D's (Discard, Deal with it, Determine future action, Deposit (file it), Direct/Distribute it) to handle information

- Read faster, remember more

- All about records management

- Data Protection and the Freedom of Information Act: working within the law

- Email: you're the boss

- Different ways of keeping up to date

- Networking.'

There is a discussion forum for employers and a short professionally produced introductory video.

Employers were asked to identify which of the iKnow skills areas were already covered by current training provision within their companies (Reedy et al. 2013). With the exception of one company, there was no current training provision in any of the six knowledge areas. The one exception identified current training provision in one area: information handling.

Comments from employers varied from:

'I could not believe the amount of "tricks" and "shortcuts" I learnt in the Finding Information section which can be used in my job on a daily basis. I never used Advanced Search in Google before or was aware of the currency converter and calculator, which all seem to be basic functions everyone in the workplace should be aware of"

to:

'The Advanced Search options were interesting but I do feel that most people won't ever explore beyond Google simple search.'

It proved difficult to involve SMEs, which produced an interesting comment:

'Small companies in a recession can't afford the time to help even though, ironically, they are the ones that need the resources most (and they are usually only too aware of that twisted dilemma).'

The small pilot study of the materials revealed that 'the "bitesize" and "mobile" nature of the materials allowed greater flexibility in the training process, and would be quite easy for staff to schedule into their working day. There was a consensus that they would "definitely" want to see a greater availability of workplace learning materials in these formats.' There were several suggested improvements including self-assessment and PDP (professional development programme) tools to enable the learner to check their learning and make a review of the content as it was felt to be 'still quite academic' (Parker 2010).

These examples show that training materials need to be linked to the aims and practices of the organisation and, if possible, to pre-existing staff development programmes. Blended learning along with more traditional instructional methods may be appropriate but information literacy training for the SME still seems to be a largely unaddressed issue.

## Summary of the chapter

The study of information literacy practices in the workplace has helped to redefine what an information source is and emphasises the social and collaborative nature of the process. Information literacy has a key role in the skills development agenda but this is insufficiently recognised by governments. Practice in the workplace is often poor and the needs of the SME in particular receive little attention. A great deal of thought needs to be given to the preparation of appropriate learning materials. Because of the varied nature of the workplace standardised materials are unlikely to be satisfactory.

# 6

# The Scottish Government Library: a case study

*Jenny Foreman and Morag Higgison*

**Abstract:** The case study describes the work of the Scottish Government Library's services – in particular, its information literacy training programme – and its strategic development work in information literacy which has included collaboration with both external and internal partners, setting up a community of practice and revision of its information literacy skills training programme. Attempts to promote an information literacy strategy for the organisation proved less successful. A major evaluation of the training programme was carried out using the Kirkpatrick model and needed improvements identified.

**Key words:** information literacy, information literacy instruction, Scottish Government Library, workplace information literacy, training, workplace learning, skills development, Kirkpatrick model, impact measurement, evaluation.

## Introduction

The Scottish Government (SG) Library's main aim is to provide its workforce with the information, skills, abilities and tools to enable the smooth running and evidence-based policy of the Scottish Government. 'Our people are our greatest economic asset. A skilled and educated workforce is essential to building our comparative advantage and to the delivery of sustainable economic growth' (Scottish Government 2007b: 2).

SG librarians provide a variety of services, from a research or literature search service, a question and answer (enquiry) service, current awareness, document acquisition and delivery service to information skills and social media awareness training for all SG staff. As a team of ten – made up of six professional information staff (currently there is no chief librarian) and four support staff – we operate as a virtual library or e-library on our intranet, whereby SG staff can access the services via their desktop PCs, email or phone. To help create an information-literate workforce and an open and transparent government, the SG Library also delivers a training programme, comprising information search skills, social media awareness and collaborative skills sessions. These training sessions aim to help SG staff search, find, evaluate, share and store information effectively as well as find out how to use social media to facilitate online collaboration with external partners, promote the SG's work and the sharing of information in general.

## Background

In Autumn 2007, SG librarians Jenny Foreman and Lesley Thomson met with John Crawford and Christine Irving – research staff at Glasgow Caledonian University who had set up the Scottish Information Literacy Project (SILP) and were undertaking research into information literacy in the workplace. They were interested in using the SG as one of their workplace examples which was encouraging for us as we hoped their research results would back up our own anecdotal and training feedback and thereby provide some concrete evidence for us to demonstrate the fairly low level of information skills within the organisation. We required evidence before embarking on writing our 'Scottish Government Information Literacy Strategy' (Foreman and Thomson 2009). In 2008 John Crawford and Christine Irving completed their research (Crawford and Irving 2009) investigating information literacy skills in the SG, a study which recognised that searching for information is a major activity in the organisation and that there was indeed a key information literacy skills deficit. Their interview-based results revealed that the SG is an information-dependent organisation and, while all the interviewees believed they had information literacy skills to a degree, some felt that they were lacking in how they evaluated and shared their information. If one examines the 'information literacy cycle' (Craig and Westwood 2009) there are seven stages involved: source, find, evaluate, combine, share, apply and question information. The research results suggested interviewees could find information reasonably well (though not necessarily very efficiently) but were not so capable at evaluating, sharing and exploiting their results. The second piece of research was carried out under the auspices of the SG Library and the Scottish Executive's Information Management Unit and was titled the *Information Use Survey*. This was a questionnaire emailed to all SG staff in 2007 which asked a whole range of information-related questions including: 'How did staff search for, use and store information within the Scottish Government?'

Both pieces of research reached the following conclusions.

## Interview-based research results

- Searching for information is a significant activity for all SG staff no matter what their position or nature of their work.

- Staff search for and use information as part of their jobs but this tends to be on a 'need to know' basis, job or task specific and driven by business needs. Formal information skills or information literacy instruction only takes place when SG staff attend the training courses delivered by the SG Library.

- There may be a link between level of work and information searching. For example, a highly qualified interviewee has both complex information needs and a clear understanding of how to address them.

- There is an introverted information culture in the SG, characterised by a tendency for civil servants to rely on internal information resources only.

- Most of those interviewed had worked in the Civil Service for some years and were therefore familiar with the system as well as with the constraints of the Civil Service culture.

## Information Use Survey results

- People emerged as the principal source of information and this is shown by the fact that 99 per cent of *Information Use Survey* responses rated 'colleagues and contacts' as 'very' or 'fairly' useful information sources.

- The Internet is heavily used – 91.6 per cent of responses from the survey alone rated the Internet as a 'very' or 'fairly' important information source in their day-to-day work. However, the level and quality of Internet searching are variable and staff could become more information literate simply by being aware of 'advanced searching' techniques.

- The profile of the SG Library in the SG is low. Those who use the service are generally 'very satisfied' with the results, but

73.3 per cent of the questionnaire respondents knew only a 'little' or 'nothing' about the services offered and 25.6 per cent had not used any of the services.

- 'It would be great if all new starts and many existing staff could have access to the same information and advice.' SG staff member's comment in the *Information Use Survey* (2007)

These valuable findings provided the evidence for Jenny Foreman and Lesley Thomson to complete the writing of the Scottish Government Information Literacy Strategy in 2009 (Foreman and Thomson 2009). The objectives of this strategy were to define a framework for embedding core transferable information literacy skills throughout the organisation at all levels, and to ensure that whenever there is learning in the SG it promotes an information-literate approach. The Strategy also aimed to promote the profile of the SG Library as a whole.

SG senior management have not yet endorsed the Scottish Government Information Literacy Strategy. Instead, they have preferred to adopt a 'subset' of information literacy, namely digital literacy, and Jenny Foreman and Lesley Thomson have been involved with others in the writing of the *Scottish Government Social Media Policy and Guidance* (which was published on 20 June 2012: *http://www.scotland.gov.uk/ About/Information/Social-Media-Policies*). This document includes the provision of training and awareness sessions on social media and digital skills by SG librarians. We are keeping a foothold regarding embedding information literacy including digital literacy skills in the organisation.

Hence, we nevertheless decided to implement certain aspects of the Scottish Government Information Literacy Strategy and the research undertaken, and as a result came up with the aims set out in the next two sections both internally with colleagues and externally with partners.

## Internal achievements

- We developed closer ties with our SG training colleagues, namely those in organisational development leadership and learning (ODLL) who are responsible for leadership and management training in the SG. We targeted the ODLL Development Advisers so that they were aware of SG Library training and could therefore promote it. We also created an SG corporate induction event, which included a session on searching skills and information about the SG Library.

- We formed a strong working relationship with the SG Finance Training Team who willingly shared generic training materials, best practice hints and tips on training, their training facilities and who also kindly agreed to provide and assess all of the SG Library trainers in Train the Trainer events. (It is worth noting that none of the SG librarians have any formal or professional training qualifications.)

- We undertook additional research within the SG Library to gather formal evidence regarding our training. This developed into an evaluating and measuring exercise which the authors delivered at the Librarians' Information Literacy Annual Conference (LILAC) 2010.

- We improved and developed our training course materials. The training team (two librarians) rewrote the materials then got additional advice and comments from the whole training team (all five librarians) so there was a unified approach and understanding of the materials when delivering the courses.

- We decided that all SG Library staff would use a signature survey via email on answering an enquiry to help promote our services as well as gather feedback on other services besides training, which had a separate questionnaire. We chose a generic tag line with a link, 'You can submit feedback on how we answered your enquiry by completing our online questionnaire here. Thank you!' (This is one of our three SG Library online questionnaires.)

- We strengthened partnerships with other SG colleagues, namely with the social researchers and analysts, as well as the Digital Communications Team where we were invited to work with them and others on the Scottish Government Social Media Policy and Guidance.

- We developed an information skills session for civil servants using social media tools in the workplace.

## External achievements

- We pursued and established partnerships with external partners, including our information literacy advocates – John Crawford and Christine Irving – the Scottish Information Literacy Project and the Chartered Institute of Library and Information Professionals in Scotland (CILIPS).

- We set up a community of practice in 2009 called 'Creating an Information Literate Scotland', a forum for all those interested in information literacy in Scotland, a place to share best practice, ideas, contacts, training materials, to have discussions and to post information about information literacy events. In 2012 the community of practice changed its name to 'Information Literacy Skills for the 21st Century' (*http://www.therightinformation.org/*

*cop/*) and received a new flurry of interest from information practitioners from all areas of work seeking to collaborate on information literacy in Scotland. (See Chapter 10 by John Crawford for further information).

- We spoke at conferences, including LILAC 2010, which was a pivotal event for us. We undertook our training evaluation research which led to us completely revising our training materials and have done so on a monthly basis updating and improving them to encompass all feedback, both from SG delegates and from the SG Library trainers.

- We improved and developed our training course feedback, which originally entailed paper forms handed out at the end of each course. Using QuestBack (the SG's preferred online questionnaire tool), we created online questionnaires for the delegates to use at the end of the course while still in the classroom. Then, three weeks later, as part of LILAC evaluation and measurement research, we sent a follow-up questionnaire asking delegates if they had put into practice anything they had learnt from the course.

## Future activities and aims (suggestions from the original research)

- To provide more flexible learning options by developing e-learning modules which will enable SG staff to access training and develop their skills at their own pace from their PCs.

- To undertake further research by investigating the information needs and evaluating the skills of complex users (e.g., analysts, policymakers, digital coordinators), and develop tailored information skills training for these areas.

- To enhance the existing information skills training programme by designing a course specifically for social researchers. This tailored course will concentrate on subject-specific resources for each social research area.

- To raise the profile of information specialists and librarians in the SG and, in particular, facilitate and support them in their role as information skills educators.

- To develop appropriate metrics for auditing the current information literacy skills of SG staff and measuring the success of the information skills training.

## SG Library: measuring and evaluating our training for LILAC 2010

In 2009 John Crawford and Christine Irving suggested that we conduct a short evaluation exercise on our training courses and then present our findings at LILAC in Limerick in March 2010. We were fortunate to be granted such an opportunity and delivered a short presentation of our research at one of the parallel sessions titled 'Scottish Government information literacy in the workplace: measuring impact' (Foreman and Higgison 2010).

The SG Library delivers a variety of training, from a 45-minute drop-in or tutorial whereby we promote and demonstrate our library resources or collaboration tools at SG staff desks, to subject-specific database training (popular with our social research staff), to current awareness like Information Monitoring courses as well as classroom-based training on information search skills and social media awareness.

We had already amalgamated the basic and advanced information search skills courses because no one was booking onto the basic courses anymore. All potential delegates considered themselves above the basic level even if we suspected they were not. (Incidentally, our results support the premise that users have 'false confidence' – as detailed by Corrall 2009 – when delegates overassess their own searching skills.)

The full list of SG Library training courses is:

- Internet Skills in the Workplace

- Social Media for Government (formerly Web 2.0 Workshop)

- Google Treasure Hunt (Advanced Google)

- Information Monitoring (current awareness and alerts)

- Discover Social Media (short presentation)

- Social Media Bites (short sessions focusing on particular social media tools)

- Information drop-ins or tailored tutorials at staff desks.

We decided to concentrate on two of our information literacy training courses for the purposes of our measuring and evaluation exercise. We chose those two courses – Internet Skills in the Workplace and the Web 2.0 Workshop – as they were the most popular and most regularly attended training sessions (two sessions delivered each month in total). Hence, we would have the relevant data to analyse and a good number of delegates to question in the three-week follow-up questionnaire and interviews. The Internet Skills in the Workplace course seeks to provide delegates with the advanced searching skills needed to effectively find information available from the Internet in the workplace, and the Web 2.0 Workshop aims to enable staff become knowledgeable and aware of using social media for collaboration and engagement in government. It is worth noting that over the years since first delivering these courses we have tailored them for our SG audience, namely civil servants, and that they are primarily work orientated.

As of 2009 when we first started evaluating our courses, a library assistant typed up the feedback from the paper questionnaires (often called 'happy sheets') onto an Excel spreadsheet, then forwarded this to the librarians to view, comment on and if necessary take action by answering any questions delegates may have and/or make any necessary changes to our training materials. The delegates would complete the paper questionnaires at the end of each course so we only gained immediate feedback revealing what their thoughts were on the day, not what they had learnt and then subsequently did or did not implement back at their desks, which as it transpired was what we were particularly interested in for our research purposes.

Although the statistics for those attending SG Library training were fairly good – in fact, the Web 2.0 Workshop – had a waiting list, this did not give any indication on the *quality* of the content of the courses, whether it was adequate, effective or even if it was required by or useful to staff to help carry out their work effectively. We realised that evaluating our course materials would be essential in identifying the success (or not) of a course and the effectiveness of the learning which was taking place (or not) and whether this had any significant impact on delegates being able to work more efficiently and effectively.

We had started gathering feedback and data from our courses in 2009; however, it was not until early 2010 that we started evaluating and measuring them with a view to presenting our findings at LILAC 2010. We planned to ascertain the following:

- Do our training courses meet the business needs? Do they enable staff to work more effectively, for example?

- What would staff like us to provide? What are their views on training content?

- What impact, if any, were we making regarding improving SG staff search skills and their understanding of the uses of social media within government?

- We needed to make sure that we were adding value to the organisation via improving staff skills, something especially pertinent in the economic climate.

- Do staff acquire knowledge and skills from the training and have they put what they have learnt into practice back at their desks?

- Do staff learn from concrete examples more than from theoretical ideas? We suspected that staff preferred examples and stories but we required evidence of this.

## Our evaluation process was divided into the following four steps

### Step 1: choosing the evaluation model

The Kirkpatrick model

As part of our collaboration with other training areas in the SG, we met with an SG colleague in ODLL to ask her advice about our evaluation exercise. ODLL is responsible for all leadership and management training in the SG. Our ODLL colleague suggested the Kirkpatrick Evaluation Method, developed by Donald Kirkpatrick for evaluating training programmes, which was first introduced in 1959, is still widely used and was well suited to our purpose. The four levels of this methodology include determining how learners react to the learning process, the success of skill acquisition by learners, the extent to which workplace behaviour changes as a result of the learning process, and measurable results, including improved efficiency towards tasks and procedures.

The four levels of Kirkpatrick's Evaluation Model (Kirkpatrick and Kirkpatrick, 2007) are given in the following four subsections.

### Level 1: reaction

How well did the learners like the learning process? As the name suggests, evaluation at this level captures the immediate reaction of the delegates about the training. It assesses learners' satisfaction with the training. While this is not an accurate measure of effectiveness, it certainly can be a filter for badly designed training. Positive reactions may or may not result in good learning but negative reactions can certainly hinder the learning process.

### Level 2: learning

What did they learn? This is the extent to which the learners gain knowledge and skills. At this level, evaluation moves beyond learner satisfaction to assess the learning that has happened in terms of new skills, knowledge or working practices. Common methods used to test this are pre-test and post-test assessments to determine the amount of learning that has occurred.

### Level 3: behaviour

What changes in staff job performance resulted from the learning process? What new capability was there to perform the newly learned skills while on the job or back at their desks? This level is a critical measure of the amount of transfer of learning or amount of application of learning at the workplace. Evaluating at this level attempts to answer the question: 'Are the newly acquired skills, knowledge or attitude being used in the everyday environment of the learner?'

### Level 4: results

What are the tangible results of the learning process in terms of reduced cost, improved quality, increased production, efficiency, etc.? At this level, evaluation is done to measure the success of the training in terms that managers can understand (i.e., increased production, improved quality, decreased costs, improved efficiency and return on investment).

## Step 2: How best should we collect our feedback? What method or combination of methods should we use?

For the purposes of our research, the authors opted to use telephone interviews and emailed questionnaires to delegates attending our two chosen courses. We demonstrate our method in Table 6.1.

## Step 3: the evaluation procedure and gathering the evidence

At both the Internet Skills in the Workplace course and the Web 2.0 Workshop, the trainers informed delegates that the authors were evaluating the course content and were seeking evidence regarding the value and practical use of the course content. It was also explained that the authors wanted to establish

**Table 6.1**  The authors' method

| Method | Purpose | Advantages | Disadvantages |
|--------|---------|------------|---------------|
| Questionnaire, survey checklist | When need to quickly and/or easily get lots of information from end users on aspects of the service/training | Can complete anonymously Inexpensive to administer Easy to compare and analyse Can get lots of data | Might not get careful feedback/ completed in a rush Wording can bias end users' responses Are impersonal Difficult to get the users' experience full story |
| Interview | Useful when want to fully understand someone's impressions or experiences, or learn more about their answers to questionnaires | Able to get full range and depth of information Develops relationship with end user Allows for flexibility Information can be given on other aspects of the service | Can take more time Can be hard to analyse and compare Can be costly Interviewer can bias client's responses |

whether staff were working more efficiently, and whether the course content was fit for purpose and fulfilled the needs of the organisation. The trainers explained the information-gathering process and informed the delegates that a librarian (the authors) would telephone first, give a quick recap or reminder of our gathering evidence exercise, before sending a questionnaire by email. Delegates were asked via an emailed questionnaire (see Appendix A) to identify the following:

- a practical example of a task they had undertaken since the course;

- the benefit of what they had learned on the course;

- the outcome (putting into practice the skills gained on the course).

The authors made contact with the delegates via an email requesting that they send their replies within one week of receiving the questionnaire (which was three weeks after attending the course). All feedback was collected into an email folder and then transferred into an Excel spreadsheet, where statistics and evidence via comments from the delegates were collated to form the basis of our findings. Using email as a means of collecting this evidence allowed the delegates a contact name should they have any further questions regarding the questionnaire. It was necessary to remind some delegates to return the questionnaire via email. This was done by phone and proved worthwhile as the majority of those who were given the reminder subsequently completed the questionnaire.

During the early stages of the evaluation exercise – October and November 2009 – response to the feedback-gathering exercise was slow but positive. At first, apart from the emailed questionnaire, there was no direct contact with the delegates from the authors. After discussion, however, the authors decided that, in order to speed up the feedback process, making a direct connection with the delegates might help. As a result, one of the authors attended each course in person at the end of a training session and met the delegates face to face to explain why they were gathering evidence and needed the delegates' help. It was emphasised that all feedback was confidential. We thought that some sort of distance would be preferable, namely a librarian who was not connected to the delivery of the course the delegates had just attended. It was also important to emphasise that we were not investigating or assessing the actual trainers in any way nor was this a means of examining the delegates' capabilities. When the authors initially telephoned, the delegate was then able to put a name to the face and recall why they were being contacted. At this stage delegates usually began to explain to the author the benefits (or not) of the new skills gained and give an example of what they were. Some delegates did ask if it was sufficient to just give the evidence by telephone, and this was agreed to. However, some delegates preferred to view the questionnaire first as it allowed them to structure their reply and gave them time to recall. If response was still slow once the initial email had been sent, the author followed up with a second phone call as a reminder and this generally resulted in delegates giving evidence by telephone. A small number of delegates did not reply to emails nor phone calls.

Examples of responses from delegates are given in the following subsection. The authors asked the following question in the questionnaire and received the following sample of replies.

### 'How do you intend to use what you have learned on the course?'

- *It will enhance my ability to carry out better Internet searches and hence be more efficient at my job.*

- *To find facts, articles, research, etc. related to my area of work.*

- *The skills covered in the course will be extremely useful for research purposes, both sourcing academic papers and reliable statistics.*

- *Working as an analyst we are also passed intelligence that we need to check further online.*

- *I intend to use these skills to search for national and international information on patient experience surveys as*

> this is the type of topics I work on as well as do more appropriate searches on various topics for my personal interests.

- *Sourcing information for briefings meetings, etc.*

- *Will enable searching to be quicker and more accurate.*

- *Will discuss with colleagues as to whether we intend to take it further.*

- *Improve our Twitter activity and consider the use of social bookmarking.*

- *To make the public and stakeholders more aware of our policies, etc.*

- *Initially for newsfeeds; however, I will now give further thought as to how my office could benefit from using social media dissemination.*

- *I need to read the handout and decide how it will work best for me.*

- *Probably to keep abreast of conversations happening online as they relate to policies I am working on.*

## Step 4: interpreting the research findings

Once the authors had gathered all the evidence from the questionnaires and the phone interviews they collated it into an Excel spreadsheet and divided the information into three categories:

- positive comments
- negative comments

- what the delegates learned and then implemented back at their desks.

There were four main findings from our research. Our training course content needs to be relevant and tailored to the user, constantly revised, subject to varied delivery methods and adequately resourced (see the following four subsections).

## Relevant and tailored to user

Learning something in context makes all the difference to whether it is learnt or not and to whether it is understood or not. We must give practical everyday work examples in our training of how new skills can be put into practice back in their work areas. Training aims and objectives need to be clearly focused. Delegates prefer to be emailed the course materials beforehand so that they know what the course will cover (holds no surprises) and what is expected of them on the course. Occasionally, delegates cancel places on the training course, explaining that the course does not meet their needs. When this happens, the SG librarians look into why and how to help.

## Constantly revised

Our training materials need to be kept up to date and relevant to SG staff and any organisational changes, so they require regular updating and revision – often on a monthly basis.

## Varied delivery methods

Our classroom-based training courses may be well attended but this method does not suit everyone. We received requests via our questionnaires for shorter training sessions and for online e-learning modules.

### Adequately resourced

Providing relevant, current and engaging training is very time consuming and entails a vast amount of staffing resources (time as well as skills and enthusiasm). Therefore, all training needs to be adequately resourced.

From a trainer's point of view it is important to consider what the delegate will learn on the course, as this will direct and focus the course content and thereby ensure that learning outcomes are clear and relevant.

Our training evaluation research confirmed what we already suspected: that we needed to ensure the following questions were asked. Since the remit and work of the SG changes and develops on a regular basis, we must adapt our training and materials to ensure:

- all course content meets the needs of the attendees to do their job effectively;

- the topics covered must be relevant and practical, not theoretical;

- those attending the training are able to apply their new skills back at their desks.

## Outcomes of the LILAC research findings

Since LILAC 2010, when we stated in our final presentation slide that we had four main aims – namely, we wanted to revise our information literacy course materials by organising a Train the Trainer event for SG librarians, improving our evaluation process, continuing to seek advice from our SG training colleagues regarding training and finding a way to tailor it specifically to SG staff needs as a whole – we have not only managed to achieve all four aims over the past two years but also included some additional ones:

- We have updated our training materials, especially the social media course, Web 2.0 Workshop, where we changed the title to Social Media for Government. We have also created new short presentations, Social Media Bites, which focus on individual social media tools and collaboration platforms. Our Internet Skills in the Workplace course has also kept up with changes regarding information skills searching. Moreover, we update where necessary the content of all our materials on a monthly basis despite this being time consuming.

- We have devised simple online questionnaires using QuestBack (the system the SG recommends for staff to use) instead of using the paper form we used before. This ensures that all feedback is recorded in Excel spreadsheets so that we can obtain statistics and keep an easy record of all comments (both positive and negative) from SG staff regarding our training. We monitor all feedback on a regular basis and thereby make any necessary changes to our course content and to the delivery of the courses.

- We have created an SG Library blog to share our training materials and as a means to receive feedback from others on how to improve them. We have subsequently posted information on our blog advertising all SG Library services not just the training (Scottish Government Library blog: *http://sglibraryservices.wordpress.com/*).

- We have undertaken delegate profiling for SG Library training. When revising our training programme we aimed to look at ways for our training to be specifically relevant. We try to have a clear idea of who will be attending the course and what work area they are in. In order to achieve this we have been able to use information that we already have, namely the information held in our internal online event booking system. We have been able to check this against names signed up to attend the training. The system records the name, details and work areas of those signed up to the courses, thus allowing us to obtain a delegate profile. This also helps organise the training content and also prepare our trainers to deliver the training at the right level for the audience. We have used this information to tailor some aspects of our courses too and make the content very specific to delegate work areas. This is especially relevant in our Keeping Up to Date sessions where we tailor information on available alerting services to specific work areas such as the SG Directorate for Housing Regeneration and Welfare.

- We have created the role of subject librarian for all the different subject areas in the SG (e.g., health and community, farming and rural affairs, environment, transport, etc.). This has enabled librarians to deliver tailored information sessions and training in their subject areas, something which our research and feedback backs up. SG staff are more likely to use their newly found skills and information if they can see the relevance and value to their work and so they prefer a subject-specific approach to training sessions.

- We have established advocates for information literacy and the SG Library. SG librarians now have contact with SG divisional business managers and training liaison officers who operate as a network to support a common approach across the organisation to developing leadership behaviours, smarter working, and learning and development in general. In promoting the SG Library to business managers, they in turn pass information onto all staff in their work area. Recently, the SG Library has also received a list of a new staff working in the SG on a monthly basis and emailing them information about the SG Library. In addition, we regularly promote the SG Library on our intranet or offer to visit work areas and demonstrate relevant Library services, training and resources, tailored specifically to their needs. We also plan to develop our contacts with divisional personal assistants who work directly with senior staff. It is hoped that this will help establish good-practice examples of senior staff using the SG Library too. In addition, we now regularly promote our training courses on our e-library intranet, with a direct link to the course description and online booking system so that it is easy for SG staff to locate and book onto these.

- We have set up an SG Library group on Yammer, the microblogging platform used internally by SG staff to communicate with each other, ask questions or comment on work-related matters or subjects of interest. The SG Library uses Yammer to promote our services, advertise our training courses, share useful pieces of information as well as answer any general questions that SG staff may post.

- We have set up a community of practice group for all staff involved in training called the 'Scottish Government Training and Development Teams' on the Knowledge Hub platform (*https://knowledgehub.local.gov.uk/*). We are using this group as a forum to share best practice, hints and tips, documents, webinar software information, training courses and ideas on all aspects of learning and development in the SG. Prior to the creation of this group, all training and development teams were working individually with minimal collaboration.

■ We have undertaken a customer journey mapping exercise to identify the key processes that our customers encounter when they interact with the SG Library. This helped us understand the needs and preferences of our customers and measure our effectiveness and customer satisfaction at each stage of contact with the SG Library. The evidence we have gathered aims to ensure that we provide an effective and efficient service to all SG staff at all times and at all levels and services.

■ We have improved our questionnaire feedback form and created three new online forms (see Appendices A–C for URLs), all of which have been extremely important in understanding our customers, what they find useful, what they have implemented back at their desks, what they do not think useful, and what they think would improve our services. There are two training questionnaires, one which delegates complete in the training room immediately after the course (Appendix D), and the other, a follow-up questionnaire, three weeks later (Appendix E). For example, we now ask SG staff: 'How did you hear about the service?' This is to discover how best to promote and advertise the SG Library. According to a recent evaluation, the most effective method of publicising our services is via our internal online training booking system on the SG intranet. 'From a colleague' and 'From an intranet article' have equal ratings. SG staff also have options of selecting via a dropdown menu, flyers and posters but these methods of publicity and promotion get no ratings at all. On investigating responses via the questionnaires, the authors have also noted that participants were far more willing to use a 'tick-box' and select from a multiple-choice menu of possible options in reply to questions rather than write their answers in a dialogue box. Therefore we plan to amend our

# Appendix A Scottish Government Library Course Feedback

*https://response.questback.com/scottishgovernment/ w5qptdgvot/*

# Appendix B Scottish Government Library Course Feedback – 3-week follow-up

*https://response.questback.com/scottishgovernment/ wdnyvtlkyh/*

# Appendix C Scottish Government Library Services Feedback

*https://response.questback.com/scottishgovernment/ svlaqcypsf/*

# Appendix D   Scottish Government Library Services Questionnaire (paper copy, no longer used)

Scottish Government Information Management Unit
*Library services*

Advanced Internet Skills – [Date] – [Location]

Thank you for attending the recent internet skills training session. We value your feedback. Please let us know what you thought and email this back to *LIBRARY*.

1.  Before attending this session, where on the below scale would you say your understanding of searching the Internet was?

| 1 | 2 | 3 | 4 | 5 |
|---|---|---|---|---|
| ☐ | ☐ | ☐ | ☐ | ☐ |

Low understanding        High understanding

2.  After attending this session, where on the below scale would you say your understanding of searching the Internet is?

| 1 | 2 | 3 | 4 | 5 |
|---|---|---|---|---|
| ☐ | ☐ | ☐ | ☐ | ☐ |

Low understanding        High understanding

3.  Did the information session meet your expectations and needs? Was there anything that was particularly relevant? If yes, please specify.

Yes ☐   No ☐

4. Please describe any areas where you would appreciate further training on a one-to-one or group basis.

   *Please leave your name and user number below or give them to the trainer*



5. We are grateful for any other comments and suggestions you may have regarding this session or any other aspect of the Library Service.

# Appendix E   Scottish Government Library Services Questionnaire email (evaluation research)

Good afternoon

*Web 2.0 Workshop (assessment of content)*

You recently attended the Web 2.0 Workshop on 29 October 2009.

   You may now have had time to put into practice some of the social media tools discussed and explored during this session. Could you please provide examples of specific tasks or occasions where you were able to use any of these new skills, the benefit gained and outcome? Listed below are a few examples:

*Task*     Task you did on the course (skill acquired)

*Benefit*  How was this useful? e.g. Communication and collaboration  I now have a better understanding of Web 2.0

*Outcome*  How did you put it into practice?

Subjects covered on the Web 2.0 Workshop are listed below and details can be found in your course manual. Please comment on as many of the four areas as you can.

|  | Task | Benefit | Outcome |
|---|---|---|---|
| An overview of Web 2.0 |  |  |  |
| Web 2.0 tools |  |  |  |
| Evaluation skills |  |  |  |
| Guidance for Government |  |  |  |

We are also evaluating the course materials (paper manual) and would welcome any additional comments you may have:

1.  Is the manual useful?

2.  Have you used the manual as a 'reference source' after the course?

3.  Would you prefer to receive the manual in paper format or electronically?

I shall contact you in three weeks to discuss these questions but would like to emphasise this is purely evaluating and assessing the course content to make sure that we are including the correct materials for the delegates and for SG business purposes.

Many thanks and look forward to talking to you but please feel free to contact me if need be beforehand.

Best wishes

# 7

# Information literacy in health management: supporting the public in their quest for health information

*Christine Irving*

**Abstract:** This chapter looks at health information policy documents and frameworks in the UK that support information literacy in healthcare with a specific focus on support for the general public. It highlights recent research findings in the UK, Sweden and Australia that support the need for health literacy skills and discusses examples of public library initiatives and activities that have emerged to assist with supporting the public in their quest for health information and the necessary information literacy skills they need.

**Key words:** information literacy, health information, health information seeking, health information literacy, health literacy, health information policies, health information frameworks, public library initiatives.

## Introduction

Health librarians play a key role in providing resources and continuing professional development (CPD) activities for health professionals, developing skills and ways in which information literacy/evidence-based practice may be used in healthcare. Whilst examples of their activities can be readily found, there is a dearth of examples relating to information literacy initiatives and activities to support patients, carers and members of the public to participate more effectively in their own healthcare.

Whilst the *Prague Declaration* (UNESCO 2003) makes no mention of health the *High-Level Colloquium on Information Literacy and Lifelong Learning* held 6–9 November 2005 in Alexandria, Egypt does identify information literacy as crucial to health. Its focus however is on: access to health information for all citizens; each country to develop an integrated education curriculum that encourages and empowers the general public to take responsibility for their own health and well-being; and encouraging and empowering 'patients and their carers to ask questions to clarify their understandings.' Information literacy is mentioned in relation to the training of healthcare practitioners, health Administrators, policymakers and 'those professionals engaged in promoting Health Information Literacy' (Garner 2005: 14–16) but not the public.

## Health information policy documents and frameworks

### Developments in Scotland – brief overview

In 2007, the Scottish Government which has devolved responsibility for health, published its health programme in *Better Health, Better Care: Action Plan* to deliver a healthier Scotland by helping 'people to sustain and improve their health, especially in disadvantaged communities, ensuring better, local and faster access to health care.' (Scottish Government 2007c: 1)

With regard to 'information for patients' the action plan called for introduction of a

'National Health Information and Support Service to provide a single shared health information online resource which brings together quality assured local and national information from the NHS and other sectors, a national health information helpline available and a network of branded health information support centres, embedded in local communities. This will involve:

○ a consistent approach to produce high quality patient information across NHS Scotland

○ information partnerships with key national voluntary organisations to maximise the benefit to patients from the high quality, patient focused information they produce

○ clearly signposted access points where people can get support to find the information they need; understand the information provided and develop the skills and confidence to use it effectively in order to become an active partner in their own care

○ a particular focus on meeting the needs of those communities and individuals who have traditionally found it harder to engage with health services.'

(Scottish Government 2007c: 44)

Following on from this is the NHS Scotland Knowledge Services Group's publication *Enabling Partnerships: Sharing Knowledge for Scotland's Health and Healthcare* which proposes a strategy for development of a National Health Knowledge Network to 'support members of the public, patients and professionals in finding health information when and where they need it, in the format they require' and 'support them in developing the skills and confidence to understand and use the information effectively' (NHSES 2008: 2). To achieve this aim NHS Education Scotland developed an Information Literacy Framework called 'Better Informed for Better Health and Better Care: A Framework to

Support Improved Information Use for Staff and Patients'. More specifically, the Framework was 'for NHS Scotland staff, partner organizations, patients, carers and members of the public who wish to further their information literacy capabilities and, consequently, contribute to health improvement and better service delivery.' (Craig 2009: 77) Information literacy was seen as supporting 'individual and organisational learning, creativity and innovation and contributes to improved healthcare delivery through a continuously evolving, reliable information base.' (Craig 2009: 78)

The Information Literacy Framework (NHSES 2009) based on an NHS information literacy model includes a series of scenarios which involves a combination of practitioners and patients. Following a piloting exercise the Framework was divided into a series of eight A5-size booklets. Each booklet is relevant to a specific information area or interest group. Of particular interest to this chapter are the following booklets/ areas:

- *Information Literacy in Healthcare*. This booklet describes several ways in which information literacy (evidence-based practice) may be used in healthcare practice. Included are examples of information literacy in action (e.g., Jim's wisdom tooth extraction, Laura checks hand hygiene procedures, Peter maintains his current awareness, Lesley learns more about surgical site infection). For more information see *http://www.infoliteracy.scot.nhs.uk/media/ 1923912/healthcare.pdf*

- *Information Literacy for Patients*. This booklet covers information literacy from the patient's point of view, intended to support patients when seeking or receiving information. It is also intended, among other things, to support self-management of long-term conditions. For more information see *http://www.infoliteracy.scot.nhs.uk/media/1923918/patients.pdf*

In addition to the Framework, online information literacy courses and an information literacy portal were produced.

In 2010 NHS Education for Scotland published *Enabling Partnerships: Sharing Knowledge to Build the Mutual NHS a Knowledge Management Strategy and Action Plan for Better Health and Better Care in Scotland 2010–2012*. Reassuringly, information skills and the Information Literacy Framework are still highlighted and two of the key messages are:

- 'We will provide information resources, technology and expertise to support NHS24 in their lead role of providing high quality patient information through the NHS Inform service.

- We will promote and develop information literacy to give people power to ask questions, find, share and use knowledge. This will support self-management and shared decision-making.'

(NHSES 2010: 3)

Unfortunately, in 2013 the online courses have been allowed to lapse and are no longer accessible. The original work has not been taken forward although the latest 'initiatives' such as Knowledge into Action, Health Literacy and Bibliotherapy are all based on the previous work. However, the term 'information literacy' is no longer used in any of the projects (Craig 2013).

## Wales

Health is a devolved responsibility for the Welsh Assembly Government. The strategy adopted by the Welsh Assembly emphasises that 'the health of the nation is not just the responsibility of the Welsh Assembly Government and the

NHS. Everyone has a part to play in improving health in Wales: health is everybody's business' (cited in Thomas n.d.: 1). In 2004 Health Challenge Wales was set up by the Welsh Assembly Government to

> '. . . empower individuals and enable them to make informed decisions which contribute to a healthier nation. The campaign encourages individuals and organisations to share responsibility for health by taking small steps to become healthier. A key part of this from the very start was the signposting of information or activities to help members of the public and organisations to improve their own health. Public libraries have a key role to play in this and the project explored how they might better provide health information to the public and support the information literacy skills required to access, evaluate and use this information.' (Thomas n.d.)

We will return to the role of public libraries and how they provide health information to the public and support information literacy skills later.

## UK

According to Marshall et al. (2012: 479), 'Information has been a key strand of UK government policy on health care since the 1990s but the emphasis has tended to be on information provision rather than use, with little attention paid to the health literacy skills of end users.' The brief review of the history of health information policy in the UK by Marshall et al. (2012: 480) shows that

> 'Information came into the health policy foreground in the United Kingdom as part of a modernization agenda for the National Health Service (NHS) in 1998, with the publication

of *Information for Health* (NHS Executive, 1998). Since then, information has been understood as a central resource for the organization and delivery of health care in the United Kingdom, with Information and Communication Technologies (ICTs) seen as having a crucial role. The NHS Constitution (Department of Health, 2010a) makes information provision a legal obligation.'

It is important to note that in 1999 responsibility for health became a devolved matter for both Scotland and Wales.

Marshall et al. (2012: 480) identify initiatives such as 'Information Prescriptions (Department of Health, 2009) [which] highlight the importance of information in long-term care' and 'key national initiatives around providing information on the Internet, including NHS Direct Online (NHS Direct, 1999) and more recently NHS Choices (Department of Health, 2008)' plus 'the UK government consultation document *Liberating the NHS: An Information Revolution* (Department of Health, 2010b) [which] sets out a vision for an "information revolution" where "people have the information they need to stay healthy ..." (p. 5)'. However, they highlight that 'despite the perceived importance of information as a vehicle for delivering effective health care, there has been little emphasis in the UK on how people find, evaluate, and use information for health; in other words on the health literacy skills of end users' (Marshall et al. 2012).

# The need for health literacy skills – research findings

## UK/England

Marshall et al. are not alone in highlighting the health literacy skills of end users. According to new research 'almost half of people are unable to properly understand medical information and instructions' (CILIP 2013: 7). The research – a study carried out by London South Bank University (LSBU) – found that

'... health literacy levels across England has shown that health information is too complex and that 42% of people aged between 16 and 65 years are unable to effectively understand and use everyday health information. This figure rises to 61% when the information also requires numeracy skills. This means between 15–21 million people across the country are not accessing the information they need to become and stay healthy.' (LSBU 2012)

Professor Gill Rowlands of the Faculty of Health & Social Care at LSBU led the research team and argues that 'this is a preventable problem, which puts an increasing pressure on an already stretched health service. Our priority now is to look at addressing the challenges uncovered in the research and to develop solutions to ensure health information is more easily understood.' Also highlighted is that 'people with low health literacy skills can have poorer health and are less likely to be able to manage illnesses or engage with health screening programmes.' (LSBU 2012)

Comparisons were made with results from the Department for Business Innovation & Skills 2011 *Skills for Life Survey: A Survey of Literacy, Numeracy and ICT Levels in England*, which measured basic skills amongst people aged between 16 and 65 in England. Over 7000 people from a cross-section of the population across England were interviewed. The study findings suggest that 'individuals associated with indicators of social exclusion are likely to have skills needs' (DBIS 2012: 275). Self-reporting ill health was amongst the indicators used. Among the Internet users selected for the ICT assessment 53 per cent searched the Internet for health-related information and 43 per cent of them did so a few times a month, whilst 7 per cent did so a few times a week (DBIS 2012: 201). Women were found to be more likely to search for health-related information than men (DBIS 2012: 200).

## Sweden

In Sweden Mårtensson and Hensing (2012: 152) found similar findings in their literature review of health literacy in 200 scientific articles published between 2000 and 2008

'A lack of health literacy may have effects at many levels, from the individual to the societal. Examples are incorrect use of medications/assistive aids, lack of knowledge in health decisions, misinterpretation of instructions or symptoms, absence from booked health care visits, unnecessary examinations or surgery, increased need of hospital treatment and security risks at home, at work or in society.'

Health literacy was said to involve the 'ability to read and the numerical skills needed to act on information or advice on health issues in ways that promote and maintain health (Ad Hoc Committee on Health Literacy for the Council on Scientific Affairs American Medical Association 1999, Williams et al. 1995, Center for Health Strategies Inc. 2000).' (Mårtensson and Hensing, 2012)

They found that 'interest in health literacy has increased during the past decade' and that

'Access to information is becoming increasingly important for individuals' health decisions. Recovery after illness, sickness absence and rehabilitation also involve decisions that are likely to be better if based on relevant information.

Furthermore, there seems to be a growing and sometimes implicit obligation on the part of individuals to search for information themselves, to understand rights and responsibilities and to make decisions in health issues (Nielsen-Bohlman et al. 2004). The purpose in this approach is to enable individuals to promote health or solve health problems by themselves or to be an active partaker and negotiator in health care interventions and decisions (Law 1998). Decisions in health issues may be complicated, as described by, e.g. Länsimies-Antikainen et al. (2010)[. H]owever, considering the increasing amount of information available about health, illness and health care[, a] crucial feature of an individual's access to and benefit of health information is his or her level of health literacy.' (Mårtensson and Hensing 2012: 151)

Whilst it is important to ensure health information is more easily understood, 'information on its own can achieve very little' and 'human contact' and 'communication' are essential (Smith and Duncan 2009 cited by Marshall et al. 2012: 488). As Yates et al. (2012) state we need to turn to 'HIL [health information literacy] research as it informs us about peoples' ways of engaging with health information (how, where, when, why, what), the challenge to public health policy is to ensure that health messages are designed and delivered in different and constantly changing ways in order to meet the diverse needs of a multifaceted community.' (Yates et al. 2012: 472)

## Supporting the public's quest for health information

Marshall et al.'s (2012: 493) study of people who were self-managing their weight found that 'the most useful sources of information for this group of people are informal rather than formal; and encountered rather than sought out' (Marshall et al. 2012: 485) and cite Kuhlthau in support of their findings as

'Kuhlthau argues people with everyday life information needs, including health-related needs, construct their information from a variety of sources over an extended period of time. She cites Bates' berry picking metaphor (Bates, cited in Kuhlthau 2008, p. 67) to illustrate that people move from one source to another and extract only certain items for use. McKenzie (2003) demonstrated similarly that, in everyday situations, people move fluidly from one type of information seeking behaviour to another, for example, from contacting a doctor to looking something up in a book to engaging in conversation with another person in a similar situation.' (Marshall et al. 2012: 485–6)

Marshall et al. (2012: 493) reported that their study

'. . . results suggest that the typical information literacy staged model needs to be developed and expanded in ways that take account of: the variety of information sources and types that people use, find useful, and need; the need for human intervention to support and supplement information; the empowering effects of peer support and participation; and the need to view people as both providers and users of information. Within the context of consumer health, a broader and more social approach to information literacy is needed to ensure a better "fit" between the provision and the use of information.'

This need for the typical information literacy–staged model, originally developed within higher education, to be developed and expanded reflects the need found in the workplace discussed in Chapter 5.

Yates et al.'s (2012) Australian study 'Exploring health information use by older Australians within everyday life', where health information literacy was understood as 'using information to learn about health' (Yates et al. 2012: 461) and 'been acknowledged as a core ingredient that can assist people to take responsibility for managing and improving their own health' (Yates et al. 2012: 460), found that older Australians used the following kinds of information to learn about their health:

- Print – brochures, magazines, books, newspapers

- Multimedia – TV, radio, YouTube, Internet searches, medical videos, photos

- Test results – laboratory tests, blood sugar machine

- Meetings – seminars, support groups, health expos [exhibitions]

- People – family, friends, childhood elders, colleagues, medical practitioners, group members

- Own body – symptoms, feelings, reaction to treatments, personal experience.

They also found that 'information is usually prioritized by such criteria as authoritative-ness, contextualization to the patient's circumstances, interactivity, and focus on the specific problem at hand:

- Medical practitioners are trusted most highly. They have the knowledge and skill to diagnose, they know your specific situation and medical history, and you choose a practitioner you can relate to. Practitioners are typically considered to be the primary source of information about health.

- People known personally (friends, support groups) are typically considered trustworthy. The advantage of people is you are able to ask questions face-to-face and obtain the viewpoint of patients who have faced similar situations.

- Text is considered relatively useful, especially if composed with your area of interest in view. Such impersonal sources are considered good for general background insights.'

(Yates et al. 2012: 470)

They argue that 'effective and efficient communication of health information includes thinking more broadly about what constitutes information and the means of transmitting that information' and that 'information literacy is not a homogenous set of skills; rather it reflects a person's experience of using information, an experience that is likely to vary across cultural and contextual boundaries, across time, and across a lifetime.' (Yates et al. 2012: 473)

They further argue that 'research into people's experiences of using information across all ages to learn about their health can support policy makers in influencing the design, use, and accessibility of health information in terms of resources, places, processes, and the way people make use of health information. As we better understand people's experiences of health information use, we can modify and design better health information delivery mechanisms and environments which support people to effectively experience and use health information.' (Yates et al. 2012: 474)

## Public library activities and initiatives

Similar to other areas outwith higher education there is relatively little literature describing actual examples of information literacy activities in public libraries related to health. However, there are reports of public library health activities.

Libraries are said to 'offer a neutral, non-stigmatised, non-clinical space, and access to individuals that can be hard to reach' and therefore seem an ideal location to help support the public's quest for health information. Museums, Libraries and Archives Council (MLA) research measured the 'overall levels and types of health and well-being related activities across English libraries. One hundred and eleven public libraries reported a total of 1,109 activities in this area, with a further 107 in preparation.' Where partnerships were found not to work well issues such as 'lack of resources in terms of funding or staff as a barrier' and a 'lack of understanding of libraries' contribution by health partners, exacerbated by different agendas, priorities or timescales.' (Anton 2010: 42).

Much of reported public library activity seems to centre on the provision of health information in the form of books, leaflets and bookmarked reliable health websites – such as NHS Choices (n.d.) and NHS Informs (2012) – and schemes such as Books on Prescription. Books on Prescription schemes are usually run in conjunction with local library services and incorporate bibliotherapy which 'can include reading for pleasure and enjoyment as well as using self help and information resources' (Eynon 2012). The Books on Prescription scheme was 'developed by Professor Neil Frude and has been established as a national scheme in Welsh libraries since 2005' (Reading Agency 2012). There is a national scheme in Ireland and books are now available on prescription across much of England and Scotland (Eynon 2012). Whilst this may be the focus of such schemes, one would hope that if you delved deeper you would find information literacy activities within the provision offered – albeit on an informal basis – implicit rather than explicit.

The Society of Chief Librarians Wales produced a report entitled *Public Libraries in Wales: Health, Wellbeing and Social Benefits* (Eynon 2012) to demonstrate the role 'public libraries have and can have in relation to health, wellbeing and social benefits.' They report that they see

'. . . the role of public libraries in relation to health and wellbeing is beginning to be recognised. This can be seen through the very successful Book Prescription Wales Scheme and our partnership work with groups such as MacMillan [*sic*] Cancer Support. However, we believe the health and social benefits provided by public library services are still often overlooked by decision makers.'

The report summarises the activities that public libraries carry out to support health, well-being and social benefits. Whilst much is related to the provision of information they state that libraries 'help reduce the burden on social care and health services by:

■ Empowering people to access and use health and wellbeing information

■ Providing free access to the internet and information resources

■ Supporting literacy, information literacy, digital literacy and health literacy

■ Helping with the prevention and early diagnosis of illness.'

Health literacy is defined as 'an individual's ability to read, understand and use healthcare information; e-health literacy is the use of the internet for information-seeking and health information distribution purposes' (Eynon 2012). The report states that 'libraries can help a person to search for health information, retrieve health information, make sense of the information and utilise this information.' An example of this is demonstrated by a Macmillian Project Report quote from a carer involved in the Carers Project run by Ebbw Vale Library, Blaenau Gwent

> 'I have been coming to the library for taster sessions on how to use the Internet. I was so nervous, I was a complete beginner, didn't know where to start. As I am a carer, it has been great to be able to come for the session when it suits me. I would never be able to commit to a class. Within a couple of weeks, I have been able to research advice and support groups for my daughter's disability. I have been able to contact other parents with similar problems. This has helped me cope with things.'

As highlighted above, searching for health information may emerge through a variety of information literacy–related activities including Internet taster sessions. Moreover, information literacy element/activities may be implicit rather than explicit. For example, public library offerings include basic computer training which includes searching the Internet for information not necessarily to meet a specific information need (Ward 2013). It could be a specific need not obviously related to health/health information. An interviewee in an Inverclyde Libraries study about information literacy in employability training, where health was a key factor for most of the participants, reported trying to find information about some prescription medicine she was taking by going to an Internet search engine and typing in the search term 'medicine' (Crawford and Irving 2012: 83). This anecdote clearly demonstrates how much support the public need in their quest for health information and the need for health information literacy activities.

There are numerous case studies that demonstrate the work of Welsh public library staff in their support of the health and well-being of the people of Wales. Activities such as 'accessing health and information from the Book Prescription Wales scheme or Macmillian cancer information services' (Library Wales 2012) along with health and well-being activities for the young and old not traditionally associated with libraries that include baby massaging, splash and rhyme time, a beauty fair and a tea dance. Whilst the information literacy element is not explicit in the case studies it could be there in a number of guises.

Staff health literacy training or availability of staff may be an issue that hinders the development of incorporating information literacy activities for the public. Many of the points made in Chapter 8 concerning the role of the public library in informal learning and the issues they face is relevant to health information literacy.

The US National Network of Libraries of Medicine's publication *Providing Health Information Services* includes 'resources that have been written and created by public librarians for use by their colleagues in answering health information questions' (NN/LM 2008) and training opportunities for providing health information services.

A UK example of public library staff receiving training can be seen in the following example.

## Health literacy partnerships in Welsh libraries

Working with NHS Direct Wales public library staff received half-day training sessions on how to access health information, and how to evaluate consumer health information on the Web.

An example of how staff went on to help their customers – the general public – is illustrated through the Blaina Library (Abertillery) engaging in partnership work with the Health Promotion Library (Cardiff). The partnership 'enabled customers to access specialist information suitable for their needs and health literacy level which has enabled them to better manage their existing health conditions and to make lifestyle changes that might prevent future problems' (Thomas n.d.: 1).

Some Books on Prescription schemes have evolved to offer more than just resources as the following examples show.

## Reading Well Books on Prescription scheme for England

In 2013 a new national Reading Well Books on Prescription scheme for England was launched. The scheme is built on the 'existing best practice to deliver a new quality assured shared approach to Books on Prescription delivery in England' providing 'self-help book-based support for adults experiencing mild to moderate mental health conditions.' The scheme available to English public library authorities from May 2013, which has been 'endorsed by the Department of Health and other health partners, aims to improve and consolidate local delivery through:

- Quality assured shared resources including core booklists, national impact evidence, training and advocacy

- Core self-help reading book collections available through all libraries

- A new integrated approach offering professionally endorsed, self-help reading alongside creative reading – our Mood-boosting Books scheme is based on evidence that stress levels can be significantly reduced by reading

- Tools to support local library/health and social care partnership working

- Signposting via NHS Choices website and other key stakeholder networks and organisations.'

(Reading Agency 2012)

Partnership work is evident with the development of the scheme being 'funded by Arts Council England, in partnership with the Society of Chief Librarians and the Reading Agency.' The scheme is supported by 'the Royal College of General Practitioners, the Royal College of Nursing, the Royal College of Psychiatrists, the British Psychological Society, the British Association for Behavioural and Cognitive Psychotherapies, the Department of Health Improving Access to Psychological Therapies programme and Mind' (Reading Agency 2012).

## East Renfrewshire's 'Health Information in Your Library'

In 2005 East Renfrewshire was involved in the first of Scotland's Books on Prescription schemes 'the Healthy Reading scheme, set up by NHS Greater Glasgow's South-East Psychosocial Services (STEPS), in liaison with Glasgow City Council, East Renfrewshire Council, GPs and other health professionals to give people with mild mental health problems speedy access to high quality psychological self-help materials' (NHSGG 2005). Today this service has developed and includes:

- *Health information points* – books on healthy living, illness, bereavement and other life issues, leaflets on health subjects and a dedicated PC where you can check out useful health websites.

- *Local health information* – health and care services in the local area, online reliable and trustworthy health information in Scotland.

- *Library staff* – to help find the information needed including books, leaflets and health websites

- *Health and well-being activities* – health activities taking place in libraries (e.g., Relaxation Clinic, therapeutic treatments, Older People's Health & Wellbeing Group.

- *Healthy Reading collection* – selected by health professionals covering a range of mental health issues such as anxiety, low mood and low self-esteem.

(ERC 2013)

Other parts of the NHS Greater Glasgow and Clyde area are included in the Healthy Reading Scheme.

### East Ayrshire Council's CHIP (Community Health Improvement Partnership)

This initiative is a mobile healthy living centre called the CHIP van, which began operations in 2001 with the aim of taking health promotion to East Ayrshire communities. It has developed over the years and delivers 'services which will improve the health of communities, support vulnerable groups and offer advice and support to individuals' (EAC 2012).

## Partnership working

Partnership working is a key element of the work being done in this area as demonstrated by the examples above – in particular, the work with the NHS and projects such as setting up Macmillan cancer information points in public libraries. Related to partnership working is funding, and it is interesting to see where some of the funding is coming from. For example, the Knowing as Healing Project is running health information literacy classes as part of the project and has been awarded Arts Enterprise funding to run these in a local public library (Grant 2013). The Knowing as Healing Project is a 'participatory action research project working with people living with irritable bowel syndrome (IBS). It is partnering undergraduate medical students with people living with IBS and the aim is to enhance health information literacy amongst participants and to synthesise biomedical knowledge with first-person illness narratives' (University of Sheffield n.d. a).

The project is part of the Storying Sheffield project that has 'worked with many different groups of people including people who are long-term users of mental health services, people with physical disabilities, older people, some who live with dementia, primary school students, new migrants to the UK, patients in secure hospitals, and others' (University of Sheffield n.d. b).

## Summary of the chapter

Whilst there are health information policies, strategies and frameworks which include health information to support the public in their quest for health information, research still identifies a need for health literacy skills. Although the public library is seen as an ideal location to help provide the support, much of it seems to focus on the provision of health information through books, leaflets and bookmarked health websites. Whilst the examples in this chapter are only a sample they seem to be representative of the activities being provided including some innovative health and well-being activities being offered. However, the challenge seems to be the need for information literacy activities relating to health/health information or health information literacy skills and competencies to be developed and encouraged within public library staff and the public. As with other information literacy activities sometimes great initiatives and projects go unnoticed; we need to share, report at conferences and write about them more.

**8**

# Employability, informal learning and the role of the public library

*John Crawford*

**Abstract:** This chapter explores further some of the issues first raised in Chapter 5 by discussing the nature of information literacy and how it is applied in ordinary people's everyday lives. In this context the use of information is strongly linked with the alleviation of disempowerment and deprivation. The use of information in such environments is unstructured and sources of information include magazines, experts, friends and random social encounters. Employability skills' development is also an important factor and it is important for information professionals to work with other relevant agencies including adult literacies trainers and community learning and development staff. Public libraries have a key role to play but there is a need for training in learning and teaching strategies and the development of appropriate learning materials. Examples of good practice from the UK and the USA are included.

**Key words:** information literacy, informal learning, lifelong learning, public libraries, employability, information literacy instruction.

## The nature of information and information literacy in informal learning

Various terms are associated with nontraditional and informal learners: lifelong learner, professional development, adult learning or literacy, nomadic learner or even the non-scholar scholar. The one thing they all have in common is that the term 'information literacy' is rarely used or accurately understood by these groups (Birdsong and Freitas 2012: 589). Although information literacy research began in the late 1980s little research has been conducted which explores information literacy within the context of everyday life (Partridge et al. 2008: 110), and in 2008 it was noted (Harding 2008) that less than 2 per cent of the literature on information literacy had any focus on public libraries. This despite the fact that it was pointed out as long ago as 1997 that 'the information needs of consumers or the general public have been wholly neglected by information researchers' (Nicholas and Marden 1997: 5).

The practice of informal information finding has been described as everyday life information seeking (ELIS) and has been defined as the process that 'people employ to orientate themselves in daily life or to solve problems not wholly connected with the performance of occupational tasks' (Savolainen 1995: 267). While this definition is quite helpful it is important to note that informal information seeking is also linked to skills and employability development. Early ELIS research studies of ordinary people's information-seeking activities were conducted in the United States in the 1970s and early 1980s and this led to further studies of topics as diverse as the role of information for hobbyists, information sharing by members of a knitting group, the information needs and behaviour of migrant Hispanic farm workers in the United States and barriers to information for battered women (Walker 2010: 43–5). Partridge et al. (2008: 111–12) consider that what they call 'community information literacy' 'encompasses a critical interest in those who are relatively disempowered in our global technological society, including women, children [and] disabled persons'. Information literacy transforms people and brings about learning. These key themes of disadvantage and empowerment will be returned to again in the course of the chapter.

The problem of disadvantage among informal learners and information users is often compounded by previous past negative experiences of library use which adult learners bring to their new learning environment (Ashcroft et al. 2007: 134), and this can be exacerbated by poor previous school performance resulting in a lack of confidence about undertaking further learning. Indeed, some adult literacies tutors interviewed in the planning of a research project (Crawford and Irving 2009) expressed considerable hostility towards scholastic education which they felt had let their clients down, and in an interview-based study of adult learners in Inverclyde in the west of Scotland (Crawford and Irving 2012) interviewees consistently reported poor school experiences and low academic achievement. Information literacy in informal environments is unusual in that it explicitly involves emotional and psychological issues, something which is less obviously evident in other forms of information literacy activity. This has important implications for training, accreditation and assessment. McNicol and Dalton (2003) found that there is a conflict between offering tentative learners a comfortable learning environment and the possibility that formal evaluation may put these learners off (i.e., changing an informal relaxed atmosphere by introducing formal connotations).

How information is perceived and used in the workplace seems tidy in comparison with the world of everyday life information seeking. This, to some extent, reflects the diverse nature of adult learners and information searching. Partridge et al. (2008: 120) believe that community information literacy research must represent the disenfranchised and 'allow the forms of information important to these communities to be recognised ... we need to recognise, and make possible the collection of information meaningful in other cultures, for example – indigenous art, stories, folk medicine, oral histories, religious culture. Indigenous knowledge of all kinds has previously been disregarded by the information world'. Pilerot and Lindbergh (2011) go further, identifying in two information literacy policy documents an 'imperialist project' which assumes that information literacy activities should be firmly based on ICT infrastructures and neglect information cultures which are based on oral communication.

Studies certainly show a lack of reliance on conventional print and electronic sources. Research into how parents find childcare information shows a preference for advice from health professionals although informal help networks consisting of family, friends and other parents are also important. Another study showed friends and professionals as the most popular sources, and friends were often preferred over relations as they were viewed as more appropriate confidants. A study of stay-at-home mothers showed that they used a wide variety of sources including books, the Internet, magazines, experts and friends. Centres for social encounters are also physical places where information is encountered. These include shopping trips and community centres. In exploiting shared social networks social stratification is a major barrier. Some parents who are better educated tend to have more reliable networks and consequently better quality information. While parents do use print and Internet sources, information found in this way is often difficult to interpret which means that professional advice must be sought (Walker 2010: 46–50).

More recognisably, conventional methods of data finding and reporting also draw attention to problems of skill and training needs. An American study of the debate on healthcare reform in online political forums analysed over 6000 postings. It showed that only 400 (6.3 per cent) cited at least one formal information source. There was evidence of statements unsupported by evidence. Of the sources used the main one was digital versions of newspapers, followed by blogs, government documents, organisation websites and broadcast news and streaming videos. Most of the streaming media appeared in YouTube videos. The study found it difficult to identify cited information sources precisely, and it was hard to quantify the objectivity and reliability of sources like blogs. One of the recommendations of the study was that public libraries should offer information literacy training (O'Connor and Rapchak 2012). This recommendation seems to be supported by an anecdote from the Inverclyde study. An interviewee reported trying to find information about some prescription medicine she was taking by going to an Internet search engine and typing in the search term 'medicine' (Crawford and Irving 2012: 83). The overall picture is of a large range of sources being used but without much discrimination or evaluation.

## Users and providers

The varied nature of users and providers illustrates the problems associated with service development in this area and eludes simple definition, but there is a clear link with deprivation. This, in turn, includes terms like digitally excluded, information poor and hard to reach. The term 'digital citizenship' has been coined to help define the issue. Digital citizenship is:

'... a series of entitlements to empower individuals and communities through the use of digital technology, where those entitlements relate to civil, political and social activity, including learning.' (O'Beirne 2010: 93)

In 2005 MORI produced a major survey which was one of the first to take a wide-ranging look at the issues of reliability of information found on the Internet and the extent to which users feel they can trust the information they find there. Issues like usage and expertise were also reviewed. Over half of the respondents were found to be Internet users. Better-off people (social classes ABC1 – upper middle class, middle class and lower middle class), those who were under 55 and those with formal qualifications and in work were more likely to use the Internet, while poorer people (social classes C2DE – skilled working class, working class and those at the lowest level of subsistence) over 55 with no formal qualifications were less likely to use the Internet. People who have never used the Internet are likely to be older, to have no formal qualifications and to be unemployed. Although, over half of Internet users (60 per cent) had been using the Internet for four years or more, only 10 per cent had received any formal training in how to use it. The term 'information poor' is closely aligned with the concept of the digital divide and refers to the ability of an individual to access information based on their socioeconomic status; it is also linked with the use of locally obtained 'information gossip' from friends and neighbours and the lack of use of official resources, most notably the public library (Walker 2010: 53–5). Social exclusion is also a factor as there is a significant overlap between poverty and exclusion. Most people below the poverty line are also socially excluded. Social class also matters. People in Social Class IV (partly skilled) and V (unskilled) are much more likely to be out of work, less likely to have qualifications and, even if working, are less likely to receive training (Muddiman et al., 2000: 4-8). Historically, public libraries have failed to engage with the socially excluded.

Identified user groups include groups whose needs are likely to overlap. These include the over-50s who may find confronting needed IT skills difficult in order to become information users. For those over 50 who do make use of the Internet the four main topics of interest are health, income, recreation and pharmaceuticals. The implied interest in health issues is dealt with in more detail in Chapter 7. However, the elderly still prefer to obtain information from people especially medical professionals and family members (Birdsong and Freitas 2012: 594–5). Another category is the long-term physically disabled who can use ICT and information to regain a 'sense of control over their lives' (Partridge et al. 2008: 115). Libraries can offer courses to immigrants to help them integrate into their new communities by giving them the opportunity to learn languages and learn about their rights, obligations and opportunities in their adopted countries (Eve et al. 2007: 398). A study of school pupils in a school in a deprived area of Glasgow found that immigrant children were heavy and demanding users of the school library and its services which they saw as a means of learning skills for use in their adopted country and also for retaining links, via the Internet, with the country they had left (McLelland and Crawford 2004). Other categories include the unemployed and those in need of employability training. Such people may have lost access to computers and Internet connections which they need to help them find jobs and learn new skills. Employability skills' development is a more complex issue than it appears. Effective personal health management is an important factor in being employable, and learning health literacy skills is useful (Crawford and Irving 2012: 85). The homeless are a category who can use information skills to look for work, find a home and deal with health issues (Birdsong and Freitas 2012: 601–2). Adult learners are a broad category who may want to develop basic literacy and numeracy skills, ICT and a range of employability skills including information literacy. Although everyday life information seeking is associated mainly with adults, low-skill young people – sometimes referred to as NEETs (not in employment, education or training) – need attention as they are likely to remain unemployed if they do not have upskilling opportunities. Finally, it should be noted that information literacy skills development in informal environments is not necessarily linked with deprivation and low skills. Family historians, amateur genealogists and local historians are keen to acquire relevant information skills and often bring with them a background of considerable expertise.

Given the large potential customer base it is not surprising that there is a wide range of providers to meet perceived needs. Much of this activity comes under the general heading of community learning and development (CLD) which now employs so many people as to be characterised as an industry. In the UK in 2010 it employed 334 041 people. This included 58 802 in Scotland and 49 452 in Wales. Most of the staff are hourly paid, seasonal or part time, and volunteering is an important part of service provision. Jobs in the industry include community development workers, community education officers, youth workers, youth support workers, youth work managers, family learning practitioners and parenting practitioners. An important group are adult literacies tutors who teach basic literacy and numeracy skills but who are also aware of the need to teach basic information skills to learners. The main skill requirements of CLD staff, apart from ICT skills, are leadership and management, partnership working, outreach skills and the ability to promote social inclusion and empower communities (SFA 2010). Careers and skills development agencies are another important group. There are various agencies in different parts of the UK. In England the National Careers Service provides a range of Web-based resources (NCS 2012) to help people career-plan and upskill. Skills Development Scotland which was created in 2008 employs over 1000 people and has three objectives: to enable people to fulfil their potential, to make skills work for employers and to be a catalyst for positive change. Its staff readily recognise the value of information literacy in skills development and are a useful group for librarians to work with. The Welsh equivalent body is Careers Wales which provides free, bilingual, impartial careers information, advice and guidance for all ages. It was set up in 2001 and aims to help individuals to move successfully into education, training and sustainable employment and make informed decisions about their careers and learning options. It provides services to young people, adults, schools and colleges, employers and parents. It offers careers information advice in about 80 careers centres, mobile units and community venues such as libraries and adult education centres (see Careers Wales 2012).

Other relevant groups include Jobcentre Plus staff who can have a role in identifying and referring potential learners to the public library, and careers centre staff who appreciate the value of information skills in career choice.

## Organisations and structures

This varied picture of users and providers raises the question of whether satisfactory organisational structures can be put in place to address the issue and, in particular, whether they can address the need for partnership and collaboration. The PuLLS Project (Public Libraries in the Learning Society) aimed to improve adults' (particularly disadvantaged adults) information literacy and active citizenship skills through informal learning by developing the concept of the public library as an open learning centre. It was a Europe-wide project which aimed to promote digital citizenship and training and reskilling of citizens for the information society, competitiveness and job creation. The Project identified three major trends:

- alignment of library goals with local, national and European policy agendas;

- increasing formalisation of what libraries have always offered (in the form of learning support and opportunities);

- partnership working with other educational providers.

These moves to standardisation at an international level are welcome. The Project also noted a small but developing role for public libraries as content providers rather than access facilitators. This is an activity which still awaits major development. The Project developed a model for open learning centres the elements of which are:

- The training of users: different types of training (individual, group, e-learning, etc.), and related issues such as the role of librarians – as trainers, teachers, guides?

- Staff issues: training of staff in new roles – a focus on ICT, presentation and communication skills.

- Physical environment within the library: a flexible, open and accessible environment which should appeal to users.

- ICT: range of equipment to be used, including video conferencing, assistive technologies, etc.

- Learning materials: a range of multimedia courses, including those delivered over the Web . . .

- Evaluation of courses and trainers: use of questionnaires and focus groups to gain user feedback; questionnaires and interviews to gain views of library partners.

- Marketing: development of marketing plans very much devolved to local levels.

- Involvement of users in designing of courses and learning materials in open learning centres.

(Eve et al. 2007)

This is a helpful list of core points but, as the review of practical activity discussed below shows, there are a lot of 'big asks' which have yet to be widely realised: development of learning materials, evaluation of courses and trainers, getting feedback from partners, effective marketing and involvement of users in designing courses and learning materials. In designing outcomes, five generic learning outcomes can be identified (Ashcroft et al. 2007: 127):

1. Increase in knowledge and understanding

2. Increase in skills

3. Change in attitudes or values

4. Evidence of enjoyment, inspiration and creativity

5. Evidence of activity, behaviour progression

Number 4 (Evidence of enjoyment . . .) should be particularly noted. The open learning agenda is a utilitarian one but, as the Inverclyde study showed (Crawford and Irving 2012: 85), it is almost impossible to separate the satisfaction of personal goals from utilitarian learning directed to employability or upskilling outcomes and, what is more, motivation to learning is as likely to come from family and friends as work-related needs.

In terms of the learning cycle McNicol and Dalton (2003) proposed a model for public libraries.

## McNicol and Dalton's cycle of learning in public libraries

- Engagement – stimulate the learner, gain attention and create a positive climate for learning

- Planning – identification of learning needs. Recollection of prior knowledge and derived identification of need for new information

- Exploration – learners undertake a process of investigation and exploration of sources of information

- Reflection – analysis, clarification, rule application, synthesis, concept formation and the identification of patterns in the collected information

- Generalization and implementation – learners make connections, validate learning and draw inferences

- Evaluation – learners are able to determine the extent of their understanding and to decide whether they need to modify their approach or change direction or refocus. This activity may lead to further enquiry.

This is a not untypical information literacy cycle model and 'identification of learning needs' certainly needs a lot of attention as this can be a very complex area, and the need may turn out not to be information literacy skills but something rather more basic. Partnership working perhaps also needs a mention. These models of activity, outcomes and learning are useful both for planning and evaluating training programmes.

Overall two points emerge: first, unlike their academic library colleagues, public librarians have rejected the role of authority figures in favour of a more empathetic supporting role and, second, partnership working is both essential and difficult to achieve. While partners (actual and potential) may have aims, values and activities which overlap with librarians, each group comes with its own agenda which has to be respected and a process of development of mutual understanding and negotiation may be necessary before progress can be made.

## The role of the public library

Since their foundation, public library services all over the world have played a role in informal and adult learning, although it is often not a recognised one. In the UK the Public Libraries and Museums Act of 1964 placed upon local authorities a duty to provide 'a comprehensive and efficient service', although what a 'comprehensive and efficient service' actually meant has never been defined. Although some services are mentioned they do not specifically include informal learning and information literacy skills training (Kelly 1977: 358–9). In an era of lifelong learning it can be suggested that this historic mission should be rediscovered, formalised and extended. As O'Beirne (2010: 8) has argued:

'Many would suggest that it is upon this informal learning, together with worthy principles of a liberal education for the masses, that the future of libraries will rest.'

However the public library has an uncertain role within local authorities, sometimes being contained within departments of leisure and recreation and sometimes situated within education departments (O'Beirne 2010: 35). To quote O'Beirne (2010: 17) again:

'There is a need for the local authority to understand the potential of the public library to contribute to the wider goals of its community in terms of school education, local regeneration, community cohesion, social inclusion and lifelong learning.'

Certainly, the public library is in a strong position to promote information literacy skills development in the community (Harding 2008: 279). Strengths within the public library service include:

- the traditional and recognised role of the public library as a place of learning;

- from a community perspective, librarians are considered to be information experts;

- the broad client base of public libraries is a strength when it comes to fostering the information literacy message;

- the public library often represents a child's first learning experience with formal information access, and from this perspective librarians are able to instil the importance and value of information and of the library as an information space;

- the public library has the ability to facilitate lifelong learning through their contact with members of the community who are interested in self-directed study or informal learning;

- the one-to-one relationship between public librarians and clients provides teachable moments (one-to-one reference training encounters);

- public librarians have been effective in forming partnerships with other stakeholders (schools, government). This places them in a prime position to advocate the information literacy message;

- as a key access point for the general public to information and ICT resources, the public library is in a strong position to provide training.

However, as has to some extent been already discussed, there are also weaknesses. The difficulty in defining learner/ stakeholder groups has already been identified. A study of the information literacy environment in Canadian public libraries (Julien and Hoffman 2008) pointed out that:

- Training remained a comparatively minor priority with little formal training given.

- Clients are learning themselves and developing information literacy skills through experience and consulting with other people for advice and help rather using formal training when offered by librarians.

- Funding dedicated to the task of information literacy was lacking.

- There was a lack of dedicated trained staff and space for training.

There is a lack of guidelines other than the general points made above and a lack of manuals of guidance or instruction. Perceptions of information literacy and information literacy practice have tended to follow library-centric models blending bibliographic instruction with a user education model (Lloyd 2010: 133) and the pedagogy and skills needed for training in public libraries have received relatively little attention.

There is a grey area between informal and formal learning provision, and it is difficult to draw a clear distinction between formal and informal learning. It is difficult to objectively measure successful training outcomes if no form of assessment is applied. It has been suggested that 'success' in a library situation depends on how learners feel about the learning experience regardless of whether they have completed a course or put their knowledge and skills to a particular purpose (McNicol and Dalton 2003). As O'Beirne (2010: 12) puts it:

> 'By far the majority of learning that takes place in a public library is informal, often intangible, untainted by a credit framework and *ipso facto* personalised and relevant to the individual. It is also, by its nature, impossible to measure and thus difficult to dismiss or to defend.'

The Inverclyde study (Crawford and Irving 2012: 85–6) of an employability training course found that the most obvious benefit of the course was one which appeared, on the face of it, to be the most difficult to quantify: confidence. All the learners and the tutor, who based his conclusion on observing the students over the period of the course, were emphatic that their self-confidence had been greatly boosted by taking part in the course which is, in itself, an important factor in employability. What constitutes success may lead to a clash of cultures between libraries and other learning organisations.

There is also the issue of library staff roles and training. Staff may feel that they are not paid enough to take on teaching roles and the performance of such tasks may not appear in their job descriptions, which might lead to disputes with relevant trade unions if they have no obligation to engage in teaching or training duties. Without proper training they may be unable to identify individual learners' needs. The issue of training/teaching styles needs to be addressed. The intellectually demanding pedagogic higher education model is hardly suitable to people who have not progressed beyond secondary education and who found that experience negative and intimidating (Ashcroft et al. 2007). What level of staffing should deliver training? Should it be restricted to professional librarians or should library assistants take part as well? Both Inverclyde Libraries and Caerphilly Library Services (Evans 2009) have used a combination of community tutors and library trainers and, while some library assistants will be keen to participate, others will see training as an additional burden for which they are neither properly trained nor rewarded.

## Public Libraries Information Offer scheme

The Society of Chief Librarians (SCL) in the UK is making progress to address the problem outlined in the previous paragraph by introducing systematic training for public library staff, a scheme known as the Public Libraries Information Offer. Sixty libraries were recruited to take part in eight pilot projects looking at how libraries can direct library users to quality Internet advice and information about finding a job, changing career or keeping healthy. In November 2010 the SCL signed up to the government's Race Online 2012 campaign which aimed, by the end of 2012, to make the UK the first country in the world where everybody can use the Internet. The SCL pledged to support 500 000 people to become digitally inclusive by the end of 2012. It hit its target within six months and by the spring of 2012 libraries had helped around 1.5 million people use the Internet (Jarvis 2012). A survey completed in June 2012 showed that in more than 3500 libraries housing over 30 000 computers, public library staff were helping new and unconfident users to navigate the World Wide Web; 80 per cent of the users surveyed through the Public Libraries Information Offer said that the support provided in libraries improved their level of understanding of online information and 70 per cent said that it had improved their online knowledge and skills. Users said they would overwhelmingly recommend their public library's online information to other people (SCL 2012).

Although collaborative working is widely viewed as necessary and is widely practised there are no formal procedures for cooperation in providing and organising training. Sector-specific skills need to be identified and brought together. Librarians and community learning and development staff, for example, can work together in the preparation of learning materials. There are relatively few evaluation instruments (this is discussed in more detail in Chapter 9) and those which exist tend to be sector specific and do not seamlessly evaluate the work of all contributors.

Public libraries are not the only agencies which provide adult skills training. Other organisations such as adult training agencies and further education colleges may be in competition for funding and service provision. They may have better ICT infrastructures, and further education colleges may have staff who have better teaching and training skills and appropriate qualifications. Unlike some other areas of library provision, this is a sector which is in direct competition with other providers.

## Links with school libraries

Finally, there is an issue which has received relatively little attention in the literature outside Scandinavia: collaboration between schools and public libraries. In Denmark a number of public libraries have undertaken joint projects with local schools. At Tranbjerg in northern Denmark the library and the local school cooperated to produce a guide to project work, aimed at pupils in lower secondary education. The exercise also helped the public library staff to learn how to support new teaching methods and assist pupils in the learning process. In another joint venture between Otterup Public Library and the local senior secondary school, Nordfyns Gymnasium, a public librarian worked 27 hours a week in the school, planning modules of project work with teachers, taking part in classroom activities, teaching information searching to both students and staff and developing a gateway to electronic resources. The aim of the project was to create a reflective learning environment to strengthen pupils' study competencies and to integrate the public library in the day-to-day teaching (Skov 2004). A more recent study (Nielsen and Borlund 2011) reported on 12 Danish high-school students' perceptions of the role of public libraries in learning, user education, information literacy and librarians' information competencies. The study showed that public librarians were good at helping pupils develop their information needs, identify sources and support them in the information search process. Pupils showed good critical skills but their information skills needed improving and they had a limited understanding of the concepts of lifelong learning and information literacy. They saw the public library as an information resource centre, a place for independent learning and a source of support and guidance. In these studies we can see public librarians benefiting from contact with scholastic education by developing learning and instructional skills and strategies.

Overall, a picture emerges not only of progress but also a need for formalisation and structuring of previously informal procedures and practices.

# Funding

Funding is a difficult and perhaps confusing topic to discuss but it is certainly true that it often comes from nonrecurrent sources outwith library budgets which in turn contributes to the sustainability issue which bedevils information literacy development as a whole. For example, at Leeds Library and Information Service the Library is a delivery partner for a Skills Funding Agency contract managed by the council's Adult Learning Department and libraries are funded to deliver ICT learning sessions to learners from deprived areas (Tutin 2012). The employability training programme at Inverclyde Libraries receives funding from the Fairer Scotland Fund (Crawford and Irving 2012: 80). Many of the staff working in community learning and development are part-time, hourly paid or seasonal workers which implies a wide range of contractual agreements.

# Physical space

Accommodation and physical space are issues which receive little attention. Much training takes place in computer suites or areas where computers are grouped which are not purpose-designed teaching and learning spaces. Although not perhaps always ideal, they do however contribute to an atmosphere of informality which is suited to the needs of the situation. Many adult learners have a background of poor formal education experiences and any learning space suggestive of the classroom situation is best avoided.

# Examples of good practice

## *Leeds Library and Information Service*

Leeds Library and Information Service has a programme of around 20 ICT learning sessions that are set out in its *Learn in the Library* booklet (LCC 2012) which is available to download. All sessions have defined learning outcomes and each session lasts for 60 or 90 minutes, depending on whether it is being delivered to an individual or a group. The learning outcomes that have been devised for a general audience have been adapted for the Service's IT for Employment sessions. In those sessions ICT skills are taught – as they relate to improving learners' employment prospects – and the outcomes have been adapted accordingly.

Sessions are arranged in response to requests. All requests for sessions are logged, everyone who makes a request for training is contacted and sessions are arranged at dates and venues which suit the learners and library staff. All sessions are delivered by librarians, many of whom have had extra training. Some librarians have achieved PTLLS at Level 3 or Level 4 (City & Guilds qualifications in Preparing to Teach in the Lifelong Learning Sector). Others have achieved Information, Advice and Guidance (IAG) Level 4 (NVQ) qualifications to help them deliver jobseekers' advice sessions. Across the Service's 40 libraries about 600 sessions are delivered every quarter to about 1000 people.

Between July and December 2011, over 500 unemployed learners attended ICT learning sessions in Leeds libraries. Almost 80 per cent of those people identified themselves as new learners. Business startup sessions, work clubs and other special events also attract a high percentage of unemployed people.

Leeds Library and Information Service offers:

- IT for Employment sessions to learn basic computer skills

- Jobseeker advice sessions to improve interview skills

- Intellectual property advice

- European employment information at our Europe Direct centre

- Networking opportunities at work clubs, inventors groups, enterprise clubs.

The Library attracts many unemployed people on to its sessions because it has a coherent offer in place. This offer can meet the needs of unemployed people because it can be adapted to meet an individual's personal goals.

More advanced sessions are also delivered from Studio12 at the Central Library. Studio12 is an 'audio visual media project providing free access to a production studio, training, accredited qualifications and an industry panel of creative professionals working in design, music, video and media arts' (LCC website). People attending Studio12 can work towards an accredited digital media qualification, based around the creation of a short animation/video and soundtrack. To achieve accreditation learners have to undertake a 30-hour OCN (Open College Network) course at Level 2. A Level 3 course is then available as a direct progression route. The course is delivered in a flexible way on a one-to-one basis and learners can attend whenever the Studio is open.

The Library is a delivery partner for a Skills Funding Agency contract managed by the council's Adult Learning Department. Libraries are funded for delivering ICT learning sessions to learners from deprived areas. Some learners are referred to the Library by Jobcentre Plus or the council's Jobshops. Studio12 has delivered numerous funded projects working with NEETs (not in employment, education or training) between 2002 and 2012. IPR (intellectual property rights) advice is a less common feature of community provision. Between October 2010 and September 2011 1337 IPR enquiries were dealt with (Tutin 2012).

## The Information Literacy Initiative (United States)

The Information Literacy Initiative (ILI) at the University of Washington Information School (Birdsong and Freitas 2012: 588–9, 600–2) provides services to populations outside traditional academic environments that are in need of either information literacy training for the first time or a refresher course on new concepts and technologies They are adult learners in need of immediately relevant education and not credits or a degree. The populations receiving training are able to learn information literacy skills that are both practical and useful, which give them the ability to find quality information for their business, professional, health, and daily needs. Participants include owners of SMEs, adults over the age of 50, and homeless women who are experiencing extreme poverty.

Face-to-face training began in late 2007 in the Denver and Boulder metro areas of Colorado. Potential trainees were reached through various nonprofit organisations. The classes were held in public libraries, small business development centres and at nonprofit organisations with computer labs. Groups receiving training included the following:

### Adults over the age of 50

Weekly classes, over a six-week period, for adults over 50 were offered through the Osher Lifelong Learning Institute (OLLI Plus) at the University of Denver and hosted by the Denver Public Library. Classes were structured with appropriate content and pace for this population, with time allotted to practise the concepts presented in each class.

## The unemployed

Classes were offered to job-seeking library users of the Boulder Public Library. Those seeking jobs have often lost access to technologies, such as computers and Internet connections, which would aid them in finding gainful employment. The classes are structured so that attendees can learn how to use cloud computing to create, find and save job-related information and how to save information on a USB drive. These are necessary skills since the use of public computers is often limited.

## Homeless women

The Gathering Place is a daytime drop-in centre for women and children who are experiencing homelessness and poverty. These women received information literacy training two to three times per month. The women used their newly acquired skills of planning, finding, analysing, staying in focus and concluding with help with a variety of issues including job seeking, finding a home, health issues and personal knowledge. They contributed to a research topic on 'How to stay healthy (emotionally, mentally, spiritually, and physically) as a woman who is temporarily without a home: What are the top survival tips?' (Birdsong and Freitas 2012: 601–2). All of the attendees who came to the class in 2009, on an ongoing basis, were able to find a home of their own and some were also able to secure employment.

## *The Welsh experience*

The Gateways to Learning initiative (see Chapter 3) was a 2-year, £2 million project, responding to the need to develop sustainable jobs following the closure of the Corus steelworks in Ebbw Vale in 2001 and directly involved libraries in employability activities. It was part-funded by the European Social Fund and ran from September 2005 to November 2007. It sought to widen participation in lifelong learning and make it more accessible, particularly to people in disadvantaged communities or circumstances. The key elements to the project were:

■ To work in partnership to develop joint protocols and catalogues enabling access to partner library loans.

■ To offer nonaccredited and accredited information literacy through one-to-one taster sessions and support for Open College Network (OCN) Levels 1–3.

The project required collaboration between 56 branch or campus libraries and learning resource centres, and provided access to more than 1.3 million books and resources through a single online search across South East Wales.

Library users were trained through one-to-one tuition to recognise when information was needed and to have the ability to locate, evaluate and use this information effectively whether from books, newspapers or the Internet.

The Gateways Project helped learners to improve core information and ICT skills based on an individual's interest or hobby and thereby demystify the entire process.

People who had never used a computer took this further to obtain Open College Network qualifications in information literacy at Levels 1, 2 and 3. Learners chose a topic of research and, with the aid of an easy-to-read booklet, compiled a portfolio of evidence to the required standard. A team of Information Literacy Coordinators taught, supported and assessed learners and provided complementary basic ICT skills training to use the Internet and software information tools.

Over a 2-year period the project worked with 2300 people, 600 of whom achieved an ONC qualification and generated further initiatives (Clark 2012a).

These included a group of people with learning difficulties who formed their own Adult Literacy Group at Blaina Library in Abertillery. This helped them in developing their reading, numeracy and information skills, which built up their confidence and supported their participation in community activities. The group emerged out of the Gateways to Learning (G2L) project and they formed their own group at the conclusion of the project. From September 2008, the group met regularly on Friday mornings and learned about using dictionaries, letter writing, using computers to research subjects of interest, using online catalogues and producing a newsletter. Group members have reviewed books they like and have devised quizzes, using library resources to find the answers. Library staff have been pivotal in the success of the project by setting up and supporting the project, by working with group members on ideas for sessions and activities and providing an informal user-friendly setting (Clark 2012b). Another initiative, run by Bettws Library, targeted young, unemployed and poorly skilled people in cooperation with Jobcentre Plus. Bettws Library has helped young people to apply for jobs, thanks to a partnership with the Youth Service and Jobcentre Plus. Bettws, largely built as a council estate in the 1960s, is where 8278 people live, a quarter of whom are under 15 years of age. There are few facilities on the estate, and the Library, which is located in the shopping precinct next door to the health centre, is a very popular place, especially with young people wanting to use the computers and meet their friends in a warm and secure environment. The Library had worked with the Youth Service for some time, but the idea of working with Jobcentre Plus was new. The project started in October 2009, was targeted at the 16–25 age group, and led to unemployed young people being able to write their own CVs, undertake job searches and apply for jobs online. Some have secured jobs. Bettws is an area of social exclusion, high unemployment and deprivation, and as such has been targeted by Jobcentre Plus. Library staff have worked hard to ensure that young people not only feel welcome, but also use the library properly.

Following previous successful collaboration in October 2009, the Youth Service asked the Library to work with them and Jobcentre Plus to develop the project.

The Library set a regular time each week for staff to assist young people in using the computers to carry out job searches, prepare their CVs, and make job applications online. The project was targeted at the 16–25 age group, as this was the group with the greatest needs; a large proportion of the participants were 16–18 years old. Many of the young people were practical rather than academic. Many of the participants had been unemployed for a long time; some had never worked; and some came from households where several generations have never worked.

Many of the participants had no idea of what a CV was, or how they could use their life experiences to support their applications.

The role of the Youth Service has been to encourage people to come forward, whilst Jobcentre Plus helped with websites, application and interview techniques. Jobcentre Plus signed 25 people onto the project, 5 of whom went into full-time work, 2 went into full-time education and 1 enrolled on a course that led to a job (Clark 2012a).

Torfaen Library and Information Service – Torfaen is a county borough in Wales – offers an example of using specialist staff. Library staff had always been very involved in helping customers with finding information and providing ICT help and guidance. In November 2009 Torfaen Library and Information Service appointed a Libraries and Learning Officer whose role was to coach and support learners in developing information literacy skills. Weekly IT drop-in sessions are held in all the libraries during which learner-led support is offered for complete beginners or those needing help with a particular task.

The role of the Learning and Libraries Officer – with support from frontline staff and the informal nature of the drop-in sessions – enabled the library service to focus on and encourage those potential learners who may not otherwise have come forward and asked for help. Information literacy has also been developed discretely through popular learning areas like family history. For example, Family History and Local History sessions have been introduced in Blaenavon Library – Blaenavon is a town within the county borough of Torfaen – to help people access genealogical information or discover more about their local area (Clark 2012a).

## Work with schools

Links between schools and public libraries is an underreported area, which is a pity as school and public library links can contribute to reader development, the development of basic 'library' skills and information literacy skills.

Midlothian Council Education and Children's Services – Midlothian is one of the 32 council areas of Scotland – has arranged school class visits to their libraries for several years and have produced guidelines and worksheets which show that, to be successful, these visits have to be highly structured and well planned to produce useful learning outcomes. These include a checklist of activities and procedures for library staff which cover all primary school years from Primary 1 to 7 (5 to 12-year-olds) and clear guidelines on the behaviour expected of pupils visiting the library. There are worksheets for pupils on using the library and understanding the differences between fiction and nonfiction books. While much of the material is at a very simple level it introduces children to library and information usage from an early age (Dryburgh 2012).

## Background to information literacy classes

In 2010 Newcastle Public Library staff visited Newcastle University Library to find out more about the services they offer and learned that first-year undergraduates arrive at the University with little or no information literacy skills. The Public Library staff decided to offer their own pre-university training sessions in Newcastle City Library as many students in the North East of England tend to stay in their local area while at university.

Learners are recruited through schools by promoting the information literacy sessions to school librarians and local school contacts. While in the two years since these sessions were set up some schools have requested repeat sessions, it has not always proved easy to make contact with the right teachers in previously uninvolved schools. Teachers are often unaware of what the public library service has to offer. Participating schools, however, often get their students to attend over a series of sessions, whereas the entire sixth form always attends. Other schools simply bring gifted and talented students who are doing extended projects as part of their A-levels (typically, they have to research and write a 5000-word project on a subject of their choice), and this is the first time they have had to cite or use references in their work. It is often the case that many of the students have never seen a library catalogue before or know how the Dewey Decimal Classification works. Moreover, they are often not aware of the advanced search on Google and/or Google Scholar and their level of knowledge in terms of searching for information and accessing good-quality information is very low.

These classes are run in group sessions of no more than 15 participants and are delivered over a one-off 2-hour period. The sessions can be tailored to what the teacher feels Years 12 or Year 13 students need and staff try and be as responsive as they can. Teachers are often unaware of the resources that the service has to offer and how they can embed information literacy into their curriculum.

Outcomes are evaluated by a simple form and feedback has been favourable, although it has been found difficult to build up a rapport with students who attend for only short 2-hour periods. Teacher support and involvement has been found to be important. It is always hard to know the students' levels of ability and to know what kind of teaching styles they are used to.

As well as sessions for school pupils the Library has also run a How to Search Google Effectively session for adults which was very well attended and had good feedback. Work clubs are provided for those looking for work and staff looking at how to include information literacy sessions in these groups. Attendees are given help with writing CVs, interview techniques and finding job advertisements. The Library also runs business sessions on how to use its online resources. These sessions are extremely popular and cover subject areas like Keynote Reports, Corporate Researcher and Know Your Market (which looks at how to search for market reports and market information) (Archer 2012).

# Learning and teaching issues

Despite their importance, the generation of learning materials, the understanding of appropriate learning and teaching styles and training and qualifications needs have received little attention. A recent study of learning objectives to support the teaching of information literacy skills makes scant reference to public libraries and notes only that material generated in higher education is inappropriate for public libraries (Graham 2011: 126). As for teaching issues O'Beirne (2010: 69) has noted:

> '... there is a lack of understanding of the use of communication and social interaction within a learning setting, which highlights the need for staff who are supporting learners at the very least to appreciate the characteristics of different learning theories and approaches. Anecdotal evidence suggests that public library staff do not have a good understanding of learning theory and are only generally aware of the learning landscape. There seems to be a prevalent view that only didactic or instructivist learning is relevant.'

Some qualifications do exist which are relevant to public library information literacy instructors and have been taken up. As mentioned earlier, at Leeds Library and Information Service some library staff have completed the PTLLS (Preparing to Teach in the Lifelong Learning Sector) course at Level 3 or 4 while others have achieved IAG (Information Advice and Guidance) Level 4 qualifications to help them deliver jobseeker advice sessions (Tutin 2012). However, a librarian who provides information literacy training courses in a public library drew attention to her own lack of formal training which she has compensated for by attending short courses and attending information literacy training sessions at a nearby university library, but the lack of training opportunities in teaching for public librarians is a handicap (Archer 2012). The Pop-i project (a collaborative noncommercial venture between Imperial College London and Bradford Library Service), which was an attempt to introduce information literacy training for public library staff, was delivered at Bradford Public Library in Yorkshire in 2005. The project used online virtual learning in a public library to train staff in the theories and practice of information literacy and assessed the outcome against generic learning outcomes. A version of the course has been successfully run on a number of occasions in Bradford. The project was further developed by the CILIP Information Literacy Group as LolliPop but attempts to promote it more widely had limited success (O'Beirne 2010: 140–2).

The most widely used teaching method is probably face-to-face small-group instruction. The American Information Literacy Initiative (ILI) provides both instructor-led programmes and self-guided instruction. Instructor-led programmes are especially useful for older people whose levels of self-confidence in using computers increases in an instructor-led environment. For the computer literate the US National Institute of Health offers a Senior Health website which has simplified easy-to-use interfaces, designed to meet the needs of the elderly. Another source for online tutorials is YouTube. Many of these tutorials are in video format and include demonstrations of the various techniques and strategies employed. An example is the Searcher in Charge series. These allow businesses and individuals to access free resources which meet their particular information literacy needs. Relevant printed sources are also available in the For Dummies series including *Job Searching Online for Dummies, Genealogy Online for Dummies* and *Internet*

*Searching for Dummies* (Birdsong and Freitas 2012: 597–9).

Leeds Library and Information Service offers a downloadable booklet *Learn in the Library* (LCC 2012) which includes sections on basic IT and Internet skills, how to use online resources, local history, family history, jobseeker skills and business resources. One of the most comprehensive products currently available is an outcome of the Welsh Information Literacy Project: the *Information Literacy Handbook* (WILP 2011a). The *Handbook* can be used both by learners and delivery staff and contains information and assessment guidance for all four information literacy units and a list of resources.

# Summary of the chapter

Informal learning, largely but not exclusively situated within the public library environment, is an evolving entity in which new organisational structures are being put together out of previously informal arrangements, although overarching policy and bureaucratic frameworks are lacking. It is heavily dependent on partnership working with other agencies but, as yet, formal structures to support this are lacking. Public librarians have shown considerable initiative in developing and coordinating service development while eschewing a role as authority figures. Issues around deprivation and empowerment and digital and social inclusion are key themes. There are staffing issues and more importance needs to be attached to the training of specialist staff who should have an appropriate variety of specialist qualifications. Learner and teaching issues are poorly understood and need further research. There are few learning and teaching materials available when a comparison is made with higher education. Appropriate standards of behaviour need to be agreed when working with children and young people.

# 9

# Value and impact

### *John Crawford*

**Abstract:** Despite much excellent work in information literacy, systematic evaluation and measurement of the impact of information literacy activity are still relatively underdeveloped. The nature of measurement and impact is discussed and the available indicators and guidelines are analysed. Methods of data collection and analysis are reviewed with a discussion of the most widely used and popular quantitative and qualitative methods. These include surveys, observation and various forms of group discussion, interviewing and phenomenographic methods. The limited number of resources available is considered and the chapter concludes with some examples of good practice in evaluation.

**Key words:** value and impact, performance indicators, information literacy, impact measurement, data collection, focus groups, interviewing, impact evaluation.

## What is impact?

The preceding chapters raise the question of how the impact of information literacy activity can be assessed, assuming of course that efforts are being made to assess it. The present study has found that, while there are excellent examples of measurement of impact, relatively little work has been done overall. Measurement of the success, or failure, of an activity always comes at the end of the process and it is all too easy to give it little attention or just ignore it altogether, although measurement of impact and using the lessons learned from it can greatly improve future performance. As will be explained below, although a wide range of rigorous procedures exist, it is still not an exact science and a range of methodologies (known as triangulation) may be needed to obtain accurate results. What is being measured may also change over time, so repeat or longitudinal studies may be needed.

In order to measure a service or part of it, it must be measured in some way. So, what forms of measurement are available and what is being measured? Some key measures are:

- *Input measures*: resources that are applied to providing a service. These include total expenditure or specific parts of it such as the materials or staffing budgets.

- *Output measures*: the products and services created by the information service. These would include issue statistics, number of inter-library loans requested and other often statistical measures of use.

(Crawford 2006b: 15–16)

Output measures, however, do not measure what the results of the activity were and how users were affected by it. Books borrowed are not necessarily read and from an information literacy perspective, while providers of information and other skills training in public libraries sometimes report formerly unemployed learners going on to employment, it is difficult to show that the learning provided by the library was solely responsible. What is needed are higher order outcomes which describe the world of impact beyond traditional performance measurement (Markless and Streatfield 2006: 21–2). Impact describes the broader influence that the information service has on the community or organisation. Impact can be interpreted as the difference made by the service in the long term. The higher levels of impact are:

- *Improved knowledge*: the user has considered the information obtained and is now more knowledgeable.

- *Changed perception*: the knowledge gained has resulted in a change in the way that the user looks at the subject. Real learning has taken place.

- *Changed world view*: the user has been transformed by the service and constructive learning has taken place which will have long-term effects.

- *Changed actions*: the user has acted in a way he/she would not have done before.

(Crawford 2006b: 19)

These are very much the kind of impacts that information literacy should achieve. The independent evaluation of the Welsh Gateways to Learning Project (Hughes and Warden 2007: 14) reported that many members would like to have seen 'softer measures' (i.e., higher order) rather than just 'process driven' measures which did not adequately reflect the difference and added value that the Project had made. However, such softer measures are difficult to quantify. All the interviewees in the Inverclyde study (Crawford and Irving 2012: 85–6) were emphatic that the main change they felt in themselves was greatly increased self-confidence as a result of attending the course. Precise quantification of increased confidence is not easily achieved.

Impact measurement may also draw attention to unexpected outcomes. The Gateways to Learning Project evaluation

(Hughes and Warden 2007: 12–13) found that prisoners greatly benefited from information literacy training as it helped to prepare them for resettlement after they had completed their sentences. Of course, unanticipated negative outcomes may also be uncovered, and it is important to be prepared to alter or develop practice in the light of evaluation. The recommendation from the above positive finding was that a targeted project should be developed in conjunction with the Prison Service, the Probation Service and relevant bodies such as the National Association for the Care and Resettlement of Offenders (NACRO). This recommendation for partner-based collaborative working draws attention to another problem, the difficulty of isolating the impact on information literacy service providers from other players. If a range of professionals are working together as an effective team – say, for example, librarians, community learning and development staff and Jobcentre Plus staff providing skills development training – it may be quite difficult to separate out the impact of the various contributors. The same might well apply to a school librarian working with teachers on an area of curriculum development.

However, good intentions are not always converted into practice. An evaluation of a national research programme by Markless and Streatfield (2006: 22–6) found that:

- There was little attempt to define terms.

- There was no framework through which to explore value and impact.

- There was a tendency to move from value and impact towards reporting and describing activities and processes.

- There was a linked tendency to escape from these problems into national surveys of activities or policies.

- There were problems with the methods chosen to gather evidence about impact.

It is all too easy to use describing what happened as a substitute for explaining why it happened. It is also important not to reinvent the wheel. Use good pre-existing research to strengthen your case and identify areas for research. It should also be noted that no research methods are immune from prejudice, experimenter bias and human error. An example of a possibly loaded question is the one quoted below: 'Why do certain information seekers rely entirely on search engines such as Google to meet their information needs? How could they be helped to change their behaviour?' (Williamson 2007: 9–10). The implication seems to be that users are somehow 'naughty' for ignoring all the expensive resources which librarians thoughtfully provide for them and their behaviour needs to be changed. Perhaps it would be more appropriate to ask why users do what they do and what lessons librarians can learn from the enquiry.

Impact measurement is not a uniform process across all kinds of information literacy activity. It would not be appropriate to describe impact evaluation in any context as 'easy' but at least it can be said that in higher education and public libraries there is a well-established externally validated culture of service evaluation. Public libraries in the UK are subject to Public Library Plus surveys while in higher education the SCONUL Satisfaction Survey is used and the American LibQUAL+ Survey. These are general satisfaction surveys, designed to give an overview picture of the services at a specific point in time and by administering the survey annually a longitudinal picture of performance can be built up. The results provide baseline data and point to topics which may require more detailed study such as information literacy service provision (Crawford 2006b: 69–76, 82–3).

In other sectors the picture is more varied. School libraries have always been a problem as they often have only one staff member with little time for anything other than 'regular' operations. More positively, they have attracted the attention of expert researchers over the past ten years or so, so a good deal of high-quality data exist which can be used for baseline and comparative data. An example is quoted below. The workplace is probably the most difficult area. Research has shown that it is impossible to objectively value information and show a clear link between the use of information and business performance. 'Information value by its very nature is subjective, dependent on the interpretation of the individual or team members who employ information in particular situations for particular purposes.' Precise accounting-based methods are not possible so it is best 'to use qualitative, but statistically reliable, methods, depending on the evaluation of knowledgeable people in the population' studied. Suggested methods are:

- Monitor how people use information and knowledge in the organisation's work.

- Record the results of initiatives and make them accessible.

- Collect examples of value added by information orientation, of risks from which it has saved the organization, and of failures and errors that could have been avoided by better use of information.

(Orna 2004: 131–5)

While it is relatively easy for imaginative workplace librarians to collect feel-good stories and cautionary tales, this is less easy to do where there is no one with responsibility for information activities. It is most difficult in SMEs where it might not even be understood that information literacy activities are taking place, let alone the need to evaluate them. Such studies as do exist tend to be one-off ones conducted by outsiders and lacking a comparative or longitudinal perspective. The activities of individuals engaging in searching for personal purposes such as health issues are again usually pursued by one-off studies.

## Indicators and guidelines

In planning impact evaluation it is important to identify criteria or indicators which inform the process. The most general one must always be the stated aims and objectives of the organisation, which information literacy must be shown to be supporting.

A performance indicator is a numerical or verbal expression derived from library statistics or other data used to characterise the performance of a library. Of the 19 or so commonly found measures used to evaluate library and information services some six are directly relevant to the measurement of impact of information literacy activities:

- Internet for public use

- number of workstations

- access to electronic information resources in the library, at home and in the workplace

- staff helpful/knowledgeable

- quality of customer care

- maintenance of equipment.

Additional relevant measures might be 'opening hours' or 'easy physical access to buildings', the latter being particularly relevant to disabled users (Crawford 2006b: 15, 22–3).

Apart from that, it is really a matter of reviewing the literature for usable measures. There is a UNESCO document on information literacy indicators (Catts and Lau 2008: 38), but it lists only very broad indicators, derived mainly from pre-existing sources, principally of the input variety such as 'Public libraries – volumes of books' or 'Library employees per 1 000 000 inhabitants' but these are of little use for measuring impact in specific situations.

Andrew Whitworth used an interpretation of Christine Bruce's 'Six frames of information literacy' (Whitworth 2011: 319–20) to analyse six information literacy policy documents. These are fairly broad and address general themes which should be common to all types of information literacy activity and focus on educational and personal and social development aspects (Table 9.1).

**Table 9.1** Christine Bruce's 'Six frames of information literacy'

| Frame | Coding categories |
|---|---|
| Content | The importance of information and IL. Drivers of the need for IL. Knowledge of information sources |
| Competency | Searching skills, anti-plagiarism, generic evaluation regimes (e.g. ensuring web page has date of publication, etc.) |
| Learning to learn | Developing metacognitive skills, independent learners |
| Personal relevance | Developing awareness of personal (not generic) filtering strategies. Awareness of context specific applications, multiliteracies |
| Social impact | The production of information intended for public use, active citizenship, solving problems |
| Relational | Awareness of holistic nature of [the] discipline, need to experience variation, iteration and dynamic definitions. Self-awareness of the process of IL itself |

To these he added a seventh 'valued collaboration', as he attributes importance to working with partners. These are useful overview indicators for policy planning. Of these the 'Relational' frame is the most challenging and the least likely to be achieved, including as it does such issues as the 'affective dimension' – the idea of pleasure being a motivator for information searching. In a subject which has a highly utilitarian content this is a challenging idea.

The model for open learning centres developed for the PuLLS (Public Libraries in the Learning Society) Project, as discussed in Chapter 8, offers a more functional list of issues to address and, although intended mainly for public libraries, can be used elsewhere. They include evaluation of:

- *The training of users*: different types of training (individual, group, e-learning, etc.) and related issues such as the role of librarians – as trainers, teachers, guides?

- *Staff issues*: training of staff in new roles, a focus on ICT, presentation and communication skills.

- *Physical environment within the library*: a flexible, open and accessible environment which should appeal to users.

- *ICT*: range of equipment to be used, including video conferencing, assistive technologies, etc.

- *Learning materials*: a range of multimedia courses, including those delivered over the Web ...

- *Courses and trainers*: use of questionnaires and focus groups to gain user feedback, questionnaires and interviews to gain views of library partners.

- *Marketing*: development of marketing plans very much devolved to local levels.

- *Involvement*: Involvement of users in designing of courses and learning materials in open learning centres.

(Eve et al. (2007: 401)

The Learning Impact Research Project (LIRP) designed five 'softer' generic learning outcomes which are much more impact related (Ashcroft et al. 2007: 127):

1.  Increase in knowledge and understanding

2.  Increase in skills

3.  Change in attitudes or values

4.  Evidence of enjoyment, inspiration and creativity

5.  Evidence of activity, behaviour progression.

Frameworks are also a useful source of indicators as they list specific information literacy skills and ascribe them to successive education levels from school to higher education and sometimes on to the workplace and lifelong learning. They usually link information literacy skill levels to school curricula and to credit and qualification frameworks thus linking them to skill levels outside the information profession. Good examples are the *Information Literacy Framework for Wales* (WILP 2011b) and the *National Information Literacy Framework Scotland* (NILFS 2009a) However, indicated skill levels should be treated as a guide and should not be interpreted too prescriptively. After all, skill levels which a 9 to 14-year-old might hope to achieve are still useful to a junior undergraduate.

## Measuring impact at a national level

Chapter 2 discussed national information literacy policies and discussed the problems associated with them: there is still disagreement about what information literacy actually means. Some policy documents are not really about information literacy but ICT, others are available only in the indigenous language, making comparative evaluation difficult, and they are rarely comprehensive, usually with a primary focus on higher education. The document on information literacy indicators produced by Catts and Lau (2008) is best seen as an introductory discussion, rather than an action plan. Andrew Whitworth identified a range of indicators for his discussion of six policy documents (Whitworth 2011). He emphasised the importance of collaboration for, to be successful, a national information literacy policy should impact all stakeholders: all education levels from early years to PhD level, the workplace, health and well-being, lifelong learning, employability and skills development, and citizenship and civil rights. The *Prague Declaration* (UNESCO 2003) and the Alexandria Proclamation (Garner 2005) lay out admirable policy guidelines, especially on citizenship, civil rights and lifelong learning, but these need to be translated into precise evaluative indicators. It is also worth looking at the activities of high-performing organisations like the National Foundation on Information Literacy to see what activities they engage in and what impact they have. Above all it is necessary to have a list of the activities in which a national information literacy policy should engage and which has some measure of international support. It is impossible to evaluate national information literacy policies until there is some measure of agreement as to what they should contain. This is discussed further in Chapter 10.

## Methods of data collection

Those new to research methods will find it useful to consult more general sources first, such as Brophy's (2006) *Measuring*

*Library Performance* which offers a painless introduction to theoretical perspectives and practical methods and Gorman, and Clayton's (2005) *Qualitative Research for the Information Professional*, one of the best introductions to qualitative methods available to librarians. Markless and Streatfield's (2006) *Evaluating the Impact of Your Library* is a detailed step-by-step guide to impact evaluation, describing all the procedures necessary for it to be comprehensive, all of which have been fully tested. It is however a painstaking and time-consuming procedure to fully implement, and many will not have the time to devote to it that it really needs.

For those with limited time wanting to integrate their working day into a useful and rewarding research process, action research is an attractive option. Action research is carried out by practitioners aiming to improve their understanding of events, situations and problems so as to increase the effectiveness of their practice. The writing of research reports and similar publications is not a primary goal (Markless and Streatfield 2006: 120). It is well suited to those attempting to carry out practical research projects, while dealing with the maelstrom of a busy working day. Moreover, it embeds research into the environment in which the practitioner is totally engaged on a daily basis (Visser 2007: 111).

Action research makes a direct link between process and impact. It is a cycle of reflecting, theorising and acting and involves the following stages:

- Identify a problem or challenge

- Gather evidence

- Interpret the evidence

- Look for ideas on what changes to make

- Make changes to the service

- Collect further evidence about the impact of changes made.

The whole process can be repeated until it is felt that enough progress has been made. Action research is especially valuable when looking at 'messy areas' where there are no clear ways forward yet. This is a helpful approach in information literacy work where, apart from higher education, much service provision is still in the developmental stage and there are few baseline data. The usual impact evaluation approach of comparing progress against a baseline begins to break down when the services provided are evolving and changing rapidly. However, because action is predicated against discovery of new evaluation data it is not a method suited to rigid planning and reporting cycles (Markless and Streatfield 2006: 120–1).

One of the few books specifically devoted to information literacy is Lipu et al.'s (2007) *Exploring Methods in Information Literacy Research*. The authors are mainly Australian academics and the chapters by and large reflect their personal experience. The book 'aims to provide an overview of approaches to assist researchers and practitioners to explore ways of undertaking research in the information literacy field.' It relies heavily on the case study method rather than straightforward explanation, which does not always make for easy reading compounded by the lack of an index. However, it describes in reasonable detail pretty much all of the research methods available, the most popular of which are briefly summarised below.

# Quantitative methods

There are two main methods of data collection, quantitative (survey) and qualitative. Quantitative methods imply the assembly and analysis of statistical data. In a library and information context this has traditionally meant a questionnaire, now usually a standardised instrument, for collecting general satisfaction data or for examining a specific issue, like the needs of disabled users. Quantitative questionnaire-based methods have certain advantages. The questionnaire can report on the views of many thousands of people and give a breadth of data not available to qualitative methods. It adopts a highly structured approach and, because it uses statistical methods and produces numerical data, its outcomes are perceived to be 'scientific' and therefore objectively correct. If well designed it gives clear-cut answers to the questions asked and, because of this and because interested parties can complete it without intervention, it appears to be neutral (Crawford 2006b: 36–7). Quantitative data are appropriate to straightforward factual information (e.g., 'what', 'who', 'how many', 'how much, 'where', 'when' information) measurable at a particular point in time. An example of questions suited to a quantitative approach would be: 'What is the extent and purpose of computer use for information seeking among a particular group of users?' However, the answers to these questions would not explain why they turned up (motivation) and what they got out of it (impact). Complex questions which involve 'why' and 'how' lend themselves to qualitative exploration. An example might be: 'Why do certain information seekers rely entirely on search engines such as Google to meet their information needs?' 'How could they be helped to change this behaviour?' (Williamson 2007: 8–9).

## Qualitative methods

Qualitative methods are designed to explore why something is happening. In library and information science they have often been seen as an addition to quantitative methods as a means of understanding the attitudes that inform the statistics. In practice, qualitative methods work in two ways:

- *When something is known about the subject.* Qualitative methods can explore the reasons behind evidence uncovered by quantitative methods. Methodologies based on direct contact with users are likely to be more revealing.

- *When the situation is not fully understood.* Qualitative methods can be used to find out what the problems actually are and, on the basis of this research, more precise research questions can be formulated. In the relatively unstructured environment of information literacy research this can be a productive approach.

Qualitative research methods have quite specific advantages (Gorman and Clayton 2005: 3–17):

- They are attuned to growing complexity in an information environment which requires flexibility and variability in data analysis.

- They facilitate the use of triangulation to enrich research findings.

- They are responsive to the need for libraries to enrich their service imperative.

- They are suited to the nonquantitative background of many information professionals.

- They fit the social nature of libraries.

For the purposes of this study three main methods of qualitative investigation are relevant:

- *Observation*: this involves the systematic recording of observable phenomena or behaviour in a natural setting.

It is particularly useful for recording unconscious patterns of behaviour which the subjects might not be aware of themselves. It can add a human dimension to statistical counts such as electronic counting of computer use which gives no idea of the interaction between computer and user which is taking place.

- *Group discussions*: the term 'group discussion' introduces what is probably the most widely used qualitative method in library and information science. This usually takes the form of 'focus groups' and they are often used to inform attitudes lurking behind previously gathered statistical survey data. The term 'focus group' has quite a precise meaning and is not just a chat round a table. They are so-called because the discussions start out quite broadly and gradually narrow down to the focus of the research.

- *Interviewing*: interviewing can obtain detailed in-depth information from subjects who know a great deal about their personal perception of events, processes and environments. It is a good way of teasing out information about complex situations and, as a one-to-one situation, it gives an opportunity to get to know and understand the subject, which is not available to other methods.

## Observation

Observing what people actually do in libraries allows users to be observed in their natural setting, and it becomes possible to study people who are unwilling or unlikely to give accurate reports on their own activity. It also enables data to be analysed in stages, as understanding of its meaning unfolds. There are two types of observation – structured and unstructured:

- *Structured observation*: a form is used in which the observer records whether specific activities take place, where and how often. A well-designed data collection method will allow space for recording unanticipated activity. However, the form must be carefully designed at the outset to allow for this. If need be, the form can be modified as the study progresses. Because this is essentially a statistical method it is often considered to be a quantitative technique.

- *Unstructured observation*: the observer records any behaviour or event which is relevant to the research question being studied. This is a much more open-ended approach and, as is the case with most qualitative research, is especially useful in exploratory research or where a situation is incompletely understood.

The skill of the observer is a key factor. On the face of it observation is an extremely easy method of data collection, but in reality the reverse is the case. Observation is a highly skilled exercise as the observer must be well enough trained to spot everything that is going on and record it accurately. Observation has disadvantages. People who are aware that they are being observed tend to change their behaviour, at least initially. Observation without consent may be considered an invasion of privacy. It is not always possible to anticipate a spontaneous event and so be ready to understand and observe it. Not all events lend themselves to observation such as those which change over time. Observation can be time consuming, and the subjectivity of the observer can also be a factor. It helps if the observer records his/her subjective reaction to the events observed (Crawford 2006b: 51–3). However, as a study from higher education shows, results can be informative. An academic library installed an 'electronic floor' on the assumption that usage of the computers would mainly be to access the library's electronic information resources and passworded databases. A further assumption was that subject librarian support would be necessary. A carefully planned observation study showed that usage of electronic information services was a small proportion of usage showing that little more than IT assistant support was needed (Crawford and Daye 2000).

## Focus groups

Once you have discovered what your users are doing you might want to ask them why they are doing it. Focus groups, the most widely used form of group discussion, are a good way to find out. They have a number of advantages:

- They allow data to be acquired quickly, facilitating rapid response to necessities for delivery changes.

- They do not require complex sampling techniques and reduce the cost of data acquisition.

- They are flexible and adaptable to a wide range of research situations.

- They are one of the few methods available for obtaining data from children or persons with limited literacy skills.

They do, however, have disadvantages. The focus group sample is not usually randomly selected, and generalisations from small focus groups to larger populations are problematic. Convenience of access to subjects may mean that an unrepresentative sample of the target population is used (Procter and Wartho 2007: 139–40). The logistics of getting the right people together in the right place at the right time should not be underestimated, and there is always the danger that the discussion will be taken over by a few dominating individuals. The facilitator, in such cases, will have to use his or her skills to draw out the less assertive members of the group. Focus groups are not very good for discussing technical issues and are best used to collect opinions on service quality.

There are a few practical tips for success. The number of people scheduled for each group should be 8 to 12. It is better to overschedule in case some do not turn up. Ample time should be allowed for discussion, although an hour will usually suffice. It is best to run three or four groups per population to get a comparative perspective. In analysing the results, it is best to look for comments or trends which are repeated over several sessions. Participants should be given some sort of reward for their time even if it is only tea, coffee and sandwiches (Crawford 2006b: 46–8).

There are a couple of other group discussion techniques which are sometimes used. A nominal group technique (NGT) in some form is quite common and many people have experienced it, albeit often without knowing they are doing so. The technique is occasionally called 'quality brainstorming' because it uses some of the techniques of brainstorming and its members do not need to be homogeneous, unlike a focus group. There are four steps:

1. Silent individual generation of ideas

2. Reporting of ideas which are written up on a board for all to see

3. Discussion to clarify and evaluate the ideas put forward

4. Individual voting on the relative importance of ideas from which a group ranking can be derived.

The advantage of NGT is that it combines both individual and group participation. Individual participation comes both at the idea generation stage and at the evaluation stage where, if participants are not convinced that the idea is good, they do not have to vote for it. The discussion of ideas and the generation of new ones form the group approach (Gorman and Clayton 2005: 151–6). It is a technique which usually generates a strong feeling of involvement.

A structured group discussion uses similar methods but eliminates individual participation. After an introductory discussion the participants begin by working in small groups to identify and prioritise key themes. The groups then come together and each group is asked to make a point which is then tested with the other groups. Agreement is reached on each point in turn and a record is kept of the discussion, which is verified towards the end of the session. Sessions last between 45 and 75 minutes and usually about 14 points emerge.

## Interviewing

Interviewing can be viewed as an extension of the meeting method. By speaking to one person it is possible to probe more deeply into the experiences and reactions of respondents. It gives a friendlier and more personal approach to the data collection process and may appeal to people who are reluctant to participate in group events. It is also a good method of collecting confidential, controversial or personal information which is unlikely to emerge in a group setting. It produces immediate responses to questions and allows interviewees to respond to open-ended questions in their own way. It also gives an opportunity to find out why people and organisations behave the way they do. It is particularly appropriate to people who cannot respond satisfactorily to other types of enquiry, such as children, immigrants and those who have difficulty in hearing or writing. As a method, however, it is open to bias because interpretation is left to the interviewer and the results may be uncritical (Gorman and Clayton 2005: 126–7).

Interviewing is a skilled, structured activity. The interviewer must have well-developed social skills and be good at putting people at their ease and persuading them to talk. He or she should talk as little as possible and concentrate on listening. There are three types of interview:

- *The structured or formal interview*: this is based on a prepared list of questions which is not deviated from. This closely resembles the administration of a questionnaire except that the interviewer is present to explain and clarify the questions.

- *The semistructured interview*: here the interviewer works from a prepared list of issues. The questions, derived from the issues, are likely to be open ended to allow the respondents to express themselves from their own perspectives.

- *The unstructured interview*: In this case the interview is informal and only the general subject is predetermined. This gives considerable scope to the interviewee to express his or her views but needs considerable skill on the part of the interviewer who must be able to subtly control digressions and tease out issues only partially examined by the respondent.

(Crawford 2006b: 50–1)

The semistructured interview is probably the most widely used method as it gives considerable freedom to the interviewee to express himself of herself while the preprepared list of issues ensures that structure and coherence is retained. It works extremely well in studying information literacy activities in public libraries, as the Inverclyde study showed. It used the 'learning life histories' methodology specially devised for the study. This approach is not in itself new as the method can be found in other work, although the exact terminology does not appear to be common. It aims to situate and understand people's learning in their life experiences including personal motivation and ambition, family life, work experience, the environment in which they live and their previous education. It takes the view that learning issues cannot be properly understood and addressed unless these factors are known. It is particularly appropriate to adult learners especially those whose previous learning experiences have been problematic (Crawford and Irving 2012: 81) (see examples below). However, a well planned and executed interview generates a huge amount of data for analysis and it can take several hours to transcribe and analyse the data from an interview lasting from an hour to an hour and a half, so it is best when planning interview-based research to keep the number of interviewees to a manageable amount (Lloyd 2007: 78). Annemaree Lloyd in her interview-based study which focused on exploring the meaning of information literacy in a fire station used 'grounded theory', a method well known to qualitative researchers, which suggests that the theory should come out of qualitative research collection data rather than being proposed at the outset (Markless and Streatfield 2006: 24). The point of grounded theory is to focus on what emerges from the data, not what has emerged from the literature. It explicitly rules out the idea of starting with a hypothesis and testing it. A grounded theory approach usually involves a mixture of observation and interviewing. This involves making observations and then noting what appear to be the key issues. This is repeated with other observations, interviews or whatever source of data is being used. Repetition of the process results in an emergent theory (Brophy 2006: 27–8). The literature is a starting point for analysis – not an end point. Annemaree Lloyd found that the librarian's traditional conception of information literacy – skills, texts and ICT – had little meaning in the workplace, and social relationships, processes and practices within context were highlighted. Information literacy in the workplace is not an individual process, but a collaborative process between experienced practitioners and novices (Lloyd 2007: 75–6, 82–3). This example shows that the findings of qualitative research can be quite profound.

Most of the research methods outlined above, as well as being well known in academia, are also widely used in the corporate environment and public services, and it is sometimes possible to work collaboratively with colleagues in other departments that have experience of research methods, such as public relations departments. However, a method which is mainly confined to academia is worth mentioning as it helps to inform understanding of what information literacy is and how it is perceived. This is 'phenomenography' which 'is a description of things, objects, experiences, facts, events or trends as they appear to us'. It is an attempt to describe the qualitatively different ways that phenomena are experienced by groups. It is sometimes explained by the metaphor of the half glass of wine which some might perceive to be half full while others think of it as half empty, depending on their point of view. The aim of phenomenography is to determine the finite number of ways the phenomenon may be experienced by participants in the research (Edwards 2007: 87–8). It is particularly applicable to information literacy given that there are still different views about what information literacy is and how it is variously conceptualised in higher education, the workplace and lifelong learning. As a technique it was deployed to great effect by Webber et al. (2005) in a higher education study which showed that interest in and understanding of information literacy varied widely across academic disciplines.

## Resources

Resources to support impact assessment and research methods are limited, but there are a couple which are worth mentioning: the Scottish Libraries and Information Council's *Building on Success: A Public Library Quality Improvement Matrix for Scotland* (SLIC 2007) which has a section on information literacy and the Museums, Libraries & Archives Council's (MLAC) GSO (Generic Social Outcomes) Toolkit which contains a section (6.1) comparing different methods of evaluation (MLAC 2008).

*Building on Success* is part of the Strategic Quality Assurance Framework which has been developed for Scottish local authorities to use in monitoring and assessing the performance of their cultural services. Although Scottish public libraries are required to provide an 'adequate' service, adequate is not defined and this approach intends to provide a clear definition of adequate service provision. It has seven quality indicators which can be measured on a scale of 6–1 (Excellent to Unsatisfactory – this is the scale used by Her Majesty's Inspectors of Education). This is an appropriate process as many public library services are involved in HMIE inspections through community learning and development and other performance review processes. The relevant indicator is the fourth – Learners' experiences. A variety of methods are identified for finding evidence, although this does not extend to a detailed review of survey and evaluation methods.

## Quality Indicator 4 – Learners' experiences – recommends inter alia . . .

- Public library services should promote and deliver learning in their communities . . .

- The services to learners should be widely publicised and regular introductory sessions should be arranged.

Entitlements to the public should include:

- Support for the development of information literacy and digital literacy to enable access and use of information services.

- Community learning and literacy classes, including taster sessions and progression through learning partnerships.

Questions to ask are:

- In what ways does the library environment promote learning?

- To what extent do staff encourage learning?

- In what ways are the needs of various learners addressed?

- What opportunities are there for progression through partnerships?

From the Scottish education world comes a parallel document. The *Improving Scottish Education* report (HMIE 2009: 73–8) offers some useful points in its review of community learning and development (CLD). It indicates the following strengths and weaknesses identified Scotland-wide:

*Strengths*

- Strong commitment to inclusion, equality and fairness

with examples of innovative and effective work with disadvantaged individuals and groups

- Learning programmes that are flexible and tailored to meet the needs of learners

- Good quality of youth work and relationships with young people

- High degree of responsiveness to the needs of adult learners

- Improvements made in community capacity building

- Partnership working remains a strength in the sector.

*Aspects for improvement*

- Demonstrating the outcomes of CLD provision and tracking improvements over time

- Ensuring that planning is needs led and outcomes focused.

While there are some useful pointers here it is interesting to note that these two documents function entirely independently of one another.

The GSO Toolkit (MLAC 2008) is a good deal more specific and 'Resource 6.1 Comparison of Different Evaluation Methods' offers a wide range of evaluation techniques, some of them little known in academia and formal research environments. It lists some 15 methods in four columns: 'Method'; 'Strengths' [advantages]; 'Things to consider' [including disadvantages] and 'May be useful for ...' [where the method is most applicable]. For example, for the first row in the table 'Outputs/statistical data', the 'Things to consider' column includes 'Not evidence of an outcome in itself'.

The methods reviewed include 'Observation' where the 'Things to consider' column includes 'Think about how you will record the observations, timing and focus of the observations, who will make the observations – a member of the team or an independent observer?'; 'Consider using an observation checklist to record what you saw or guide to code and identify certain behaviour'. In the fifth row of the table 'Letters/emails', the 'Things to consider' column includes 'Unpredictable and ad hoc source of collecting GSO outcomes'; 'Useless unless properly analysed'. Methods less well known to the library and information world include 'Drawings' (row 10 of table) which 'Are useful when writing skills are limited and may be more "fun" and engaging' (column 2 of the table). The 'Things to consider' column includes 'These are challenging to interpret without questioning and mediation' but notes under the 'May be useful for ...' column 'Works well as a way for children to feedback on what they most enjoyed about the experience ...'

All in all this is a useful checklist of both well-known and less familiar methods conveniently summarising all the advantages and disadvantages of each method and in what situations they are most applicable. 'Resource 6.3 Using the Mosaic Approach to Plan Your Evaluation – Scenario Activity' gives an example of a practical scenario and 'Resource 6.6 A Note on Ethics' offers some tips on this important issue.

## Examples of impact and evaluation

### Information literacy in employability training: the experience of Inverclyde Libraries
(Crawford and Irving 2012).

This study evaluated an employability training programme provided by Inverclyde Libraries in West Central Scotland and the role of information literacy within the training programme. The programme was found to be a success and had greatly increased the confidence of learners. It was recommended that the course be developed further to endow learners with the expertise to develop employability and workplace decision-making skills. There were a number of recommendations for improvement including:

- Improving recruitment with more regularised procedures

- Need to focus on health and financial literacies

- Improve course scheduling and planning

- Include information on copyright and Internet safety issues.

Inverclyde Libraries found this evaluation extremely useful. At the time evaluation was taking place the service was trying to implement a strong information literacy agenda, and the classes run in partnership with community learning and development (CLD) were some of the first to have a clear information literacy focus. By being able to see feedback from one-to-one interviews staff were able to understand their learner's needs better than through standard evaluation forms. In the years following the evaluation staff have adapted the courses to run at different times and in different formats to allow them to reach the people best served by them. As a result of the evaluation Inverclyde has developed in-house information skills courses which focus on a variety of topics including health, finance and employability. Learners are encouraged to use online reference services and staff plan to instil high-quality information-seeking skills in their learners. Internet safety and copyright issues are now included in various digital participation projects that the service now runs (McNamara 2012).

## Derbyshire Libraries. Local Strategic Partnership (LSP) Living Literacy Project Key Stage 3: Bolsover Library: evaluation report

The intention of the project was to help children understand what information literacy means and how it works in practice. The target for the project was:

'To raise standards in English, maths, ICT and science in secondary education so that:

○ By 2007 85% of 14 year olds achieve level 5 or above in English, maths and ICT (80% in science) nationally, sustained to 2008

○ By 2008, in all schools, at least 50% of pupils achieve level 5 or above in each of English, maths and science.'

The project also links to the Libraries and Heritage Division vision statement and helps to deliver on one of Derbyshire County Council's key priorities:

'To *improve access and encourage participation in leisure, recreation, information, learning and culture.*'

The anticipated outcomes were for students at the end of the session to be able to:

- Read and understand maps

- Access information using IT resources and identify relevant material

- Use a public library effectively

- Use digital multimedia.

These were to be achieved in readiness for a morning tour of the town of Bolsover during which students noted and photographed historic buildings. This was followed by a 2-hour session using library resources and a short piece of work. Another event was the visit to a nature reserve followed by a session using library resources. In all 101 students participated. The project was evaluated using the MLA's Inspiring Learning Framework referred to above and employing questionnaires which were administered to both students and teachers. The evaluation was very positive, although there were some differences in responses due to the differing abilities of students. It was concluded that:

- The evaluation showed that aims and objectives were met.

- The full day's session at the library yielded the most positive responses from both pupils and staff.

- The diversity of the day stimulated creativity and involvement from pupils of all abilities.

- The majority of pupils and staff enjoyed the day which helped to change perceptions of the library and what it could offer.

- All the teachers would recommend the day to colleagues.

- One of the teachers from one of the participating schools felt the programme ought to be added to the curriculum.

The main recommendation was that there should be improved communications between library staff and teachers, but library staff should find out in advance the ability levels of pupils to help with the planning of the day and the creation of appropriate worksheets (Petersen et al. 2007).

## Gateways to Learning

Gateways to Learning (Gateways) was a 2-year, £2 million project, which was developed in response to the need to develop sustainable jobs following the closure of the Corus steelworks in Ebbw Vale in South Wales in 2001. It ran from September 2005 to November 2007 and sought to widen participation in lifelong learning and make it more accessible, particularly to people in disadvantaged communities or circumstances. There were four elements to the project:

- To work in partnership to develop joint protocols between partner libraries (e.g., on borrowing rights)

- To develop a joint catalogue between eight partner libraries in South East Wales

- To develop a library card enabling access to partner library loans, which would be requested from and delivered to the client's local library

- To offer nonaccredited and accredited learning in information literacy through one-to-one taster sessions and support for OCN (Open College Network) Levels 1–3.

It was the subject of an independent evaluation which aimed to assess the qualitative impact and benefits of the project, its success in meeting its objectives and its management. It was based on interviews with key participants – 9 project staff, 8 Strategic Management Committee members, 29 library staff, and 59 beneficiaries. With a total of 105 participants it was clearly a major project. Although it was large and complex, it was well managed and its achievements were impressive. Findings included:

- User satisfaction among learners with Gateways was over 90 per cent.

- Gateways addressed the skills deficit of many of its clients – identifying relevant help for people with basic literacy needs;

241

providing one-to-one sessions for people needing help with using a computer and email; and supporting people in learning how to locate and use information to meet their needs as citizens, purchasers and learners.

- Gateways enhanced clients' image of the library and enabled them to use library resources more effectively.

- Gateways raised the profile of and esteem for libraries amongst other parts of the local authority, decision makers and politicians; it embedded information literacy as part of the culture of libraries.

- Gateways helped 600 people to learn about computers, identify, select and manage the information obtained and clients have gained a qualification they did not have before.

- Gateways helped prisoners to be more aware of information and its importance in their lives, to use information more discriminatingly and to value libraries as a 'gateway to living'.

- An OCN in Information Literacy helped would-be students to progress seamlessly into further or higher education, gaining accredited training and essential learning skills.

- The free accredited qualification in Information Literacy has begun to benefit people wanting to find a job.

Clearly the project demonstrated the value of information literacy in skills development and employability.

The lessons learned and issues raised by the Project included:

- Libraries need to continually find ways of broadening the contexts in which they support citizens' information literacy skills (e.g., through closer relationships with community development, regeneration and economic participation).

- Gateways was less successful in attracting clients 20 years or older who were not active participants in education, employment or training.

- It was not possible to clearly identify the impact of Gateways on participants' progression to lifelong learning.

- Adapting to the regime of the prison service required additional arrangements being made initially, but produced substantial benefits.

As some of these points have surfaced in other studies, they are not perhaps unexpected.

## Student learning through Ohio School Libraries
(Todd and Kuhlthau 2004)

This report is an overview of key findings from the *Student Learning through Ohio School Libraries* research study. It studied 39 school libraries across Ohio and sought to understand how students benefit from school libraries. The schools chosen to participate were selected on the basis of providing an 'effective school library program' rather than randomly selected. This meant that they met a series of national and international guidelines. The research collected data from the students themselves, rather than from school staff which had been the method used in previous state-wide studies. Questionnaires in this study were administered to both students and staff, although both questionnaires had sections where respondents could write down their own thoughts, thus generating qualitative data.

The results were extremely positive and the researchers concluded that 'The study portrays effective school libraries across Ohio as dynamic agents of student learning and student achievement.' It was found that the school library and librarian-trained students in both search and research methods helped students to develop 'information literacy scaffolds [...] to construct and effectively demonstrate new knowledge and understanding.' The school library helped students to get good grades, particularly on research projects and assignments. It also found that the school library played a role in fostering independent reading, although it was more successful with lower grade than higher grade pupils. The study found that the school library supported 'just-in-time learning' as the students seemed to have many 'information crises' when they needed information fast and support with technological issues – a phenomenon not unknown in higher education as well. The involvement of the professional school librarian was a personal touch that mattered a good deal to students who valued such personal engagement with them. While such studies are to be welcomed, providing as they do objective evidence of what many school librarians are subjectively well aware of, restricting the research to school libraries already known to perform well perhaps produces a more optimistic result than a sample chosen at random might.

## Summary of the chapter

Measurement of impact is a potentially complex process, made more difficult by differences in conceptualisation of what information literacy is and how it takes place in practice in particular sectors. Impact assessment at the national level is the most challenging area and least tackled, reflecting the relative attention given to national information literacy policymaking as a whole. For activity in a range of sectors, both quantitative and qualitative methods are available, although it is probably better to use qualitative methods which are more suited to the as yet relatively unstructured nature of the process. Group discussion methods and interviewing are likely to produce substantial but manageable amounts of data and – as they are widely used both within and outside the information profession – they are likely to be understood by participants. Higher education and public libraries are the types of library most likely to be able to deploy the necessary expertise, but independent studies are a valuable additional source of information. The literature should always be searched for comparative data before undertaking research. There is a dearth of guidance documents in the topic area.

# Part 3
# Policymaking and issues for the future

# 10

# Review and issues for the future

*John Crawford*

**Abstract:** This final chapter considers the content of previous chapters and endeavours to draw out key points and general policy issues. These focus around the need to extend the scope of information literacy, the difficulties inherent in doing so and the need to develop rigorous evaluation strategies. The chapter discusses the need for national information literacy policies and suggests a range of issues and activities which might inform such policies.

**Key words:** information literacy, information literacy policymaking, information policy, national information literacy policies, digital participation.

## A review of issues

Even a cursory review of the evidence demonstrates that historic factors lie behind the contemporary debate. There has been little agreement about what information actually is, and people's views are influenced by education, experience, personal agendas and issues of technology. The role of government has always been poorly defined, and government engagement with information issues has been intermittent and frequently vestigial. Similarly, the relationship between governments and information organisations has often been weak and frequently nonexistent. Information organisations have not always cooperated harmoniously, and in a historical context information literacy is invisible.

To understand information literacy it is necessary to contextualise it within the modern information society which has been defined as a 'society in which the creation, distribution and treatment of information have become the most significant economic and cultural activities' (UNESCO 2009: 123–4). An information society also covers many related sectors which include industrial and economic policy, technology policy, telecommunications policy and a huge sector: social issues and policies that comprise e-government, education, e-health, media policy and cultural issues within which much of the material of information literacy lies. However, what information actually is remains a variable concept.

There has been much debate about the definition of information literacy, but it comprises a complex mixture of factors, much influenced by key documents, such as the groundbreaking *Presidential Committee on Information Literacy: Final Report* (ACRL 1989), the implications of which are still with us today. The *Prague Declaration* (UNESCO 2003) and the Alexandria Proclamation (Garner 2005) extended the debate to include economic development, effective citizenship, lifelong learning and critical thinking. A more recent focus on the workplace and informal learning has led to the redefinition of what an information source is and emphasises the social and collaborative nature of the process. Information literacy has a key role to play in the skills development agenda and in combating social deprivation and disadvantage which moves it a long way from the earlier view of information literacy, deriving mainly from higher education, which saw information literacy skills development as primarily an individual activity focusing around print and online sources. To understand information literacy today we have to include not only the evaluation and use of traditional 'library' sources but also social policy issues, relating to the relief of inequality and disadvantage, skills development for a post-industrial society, critical thinking and lifelong learning, an activity which information literacy informs and supports. There are also the issues of digital literacy, school and higher education curricula, early-years' learning, health issues, the dynamics of the workplace, learning and teaching skills and strategies with an increasing emphasis on teaching and learning in informal situations. The role of ICT and digital agendas is a potential source of confusion, not least among key decision makers in politics, civil services and NGOs. In an information society, information flows through ICT, and it can be difficult to distinguish between the two. The increasing interest of governments in many countries in these issues is both a threat and an opportunity. As Jenny Foreman and Morag Higgison point out in their case study (Chapter 6), Scottish Government senior management did not endorse the *Scottish Government Information Literacy Strategy* which they authored with the help and support of the Scottish Information Literacy Project. Instead, senior management preferred to adopt a 'subset' of information literacy, namely digital literacy. On the other hand, digital literacy or digital participation represents a considerable opportunity for public librarians to engage in training and support activities in cooperation with other agencies such as community learning and development bodies and Jobcentre Plus. Unfortunately, digital participation is viewed by some governments as meaning principally access and infrastructure issues rather than usage and skills training and development. In Canada a major initiative was Connecting Canadians – an attempt by the Canadian Government to connect Canada's citizens to the Internet; however, it emphasised technological access and connections over human needs which led to an intense need for public librarians to promote information literacy to the public. This has, in turn, led to proposals for more information literacy instruction from public libraries and for more government support to make this possible. Similarly, Connect Australia set out to improve broadband services in regional, rural and remote areas. However, an impact investigation of this service found that there was a major disconnect between the development of these services by the government and library patrons' use of them. In both countries there is technology to make the Internet widely available, but the real need is promotion of information literacy instruction among their citizens (Gilton 2012: 41–2). In Chapter 7 we saw a real need for health information literacy training and support for the public and public library staff. Whilst there are some visible examples of such activities, we need many more in order to meet the needs of the public and achieve the importance outlined in government health information policies. This growing perceived need for information literacy training by public librarians raises important questions about staff structure and training. Do the staff structures of public libraries need to be modified to meet this new challenge and do new training needs have to be identified and addressed? Do public librarians need to be as well versed in learning and teaching theory as their counterparts in higher education but with additional skills in developing supportive learning environments for people with poor, negative or limited previous learning experiences?

As York University Librarian Stephen Town has pointed out, the road to information literacy activity takes place in three stages: a nation perceives a need for competitive reasons to be a player in the global knowledge economy. This, in turn, suggests a need for the upskilling of its population to work effectively in this sort of economy, resulting in a national 'learning agenda'. The 'learning agenda' also tends to become explicitly associated with the skills of citizens, the development of these skills within educational programmes and their subsequent application in the workplace. Third, the growth of digital media and communications results in widespread information overload, leading to the need for both individuals and corporations to have effective information and knowledge management. This sequence tends to run from national concern to process analysis to products for developing information literacy (Town 2003: 86). However, somewhat surprisingly, it is the third of these three factors which has received the most attention and usually in higher education. There is a clear need for information literacy training and training materials to be developed for use in the workplace and in informal learning environments, and in these areas collaboration with other agencies is a good idea. The Scottish Government information service staff, for example, plan their training work in conjunction with training agencies within the Scottish Government. Information literacy policymaking is less visible and often subsumed in documents concerned with ICT policy. Documents with 'information literacy policy' prominently displayed on the title page are a comparative rarity. There is no agreed template for information literacy policy documents. As Chapter 3 shows, while there are helpful advocacy documents, some produced over ten years ago, there is little evidence as to what impact they have had and there are no agreed tools for impact assessment. Attempts to derive generally applicable indicators from pre-existing sources (Catts and Lau 2008: 38) have proved problematical, and a further attempt to develop adult information literacy indicators from relevant international surveys was unsuccessful (Catts 2012).

A content analysis of articles in 'the top 10 [library and information science] journals' (Aharony 2011) yields useful data and offers pointers to the future, although the chosen 'top 10' shows a bias to science and computing-related journals which are less favoured by those reporting on information literacy research and development work. The survey covers articles published in 2007–8 and found that most of the authors originated in North America or Europe with a few emanating from South America or Africa. Of the various categories identified 'social information science' was found to be one of the three largest categories. This includes topics familiar to information literacy: information needs of different cultures, self-help sources, health information centres and social information banks. The category 'information/learning society' comprised more than 10 per cent of items and included information society, information literacy and lifelong literacy. Information literacy has an important place in research and publication and, although major contributions to information literacy have come from Australasia and Mexico, North America and Europe dominate and may continue to do so for the foreseeable future.

## What is to be done?

While considerable progress has been made in moving information literacy from a 'library centric' model to one which is more society and community based, not enough has been done to integrate information literacy policymaking into public advocacy, and indeed information literacy policymaking as a distinctive systematic activity scarcely exists. ICT infrastructural and digital participation issues have achieved a much higher profile. It is difficult to see how much progress can be made without well-funded centrally led strategies which can coordinate and support the many disparate initiatives which take place. There has been much debate as to whether information literacy activity should be a top-down activity or a bottom-up one, in which it has hoped that numerous local and disparate activities will somehow coalesce into a coherent whole. However well intentioned the latter approach might be, it has not achieved high-profile results. Woody Horton, an expert in information literacy advocacy, champions the top-down approach (Horton 2011). A national agency of some sort, in all countries, is needed to develop initiatives and support those who are already making them at a regional or local level. The American National Forum on Information Literacy is a possible model for all but expert national organisations need to be staffed and funded, although much can be achieved by a small number of people, as the Welsh Information Literacy Project has shown. Such an agency might be led by the country's principal information organisation or at least have strong links with it. The primary motivation for setting up such an agency would almost certainly have to come from the country's principal information organisation, as it is unlikely that any other body would have the expertise or will to do it. What would such an agency do?

Its first task would be to raise funding to support its activities and this must be an ongoing concern. Collaborative working with other bodies is essential and this applies to fundraising which should be sought in cooperation with universities and research bodies, charities including those concerned with deprivation issues, educational organisations and curriculum development agencies, relevant professional bodies, employers and employee organisations, chambers of commerce and skills and training agencies. It should have the support of the relevant government department which would probably be a ministry of education or a ministry of lifelong learning. Collaborative working brings problems with it. Every organisation has its own distinctive aims and objectives and, while these may overlap with information literacy, they will not be the same. It is important to respect other's aims and objectives and show how information literacy can inform and support them. Its first and principal task should be the development of an information literacy policy in cooperation with the above bodies. Policymaking must be realistic and should develop strands that have appeal outside the information sector and are likely to attract funding. Particular attention should be paid to a country's social and educational policies, and then policy and action should be mapped against them by including topics that appeal both to government and the public. Internet safety and IPR issues are obvious examples. Policymaking should recognise and work with innovative learning and teaching agendas which recognise independent learning and those who promote them, as they are likely to be sympathetic to lifelong learning. An information literacy policy is however a process – not an event – and it needs to be modified and developed as new needs emerge. As an Irish study points out, the information literacy landscape is constantly changing (Connolly et al. 2013). For this reason documentation should be Web based and evolving, rather than a fixed printed document. Advocacy and lobbying, carried out in partnership with other agencies, should draw on and enhance existing policies or, as Woody Horton puts it, 'Link information literacy to specific long-standing goals and rewards' (Horton 2011: 273). It is important to bring together all information sectors to achieve a process of cross fertilisation so that different sectors can learn from one another. Librarians working in higher education probably have the best developed skills in learning and teaching, thanks to links with academic departments and educational development units and hence are well placed to support other sectors. They could pass on their skills to other sectors. It is important that a national information literacy agency should support regional and local initiatives within the state by giving advice and guidance and acting as a link to relevant agencies and behaving as a critical friend. It could well undertake evaluation work and one of its tasks might be to devise evaluation strategies. Cross-sectoral and collaborative working implies a community of practice. This might be Web based or consist of face-to-face meetings or, more probably, a combination of both. It should be a forum for the exchange of ideas and discussion of possible developments. Research projects relevant to the agency's policies should be undertaken, preferably in conjunction with relevant partners, both within and beyond the information sector. These will build up the agency's expertise and provide a base of knowledge to further develop policy and activity. The Scottish Information Literacy Project, for example, was founded with the sole time-limited aim of developing an information literacy framework linking secondary and tertiary education but soon found, through a process of action research, that its remit needed to be widened to include the workplace, lifelong and informal learning.

Through collaboration with partners exemplars of good practice and case studies should be collected and placed on the agency's website. These will both encourage and give status to those who have contributed them and will provide material which other partners can learn from and use and develop themselves. It can also provide data to inform policy development and future action points. Communication is important and the agency should write up and publish by whatever means are appropriate the results of its work. These might include a blog and other forms of social media, reporting at conferences and publication in appropriate journals. It should also organise conferences where its staff and partners can present papers and outside experts can be invited to contribute.

It should also undertake evaluation activity and develop evaluative criteria. As these are currently underdeveloped, this is an important function.

If a national information literacy programme is impossible, then activity by a professional body is another possibility. This is probably the most favoured option. However, information literacy then has to take its place with a multiplicity of other information concerns. Time and resources are always constraints and information literacy has to compete with other priorities. A third and probably the cheapest option is to form a community of practice. Most of its work will probably be online but face-to-face meetings are also possible. An existing example is *Information Skills for a 21st Century Scotland* (SLIC 2012). This involves an online community of practice which is open to everyone both within and outside the information profession, primarily in Scotland but also elsewhere. The community is open to everyone who is interested in information literacy, associated skills and competencies and wants to share practice, contribute to the community's knowledge of information literacy activities, and contribute case studies and news, reports of conferences and events and information about new research. One of the community of practice's key tasks is to further develop the Information Literacy Framework Scotland by enriching it in the areas where it is still underdeveloped. Another area requiring attention is the identification and addressing of training needs, preferably in conjunction with the relevant professional body.

A recent report from the Republic of Ireland recommends a similar approach (Connolly et al. 2013). Its results derived from data collected from 26 information literacy experts including 7 from outside Ireland. There are two principal recommendations:

- The setting up of a high-level advocacy committee, composed of leading figures within the profession in Ireland (high-level strategists and managers).

- A practitioner-led community of practice, composed of innovative practitioners, who manage and implement information literacy programmes throughout Irish libraries.

According to the Irish report (Connolly et al. 2013):

'The high level advocacy committee would operate both within and outside the profession: Within the library profession, a high-level advocacy committee would provide a framework that supports and facilitates the work of the community of practice.

Outside the library profession, a high-level advocacy committee would liaise with other national library organisations, collaborate with non-library groups whose information literacy goals are aligned with those of libraries, and lobby local and national government agencies to support information literacy initiatives across public life.'

The information literacy community of practice would have both online and offline components and would provide one online centralised resource for information literacy practice in Ireland. An online community would be a repository for information literacy literature, an opportunity for networking and sharing knowledge, an opportunity to communicate with peers and be home to a greater sense of inclusion for practitioners in small or remote organisations. Regional groupings outside the Dublin area are also proposed. Research, collaboration and continuing professional development are also recommended. This model is in part derived from the Scottish and Welsh experience and could be applied much more widely.

While formal education is not central to this study there are relevant issues. As Chapter 4 points out, lifelong learning means just that, but little work was done in earlier years in primary schools or nursery education. What is more, this is an age group with whom librarians have had little engagement. As the chapter shows, information literacy skills can be taught at nursery and early years in primary schools. However, it is difficult to make progress if teachers are not trained in information literacy skills, in addition to which there is, as yet, little interest in information literacy in departments of education. Vigorous advocacy campaigns directed at departments of education and senior teachers are needed. The Welsh Information Literacy Project is addressing this issue. Meetings have been held with head teachers and deputy heads in different parts of Wales and, at the time of writing, two case studies are to take place in two secondary schools. Contact has also been made with two teacher training colleges to highlight the importance of information literacy to student teachers before going out on school placements (Eynon 2013). It is also desirable that information literacy outcomes should be written into national school curricula. As Chapter 8 shows, links between schools and public libraries are also important, but it is equally or more important for teachers and librarians to cooperate, plan carefully and link activities to school curriculum outcomes.

As with all information literacy activities we need to share, report at conferences and write about them more – for sometimes great initiatives and projects go unnoticed.

Information literacy is an information ideology with huge potential but has many challenges to face as well.

# References

Abell, A. and Skelton, V. (2005) Intellectual linking: making sense of the dots. *Library & Information Update*, **41**(1/2), 44–5.

ACRL (1989) *Presidential Committee on Information Literacy: Final Report*. Chicago: Association of College & Research Libraries.

Aharony, N. (2011) Library and information science research areas: a content analysis of articles from the top 10 journals 2007–8. *Journal of Librarianship and Information Science*, **44**(1), 27–35.

Ahlgren, L. (2007) Learning in small and medium sized enterprises in Scotland. Conference proceedings 22–24 July 2007. *The times they are a-changing: researching transitions in lifelong learning*. Centre for Research in Lifelong Learning, CD-ROM format.

ALA (1989) *Presidential Committee on Information Literacy: Final Report*. Chicago: American Library Association. Available from: *http://www.ala.org/ala/mgrps/divs/acrl/publications/whitepapers/presidential.cfm* [accessed 10 January 2012].

ALA (2001) *A Library Advocate's Guide to Building Information Literate Communities*. Chicago: American Library Association.

ALIA (2003) *A Library Advocate's Guide to Building Information Literate Communities*. Canberra: Australian Library and Information Association.

ALIA (2006) *Statement on Information Literacy for All Australians*. Available from: *http://www.alia.org.au/policies/information.literacy.html* [accessed 23 November 2011] [Australian Library and Information Association].

AMA (1999) Health literacy: Report of the Council on Scientific Affairs, American Medical Association. *JAMA (Journal of the American Medical Association)*, **281**, 552–7.

Anton, S. (2010) Contributing to health and well-being: the public library partnership. *Library & Information Update*, August, 42–3.

Archer, A. (2012) Email communication, 11 April 2012.

Ashcroft, L., Farrow, J. and Watts, C. (2007) Public libraries and adult learners. *Library Management*, **28**(3), 125–38.

Ballantyne, L. (2008) *Real and Relevant: Information Literacy Skills for the 21st Century Learner*. Available from: *http://wayback. archive-it.org/1961/20100625210259/http://www.ltscotland.org. uk/slf/previousconferences/2008/seminars/a2e.asp* [accessed 24 August 2010].

Bandura, A. (2010) Self-efficacy: abstract. *Corsini Encyclopedia of Psychology*. Available from: *http://onlinelibrary.wiley.com/doi/ 10.1002/9780470479216.corpsy0836/abstract* [accessed 1 February 2013].

Basili, C. (2011) A framework for analysing and comparing information literacy policies in European countries. *Library Trends*, 60(2), 395–418.

Batool, S.H. and Mahmood, K. (2012) Teachers' conceptions about information literacy skills of school children. *Pakistan Journal of Library & Information Science*, **13**. Available from: *http:// pu.edu.pk/images/journal/pjlis/pdf/pjlis-13-batool.pdf* [Accessed 22 January 2013].

Bawden, D. (2001) Information and digital literacies: a review of concepts. *Journal of Documentation*, 57(2), 218–59.

Beautyman, W. (2012a) The road to information literacy: an ethnographic investigation into the cognitive and affective characteristics of key stage 2, primary school children. Doctoral thesis, Northumbria University.

Beautyman, W. (2012b) The road to information literacy: primary school children and their information seeking behaviour. Paper presented at *LILAC 2012*. Available from: *http://www. slideshare.net/infolit_group/beautyman* [accessed 17 January 2013].

BID (2011) *Medien- und Informationskompetenz – immer mit Bibliotheken und Informationseinrichtungen!* Berlin: Bibliothek & Information Deutschland. Available from: *http://www. bideutschland.de/download/file/BID_Positionspapier_Medien-% 20und%20Informationskompetenz_Enquete_Internet.pdf* [accessed 10 January 2012].

Birdsong, L. and Freitas, J. (2012) Helping the non-scholar scholar: information literacy for life-long learners. *Library Trends*, 60(3), 588–610.

Black, A. (2007) Arsenals of scientific and technical information: public technical libraries in Britain during and immediately after World War 1. *Library Trends*, 55(3), 474–89.

Black, A., Muddiman, D. and Plant, H. (2007) *The Early Information Society: Information Management in Britain before the Computer*. Aldershot: Ashgate.

Black, A., Pepper, S. and Bagshaw, K. (2009) *Books, Buildings and Social Engineering*. Aldershot: Ashgate.

Boekhorst, A. (2009) *Primary School Projects*. Available from: *https://www.jiscmail.ac.uk/cgi-bin/webadmin?A2=ind0905&L= lis-infoliteracy&P=R1124&1=lis-infoliteracy&9=A&J=on&d= No+Match%3BMatch%3BMatches&z=4* [accessed 16 January 2013].

Boud, D., Cohen, R. and Walker, D. (1985) *Reflection: Turning Experience into Learning*. London: Kogan Page.

Brookes, C. (2006) The legacy of lifelong learning. *RSA Journal*, 20 February 2006, 34–9.

Brophy, P (2006) *Measuring Library Performance: Principles and Techniques*. London: Facet.

Brown, A. (2009) *Higher Skills Development at Work*. London: Economic and Social Research Council, Teaching and Learning Research Programme.

Bruce, C.S. (1997) *The Seven Faces of Information Literacy*. Adelaide: AUSLIB Press.

Byron, T. (2008) *Safer Children in a Digital World* (report of the Byron Review). London: Department for Children, Schools and Families/Department for Culture, Media and Sport.

Careers Wales (2012) *Careers Wales*. Available from: *http://www. careerswales.com/aboutcareerswales/server.php?show=nav.5334* [accessed 2 April 2012].

Catts, R. (2012) Indicators of adult information literacy. *Journal of Information Literacy*, 6(2), 4–18. Available from: *http:// ojs.lboro.ac.uk/ojs/index.php/JIL/article/view/PRA-V6-l2-2012-1* [accessed 14 January 2013].

Catts, R. and Lau, J. (2008) *Towards Information Literacy Indicators*. Paris: UNESCO.

Center for Health Strategies Inc. (2000) *What Is Health Literacy?* (Fact Sheet). Princeton, NJ: Center for Health Care Strategies.

Chang, Y., Zhang, X., Mokhtar, A.I., Foo, S., Majid, S., Luyt. B. et al. (2012) Assessing students' information literacy skills in two secondary schools in Singapore. *Journal of Information Literacy*, 6(2). Available from: *https://ojs.lboro.ac.uk/ojs/index. php/JIL/article/view/PRA-V6-I2-2012-2/1718* [accessed 22 January 2013].

Cheuk, B. (2008) Delivering business value through information literacy in the workplace. *Libri*, **58**, 137–43.

Childers, T. and Post, J.A. (1975) *The Information-poor in America*. Lanham, MD: Scarecrow Press.

Chu, S.K.W. (2012) Assessing information literacy: a case study of Primary 5 students in Hong Kong. *School Library Research*, **15**. Available from: *http://www.ala.org/aasl/sites/ala.org.aasl/files/content/aaslpubsandjournals/slr/vol15/SLR_Assessing Information Literacy_V15.pdf* [accessed 22 January 2013].

CIBER (2008) *Information Behaviour of the Researcher of the Future*. Available from: *http://www.jisc.ac.uk/media/documents/programmes/reppres/gg_final_keynote_11012008.pdf* [accessed 25 January 2013].

CILIP (2004) *Information Literacy Definition*. London: Chartered Institute of Library and Information Professionals. Available from: *http://www.cilip.org.uk/get-involved/advocacy/learning/information-literacy/Pages/definition.aspx* [accessed 1 December 2011].

CILIP (2009) *An Introduction to Information Literacy*. Available from: *http://www.cilip.org.uk/get-involved/advocacy/information-literacy/pages/introduction.aspx* [accessed 1 March 2012] [Chartered Institute of Library and Information Professionals].

CILIP (2013) Health literacy skills need to be improved. *CILIP Update*, **3**, January, 7.

Clark , C. (2012a) Email communication, 8 February 2012.

Clark , C. (2012b) Email communication, 8 February 2012.

Connolly, A., Curran, L., Lynch, A. and O'Shea, S. (2013) BILI: building information literacy in Ireland. *Library and Information Research*, **37**(114), 37–54.

Cooke, L. and Greenwood, H. (2008) 'Cleaners don't need computers': bridging the digital divide in the workplace. *Aslib Proceedings*, **60**(2), 143–57.

Corrall, S. (2009) *Information Literacy: The Case for Strategic Engagement*. Available from: *http://www.slideshare.net/cilr/information-literacy-the-case-for-strategic-engagement* [accessed 8 January 2013].

Craig, E. (2009) Better informed for better health and better care: An information literacy framework to support health care in Scotland. *Health Information and Libraries Journal*, **26**(1), 77–80. Available from: *http://onlinelibrary.wiley.com/doi/10.1111/j.1471-1842.2008.00837.x/pdf* [accessed 6 February 2013].

Craig, E. (2013) NHS Scotland Information Literacy Framework. Email communication, 26 February 2013.

Craig, E. and Westwood, R. (2009) *What Is Information Literacy and Why Does It Matter.* Available from: *http://www.info literacy.scot.nhs.uk/media/1923903/bgbooklet.pdf* [accessed 9 November 2009].

Crawford, J. (2006a) The use of electronic information services and information literacy: a Glasgow Caledonian University study. *Journal of Librarianship and Information Science,* **38**(1), 33–44.

Crawford J. (2006b) *The Culture of Evaluation in Library and Information Services.* Oxford: Chandos.

Crawford, J.C. and Daye, A. (2000) A survey of the use of electronic services at Glasgow Caledonian University Library. *The Electronic Library,* **18**(4), 255–65.

Crawford, J. and Irving, C. (2007) Information literacy, the link between secondary and tertiary education project and its wider implications. *Journal of Librarianship and Information Science,* **39**(1), 17–26.

Crawford, J. and Irving, C. (2009) Information literacy in the workplace: a qualitative exploratory study. *Journal of Librarianship and Information Science,* **41**(1), 29–38. Available from: *http://lis.sagepub.com/cgi/content/abstract/41/1/29?etoc* [accessed 13 February 2012].

Crawford, J. and Irving, C. (2012) Information literacy in employability training: the experience of Inverclyde Libraries. *Journal of Librarianship and Information Science,* **44**(2), 79–89.

Crawford, J., De Vicente, A. and Clink, S. (2004) Use and awareness of electronic information services by students at Glasgow Caledonian University: a longitudinal study. *Journal of Librarianship and Information Science,* **36**(3), 101–17.

Crawford, J., Irving, C., Thomson, L. and Foreman, J. (2008) The use of information by Scottish Government staff. *Library & Information Update,* December, 48–9.

DBIS (2012) *The 2011 Skills for Life Survey: A Survey of Literacy, Numeracy and ICT Levels in England.* Available from: *http://www.gov.uk/government/uploads/system/uploads/attachment_data/file/36000/12-p168-2011-skills-for-life-survey.pdf* [accessed 29 January 2013] [Department for Business Innovation & Skills].

DCMS (2009) *Digital Britain*. London: Department for Culture, Media and Sport. Available from: *http://www.culture.gov.uk/what_we_do/broadcasting/5944.aspx* [accessed 19 January 2012].

DCMS/BERR (2009) *Digital Britain: The Interim Report*. Available from: *http://webarchive.nationalarchives.gov.uk/+/http://www.culture.gov.uk/images/publications/digital_britain_interimreport jan09.pdf* [accessed 25 January 2013] [Department for Culture, Media and Sport/Department for Business Enterprise and Regulatory Reform].

De Saulles, M. (2007) Information literacy amongst UK SMEs: an information policy gap. *Aslib Proceedings*, **59**(1), 68–79.

DfEE/QCA (2010) *National Curriculum Primary Handbook*. Available from: *https://orderline.education.gov.uk/gempdf/184962383X.PDF* [accessed 24 January 2013] [Department for Education and Employment/Qualification and Curriculum Authority].

DfES/DWP (2005) *Skills, Getting on in Business, Getting on at Work* (3 vols). London: Department for Education and Skills.

DH (2008) *NHS Choices*. Available from: *http://www.nhs.uk* [accessed 1 December 2011] [Department of Health].

DH (2009) *Information Prescriptions*. Available from: *http://www.informationprescriptions.info/* [accessed 1 December 2011] [Department of Health].

DH (2010a) *The NHS Constitution*. Available from: *www.nhs.uk/choiceintheNHS/Rightsandpledges/NHSConstitution/Documents/nhs-constitution-interactive-version-march-2010.pdf* [accessed 1 December 2011] [Department of Health].

DH (2010b) *Liberating the NHS: An Information Revolution*. Available from: *http://www.dh.gov.uk/prod_consum_dh/groups/dh_digitalassets/@dh/@en/documents/digitalasset/dh_120598.pdf* [accessed 1 December 2011] [Department of Health].

DIUS (2009) *Skills for Life*. London: Department for Innovation, Universities & Skills.

Doyle, C.S. (1994) *Information Literacy in an Information Society: A Concept for the Information Age*. Syracuse: ERIC Clearinghouse.

Dryburgh, R. (2012) Email communication, 11 April 2012.

Dubber, G. (2008a) *Cultivating Curiosity Information Literacy Skills and the Primary School Library*. Swindon. School Library Association.

Dubber, G. (2008b) *A Primary School Information Skills Toolkit*. Swindon. School Library Association.

EAC (2012) *Community Health Improvement Partnership (CHIP)*. Available from: *http://www.east-ayrshire.gov.uk/Community LifeAndLeisure/ServicesAndAdviceForOlderPeople/ActivitiesFor OlderPeople/CHIP.aspx* [accessed 14 February 2013] [East Ayrshire Council].

Education Scotland (2009a) Literacy across learning. Available from: *http://www.educationscotland.gov.uk/learningteachingand assessment/learningacrossthecurriculum/responsibilityofall/ literacy/index.asp* [accessed 25 January 2013].

Education Scotland (2009b) *Literacy and English*. Available from: *http://www.educationscotland.gov.uk/learningteachingand assessment/curriculumareas/languages/litandenglish/index.asp* [accessed 25 January 2013].

Education Scotland (2009c) *Principles and Practice: Literacy across Learning*. Available from: *http://www.educationscotland.gov.uk/ learningteachingandassessment/learningacrossthecurriculum/ responsibilityofall/literacy/principlesandpractice/index.asp* [accessed 25 January 2013].

Education Scotland (n.d.) *About Early Years*. Available from: *http:// www.ltscotland.org.uk/earlyyears/about/index.asp* [accessed 1 March 2012].

Edwards, S.E. (2007) Phenomenography: 'Follow the yellow brick road'! In: S. Lipu, K. Williamson and A. Lloyd (Eds), *Exploring Methods in Information Literacy Research* (Topics in Australasian Library and Information Studies No. 28). Wagga Wagga: Centre for Information Studies, Charles Sturt University, pp. 87–110.

Eraut, M. (2000) Non-formal learning and tacit knowledge in professional work. *British Journal of Educational Psychology*, 70, 113–36.

Eraut, M. (2007) University–work transitions: what counts as knowledge and how do we learn it? In: M. Eraut, G. Wisker and J. Barlow (Eds), *Making Teaching More Effective: Articles from the Learning and Teaching Conference 2006*. Brighton: University of Brighton Press.

Eraut, M., Harrison, R., Reeve, F., Hanson, A. and Clarke, J. (2002) Learning from other people at work. In: R. Harrison, F. Reeve, A. Hanson and J. Clark (Eds), *Supporting Lifelong Learning: Perspectives on Learning*. London: Routledge, pp. 127–45.

ERC (2013) *Health Information in Your Library*. Available from: *http://www.eastrenfrewshire.gov.uk/index.aspx?articleid=2192* [accessed 14 February 2013] [East Renfrewshire Council].

Evans, G. (2009) Information literacy in public libraries: the lifelong learning agenda. PowerPoint presentation. Available from: *http://www.slideshare.net/cirving/information-literacy-a-public-library-view* [accessed 4 April 2012].

Eve, J., De Groot, M. and Schmidt, A. (2007) Supporting lifelong learning in public libraries across Europe. *Library Review*, 56(5), 393–406.

Eynon, A. (2013) Welsh Information Literacy Project. *Library and Information Research*, 37(114), 17–22.

Eynon, K. (2012) *Public Libraries in Wales: Health, Wellbeing and Social Benefits.* Cardiff: Society of Chief Librarians. Available from: *http://www.goscl.com/public-libraries-in-waleshealth-well being-and-2/* [accessed 19 February 2013].

Felstead, A., Fuller, A., Unwin, L., Ashton, D, Butler, P. and Lee, T. (2005) Surveying the scene: learning metaphors, survey design and the workplace context. *Journal of Education and Work*, 18(4), 359–83.

Ferguson, S. (2009) Information literacy and its relationship to knowledge management. *Journal of Information Literacy*, 3(2), 6–24. Available from: *http://ojs.lboro.ac.uk/ojs/index.php/JIL/article/viewArticle/PRA-V3-I2-2009-1* [accessed 18 February 2012].

Foreman, J. and Thomson, L. (2009) Government information literacy in the 'century of information'. *Journal of Information Literacy*, 3(2). Available from: *http://ojs.lboro.ac.uk/ojs/index. php/JIL/article/view/PRA-V3-I2-2009-5* [accessed 8 January 2013].

Foreman, J. and Higgison, M. (2010) Scottish Government information literacy in the workplace: measuring impact. Paper presented at *LILAC 2010*. Available from: *http://www.lilac conference.com/dw/programme/parallel_sessions_detail_3.html#41* [accessed 6 January 2013].

Garner, S.D. (2005) *High-Level Colloquium on Information Literacy and Lifelong Learning.* Available from: *http://www. ifla.org/publications/high-level-colloquium-on-information-literacy-and-lifelong-learning* [accessed 22 January 2013].

Gerber, R. (1998) How do workers learn in the workplace? *Journal of Workplace Learning*, 16(1/2), 22–33.

Gilton, D.L. (2012) *Lifelong Learning in Public Libraries: Principles, Programs, and People.* Lanham, MD: Scarecrow Press.

Gorman, G.E. and Clayton, P. (2005) *Qualitative Research for the Information Professional: A Practical Handbook*, Second Edition. London: Facet.

Graham, N. (2011) Are we sharing our toys in the sandpit? In: G. Walton and A. Pope (Eds), *Information Literacy: Infiltrating the Agenda, Challenging Minds*. Oxford: Chandos.

Grant, V. (2013) Health information literacy activities in Public Libraries. Email communication, 15 February 2013.

Guile, D. and Young, M. (2002) Beyond the institution of apprenticeship: towards a social theory of learning as the production of knowledge. In: R. Harrison, F. Reeve, A. Hanson and J. Clark (Eds), *Supporting Lifelong Learning: Perspectives on Learning*. London: Routledge, pp. 146–62.

Hadley, S. and Hacker, K. (2007) Embedding information literacy into staff development in an acute National Health Service (NHS Trust). *Journal of Information Literacy*, 1(2). Available from: *http://ojs.lboro.ac.uk/ojs/index.php/JIL/article/view/20* [accessed 20 February 2012].

Haras, C. and Brasley, S.S. (2011) Is information literacy a public concern?: a practice in search of a policy. *Library Trends*, 60(2), 361–82.

Harding, J.N. (2008) Information literacy and the public library: we've talked the talk but are we walking the walk? *Australian Library Journal*, 56, 48–62.

Head, A. (2012) *How College Graduates Solve Information Problems Once They Join the Workplace* (Project Information Literacy Research Report). Available from: *http://projectinfolit. org/pdfs/PIL_fall2012_workplaceStudy_FullReport.pdf* [accessed 14 November 2012].

Herring, J.E. (1996) *Teaching Information Skills in Schools*. London: Library Association.

Herring, J. (2012) *Japanese Translation, Lifting and Planting Bulbs and Boogie Woogie!* Available from: *http://jherring.wordpress. com/2012/11/09/japanese-translation-lifting-and-planting-bulbs-and-boogie-woogie/* [accessed 17 January 2013].

Herring, J.E. (n.d.) *PLUS Model*. Available from: *http://athene. riv.csu.edu.au/~jherring/PLUS%20model.htm* [accessed 22 January 2013].

HKHE (2013) *Hong Kong's Higher Education System*. Available from: *http://studyinhongkong.edu.hk/eng/01hkesystem.jsp* [accessed 22 January 2013].

HMIE (2009) *Improving Scottish Education.* Livingston: HM Inspectorate of Education. Available from: *http://www. educationscotland.gov.uk/Images/ise09_tcm4-712882.pdf* [accessed 20 September 2012].

Horton, F.W. (2008) *Understanding Information Literacy: A Primer.* Paris: UNESCO.

Horton, F.W. (2011) Information literacy advocacy: Woody's ten commandments. *Library Trends,* **60**(2), 262–76.

Hughes, K. and Warden, M. (2007) *An Evaluation of the Gateways to Learning Project: The Contribution of Public and Academic Libraries in Gwent to Information Literacy, Learning, and Training* (final report). Caerphilly: Katherine Hughes Associates.

Irving, C. (2006) *The Role of Information Literacy in Addressing a Specific Strand of Lifelong Learning: The Work Agenda* (research article). Edinburgh: Learning and Teaching Scotland. Available from: *http://www.caledonian.ac.uk/ils/documents/Information Literacyintheworkplacearticle.pdf* [accessed 23 February 2012].

Irving, C. (2007a) The role of information literacy in addressing a specific strand of lifelong learning: the work agenda. MSc work-based learning project, Glasgow Caledonian University.

Irving, C. (2007b) Information literacy in the workplace: a small exploratory study. Paper presented at *Information: Interactions and Impact (i3), The Department of Information Management, Aberdeen Business School, The Robert Gordon University, Aberdeen.*

Irving, C. (2009) Collecting case studies/exemplars of good practice to enrich the National Information Literacy Framework (Scotland). *Library and Information Research,* **33**(105), 10–18. Available from: *http://www.lirgjournal.org.uk/lir/ojs/index.php/ lir/article/view/206/271* [accessed 25 January 2013].

Irving, C. (2010a) The Curriculum for Excellence: knowledge, engagement and contribution by Scottish school librarians. *The School Librarian,* **58**(3), 142–4.

Irving, C. (2010b) *Early and First Level CfE Experiences and Outcomes Linked to Information Literacy.* Available from: *http://curriculumforexcellence.pbworks.com/w/page/24176354/ Early%20and%20First%20Level%20CfE%20Experiences%20 and%20Outcomes%20linked%20to%20information%20 literacy* [accessed 25 January 2013].

Irving, C. (2011) National Information Literacy Framework (Scotland): pioneering work to influence policy making or tinkering at the edges. *Library Trends,* **60**(2), 419–39.

Irving, C. (2012) Case study: engaging and influencing policy and curriculum – the Scottish Information Literacy Project experience. In: C. Rankin and A. Brock (Eds), *Library Services for Children and Young People: Challenges and Opportunities in the Digital Age*. London: Facet, pp. 49–62.

Irving. C. and Crawford. J. (2006) Begin at school. *Library + Information Update*, 5(1/2), 38–9.

Jackman, L.W. (2012) *National Forum on Information Literacy's Gubernatorial Proclamation Campaign*. Available from: *http://teacherlibrarian.ning.com/profiles/blogs/national-forum-on-information-literacy-s-gubernatorial?xg_source=activity* [accessed 29 February 2012].

Jackson, A. (2010) Just enough education to perform: information skills, professionalism and employability. Paper presented at *LILAC 2010*. Available from: *http://www.lilacconference.com/dw/programme/parallel_sessions_detail_4.html#13* [accessed 9 February 2012].

Jarvis, E. (2012) Email communication, 12 November 2012.

Julien, H. and Hoffman, C. (2008) Information literacy training in Canada's public libraries. *Library Quarterly*, 78(1), 19–41.

Keenan, P. and McDonald, N. (2009) The stuff beyond Google (Presentation C1). Available from: *http://conferences.alia.org.au/online2009/docs/PresentationC1.pdf* [accessed 15 November 2012].

Kelly, T. (1977) *A History of Public Libraries in Great Britain, 1845–1975*. London: Library Association.

Kirkpatrick, D.L. and Kirkpatrick, J.D. (2007) *Implementing the Four Levels: A Practical Guide for Effective Evaluation of Training Programs*. San Francisco, CA: Berrett-Koehler Publishers.

Kuhlthau, C.C. (2008) From information to meaning: Confronting challenges of the twenty-first century. *Libri*, 58(2), 66–73.

Lave, J. and Wenger, E. (2002) Legitimate peripheral participation in communities of practice. In: R. Harrison, F. Reeve, A. Hanson and J. Clark (Eds), *Supporting Lifelong Learning: Perspectives on Learning*. London: Routledge, pp. 111–26.

Law, M. (1998) *Client-Centered Occupational Therapy*. Thorofare, NJ: SLACK Inc.

Library Wales (2009) *Schools Case Studies: NLW*. Available from: *http://librarywales.org/en/information-literacy/case-studies/schools/* [accessed 24 January 2013].

Library Wales (2012) *The First Incomplete Field Guide to Wellbeing in Libraries*. Available from: *http://librarywales.org/fileadmin/*

*documents/toolkit/Marketing/Get_Libraries/Wellbeing_in_
Libraries_ENGLISH_FINAL.pdf* [accessed 20 February 2013].

Lipu, S., Williamson, K. and Lloyd, A. (Eds) (2007) *Exploring
Methods in Information Literacy Research* (Topics in
Australasian Library and Information Studies No. 28). Wagga
Wagga: Centre for Information Studies, Charles Sturt University.

LLC (2012) *Learn in the Library*. Available from: *http://www.
leeds.gov.uk/docs/Learn%20in%20the%20library%20booklet.
pdf* [accessed 30 April 2012] [Leeds City Council].

Lloyd, A. (2007) Understanding information literacy in the
workplace: using a constructivist, grounded theory approach.
In: S. Lipu, K. Williamson and A. Lloyd (Eds), *Exploring
Methods in Information Literacy Research* (Topics in
Australasian Library and Information Studies No. 28). Wagga
Wagga: Centre for Information Studies, Charles Sturt
University, pp. 67– 86.

Lloyd, A. (2009) Informing practice: information experiences of
ambulance officers in training and on-road practice. *Journal of
Documentation*, 65(3), 396–419.

Lloyd, A. (2010) *Information Literacy Landscapes*. Oxford:
Chandos.

Lloyd, A. (2011) Trapped between a rock and a hard place: what
counts as information literacy in the workplace and how is it
conceptualized? *Library Trends*, 60(2), 277–96.

LSBU (2012) *Research Led by LSBU Academic Professor Gill
Rowlands Highlights the Need to Simplify Health Information.*
Available from: *http://www.lsbu.ac.uk/php5c-cgiwrap/hscweb/
cm2/public/news/news.php?newsid=115*
[accessed 29 January 2013] [London South Bank University].

Lundh, A. and Alexandersson, M. (2012) Collecting and compiling:
the activity of seeking pictures in primary school. *Journal of
Documentation*, 68(2), 238–53. Available from: *http://www.
emeraldinsight.com/journals.htm?articleid=17019400&show=
abstract* [accessed 22 January 2013].

Länsimies-Antikainen, H., Laitinen, T., Rauramaa, R., and Pietilä,
A.M. (2010) Evaluation of informed consent in health research: A
questionnaire survey. *Scandinavian Journal of Caring Science*, 24,
56–65.

Markless, S. and Streatfield, D. (2006) *Evaluating the Impact of Your
Library*. London: Facet.

Marshall, A., Henwood, F. and Guy, E.S. (2012) Information and
health information literacy in the balance: findings from a study

exploring the use of ICT's in weight management. *Library Trends*, 60(3), 479–96.

Mårtensson, L. and Hensing, G. (2012) Health literacy – a heterogeneous phenomenon: a literature review. *Scandinavian Journal of Caring Sciences*, 26(1), 151–60. Available from: *http://onlinelibrary.wiley.com/doi/10.1111/j.1471-6712.2011.00900. x/full* [accessed 13 February 2013].

May, J. (2013) Email communication, 8 February 2013.

McKenzie, P.J. (2003) A model of information practices in accounts of everyday-life information seeking. *Journal of Documentation*, 59(1), 19–40.

McLelland, D. and Crawford, J. (2004) The Drumchapel Project: a study of ICT usage by school pupils and teachers in a secondary school in a deprived area of Glasgow. *Journal of Librarianship and Information Science*, 36(2), 55–67.

McNamara, S. (2012) Email communication, 15 June 2012.

McNicol, S. and Dalton, P. (2003) *Public Libraries: Supporting the Learning Process*. Birmingham: Centre for Information Research, University of Central England. Available from: *http://www. ebase.bcu.ac.uk/cirtarchive/projects/past/public_libraries.htm* [accessed 20 March 2012].

Meadows, J. (2008) Fifty years of UK research in information science. *Journal of Information Science*, 34(4), 403–14.

Microsoft Research (2008) *Information Age*, January 2008.

Milne, C. (2004) University of Abertay, Dundee. In: SCONUL (Ed.), *Learning Outcomes and Information Literacy*. London: Higher Education. Available from: *http://www.heacademy.ac.uk/assets/ documents/resources/database/id515_learning_outcomes_and_ information_literacy.pdf* [accessed 15 August 2013] [Society of College, National and University Libraries].

MLAC (2008) *Inspiring Learning: An Improvement Framework for Museums, Libraries and Archives*. Available from: *http://www. inspiringlearningforall.gov.uk/toolstemplates/genericsocial/* [accessed 20 September 2012] [Museums, Libraries and Archives Council].

Moore, R. and Moschis, G. (1978) Consumer information use: Individuals vs. social predictors. Paper presented at *Association for Education in Journalism Annual Convention, Seattle, Washington*. Available from: *www.eric.ed.gov/ERICWebPortal/ contentdelivery/servlet/ERICServlet?accno=D158321* [accessed 1 December 2011].

MORI (2005) *Understanding the Audience*. London: MORI Social Research Institute.

Muddiman, D. (2003) Red information scientist: the information career of J. D. Bernal. *Journal of Documentation*, 59(4), 387–409.

Muddiman, D. (2007) Science, industry and the state: scientific and technical information in early twentieth century Britain. In: A. Black, D. Muddiman and H. Plant (Eds), *The Early Information Society: Information Management in Britain before the Computer*. Aldershot: Ashgate.

Muddiman, D., Durrani, S. and Dutch, M. (2000) *Open to All? The Public Library and Social Exclusion, Vol. 1: Overview and Conclusions*. London: Resource.

NCS (2012) *National Careers Service*. Available from: *https:// nationalcareersservice.direct.gov.uk/Pages/Home.aspx* [accessed 4 April 2012].

NFIL (2012) *Information Literacy*. Wikipedia. Available from: *http://en.wikipedia.org/wiki/Information_literacy* [accessed 13 January 2012] [National Forum on Information Literacy].

NHS Choices (n.d.) *Your Health, Your Choices*. Available from: *http://www.nhs.uk/* [accessed 7 February 2013].

NHS Direct (1999) *NHS Direct*. Available from: *http://www. nhsdirect.nhs.uk* [accessed 1 December 2011].

NHS Executive (1998) *Information for Health: An Information Strategy for the Modern NHS 1998–2005*. London: Department of Health.

NHS Informs (2012) *Scotland's Health Information Service*. Available from: *http://www.nhsinform.co.uk/* [Accessed 7 February 2013].

NHSES (2008) *Enabling Partnerships: Sharing Knowledge for Scotland's Health and Healthcare*. Available from: *http://www. healthscotland.com/uploads/documents/8394-14032_NES_ Leaflet_6pp_split_A5_final_41.pdf* [accessed 7 February 2013] [NHS Education for Scotland].

NHSES (2009) *Information Literacy Framework*. Available from: *http://www.infoliteracy.scot.nhs.uk/information-literacy-frame work.aspx* [accessed 8 February 2013] [NHS Education for Scotland].

NHSES (2010) *Enabling Partnerships: Sharing Knowledge to Build the Mutual NHS: A Knowledge Management Strategy and Action Plan for Better Health and Better Care in Scotland 2010–2012*. Available from: *http://www.knowledge.scot.nhs.uk/uploads/*

*Enabling_Partnerships.pdf* [accessed 7 February 2013] [NHS Education for Scotland].

NHSGG (2005) *Launch of Scotland's First Book Prescription Scheme*. Available from: *http://www.nhsgg.org.uk/content/default.asp?page=s1192_3&newsid=2251* [accessed 14 February 2013] [NHS Greater Glasgow and Clyde].

Nicholas, D. and Marden, M. (1997). The information needs of parents. *Aslib Proceedings*, 49(1), 5–7.

Niederdeppe, J. (2008) Beyond knowledge gaps: Examining socioeconomic differences in response to cancer news. *Human Communication Research*, 34(3), 423–447.

Nielsen, B.G. and Borlund. P. (2011) Information literacy, learning, and the public library: a study of Danish high school students. *Journal of Librarianship and Information Science*, 43(2), 106–19.

Nielsen-Bohlman, I., Panzer, A.M. and Kindig, D.A. (Eds) (2004) *Health Literacy: A Prescription to End Confusion*. Washington, DC: National Academic Press.

NILFS (2007) *A National Information Literacy Framework Scotland* (Draft). Available from: *http://www.therightinformation.org/storage/documents/DRAFTINFORMATIONLITERACY FRAMEWORK1h.pdf* [accessed 1 February 2013] [National Information Literacy Framework Scotland].

NILFS (2009a) Available from: *http://www.therightinformation. org/framework-home/* [accessed 25 January 2013] [National Information Literacy Framework Scotland].

NILFS (2009b) *Exemplars*. Available from: *http://www.theright information.org/temp-exemplars/* [accessed 25 January 2013] [National Information Literacy Framework Scotland].

NILFS (2009c) *Information Literacy Model: ExPLORE*. Available from: *http://www.therightinformation.org/temp-exemp-explore/* [accessed 25 January 2013] [National Information Literacy Framework Scotland].

NILFS (2009d) *North Ayrshire Information Literacy Toolkit*. Available from: *http://www.therightinformation.org/temp-exemp-northayrshire/* [accessed 25 January 2013] [National Information Literacy Framework Scotland].

NILFS (2009e) *Aberdeenshire's Schools Toolkit for Information Literacy*. Available from: *http://www.therightinformation.org/temp-exemp-aberdeenshire/* [accessed 25 January 2013] [National Information Literacy Framework Scotland].

NN/LM (2008) *Providing Health Information Services*. Available from: *http://nnlm.gov/outreach/community/onsite.html* [accessed

20 February 2013] [National Network of Libraries of Medicine (US)].

O'Beirne, R. (2010) *From Lending to Learning: The Development and Extension of Public Libraries*. Oxford: Chandos.

O'Connor, L. and Rapchak, M. (2012) Information use in online civic discourse: a study of heath care reform debate. *Library Trends*, 60(3), 497–521.

Ofcom (2009) *Report of the Digital Britain Media Literacy Working Group*. London: Ofcom. Available from: *http://stakeholders.ofcom.org.uk/market-data-research/media-literacy/medlitpub/media_lit_digital_britain/* [accessed 15 February 2012].

Oman, J.N. (2001) Information literacy in the workplace. *Information Outlook*, 5(6). Available from: *http://www.sla.org/content/Shop/Information/infoonline/2001/jun01/oman.cfm* [accessed 15 February 2012].

Open University (2010) *iKnow: Information and Knowledge at Work*. Available from: *http://www.open.ac.uk/iknow* [accessed 15 February 2012].

Orna, E. (1999) *Practical Information Policies*, Second Edition. Aldershot: Gower.

Orna, E. (2004) *Information Strategy in Practice*. Aldershot: Gower.

Orna, E. (2008) Information policies: yesterday, today and tomorrow. *Journal of Information Science*, 34(4), 547–65.

Parker, J. (2010) Email communication to Christine Irving, 29 April 2010.

Partridge, H., Bruce, C. and Tilley, C. (2008) Community information literacy: developing an Australian research agenda. *Libri*, 58, 110–22.

Petersen, C., Matkin, K. and Howard, C. (2007) *LSP Living Literacy Project Key Stage 3: Bolsover Library: Evaluation Report*. Derby: Derbyshire County Council.

Pilerot, O. and Lindbergh, J. (2011) The concept of information literacy in policy-making texts: an imperialist project? *Library Trends*, 60(2), 338–60.

Pinto, M., Cordon, J.A. and Diaz, R.G. (2010) Thirty years of information literacy (1977–2007): a terminological, conceptual and statistical analysis. *Journal of Librarianship and Information Science*, 42(1), 3–19.

Procter, L. and Wartho, R. (2007) Using focus groups in a mixed method approach to evaluate student learning in an information literacy embedding project. In: S. Lipu, K. Williamson and A. Lloyd (Eds), *Exploring Methods in Information Literacy*

*Research* (Topics in Australasian Library and Information Studies No. 28). Wagga Wagga: Centre for Information Studies, Charles Sturt University, pp. 133–48.

Puttick, K. (2011) 'Enquiring minds' and the role of information literacy in the design, management and assessment of student research tasks. In: G. Walton and A. Pope (Eds), *Information Literacy: Infiltrating the Agenda, Challenging Minds*. Oxford: Chandos.

Reading Agency (2012) *Reading Well*. Available from: *http://reading agency.org.uk/adults/quick-guides/reading-well/* [accessed 14 February 2013].

Reedy, K., Mallett, E. and Soma, N. (2013) iKnow: information skills in the 21st century workplace. *Library and Information Research*, 37(114), 105–22.

Rowlands, I., Nicholas, D., Williams, P., Fieldhouse, M., Gunter, B. Withey, R. et al. (2008) The Google Generation: the information behaviour of the researcher of the future. *Aslib Proceedings: New Information Prospective*, 60(4), 290–310.

Savolainen, R. (1995) Everyday life information seeking: approaching information seeking in the context of 'way of life'. *Library and Information Science Research*, 17(3), 259–94.

SCL (2012) *Survey Reveals Librarians Second Only to Doctors in Public Trust*. Available from: *http://www.goscl.com/public-libraries-information-offer-publishes-final-evaluation/evaluation-final-12-06-15-nio-final-report-v-0/)%20* [accessed 14 September 2012] [Society of Chief Librarians].

SCONUL (2011) *The SCONUL Seven Pillars of Information Literacy: Core Model for Higher Education*. Available from: *https://www.sconul.ac.uk/groups/information_literacy/publications/coremodel.pdf* [accessed 18 October 2012] [Society of College, National and University Libraries].

Scottish Government (2007c) *Better Health, Better Care: Action Plan*. Available from: *http://www.scotland.gov.uk/Resource/Doc/206458/0054871.pdf* [accessed 8 February 2013].

Scottish Government (2007b) *Government Economic Strategy*. Edinburgh: Scottish Government. Available from: *http://www.scotland.gov.uk/Resource/Doc/202993/0054092.pdf* [accessed 22 November 2012].

Scottish Government (2007a) *Skills for Scotland: A Lifelong Skills Strategy*. Edinburgh: Scottish Executive. Available from: *http://www.scotland.gov.uk/Resource/Doc/197204/0052752.pdf* [accessed 1 February 2013].

Scottish Government (2007a) *Skills for Scotland: A Lifelong Skills Strategy*. Edinburgh: Scottish Government. Available from: *http://www.scotland.gov.uk/Publications/2007/09/06091114/0* [accessed 9 February 2012].

Scottish Government Library blog. Available from: *http://sglibraryservices.wordpress.com/* [accessed 6 January 2013].

Scottish Parliament (2005a) *Public Petitions Committee: e-Petitions Information Literacy*. Available from: *http://archive.scottish.parliament.uk/business/petitions/docs/PE902.htm* [accessed 25 January 2013].

Scottish Parliament (2005b) *Public Petitions Committee: e-Petitions Information Literacy*. Available from: *http://archive.scottish.parliament.uk/business/petitions/pdfs/PE902.pdf* [accessed 25 January 2013]

Scottish Parliament (2006) *Public Petitions Committee Official Report 15 November 2006: Information Literacy (PE902)*. Available from: *http://archive.scottish.parliament.uk/business/committees/petitions/or-06/pu06-1802.htm* [accessed 25 January 2013].

SFA (2010) *Finding Out about Community Learning and Development*. Available from: *http://readingroom.skillsfundingagency.bis.gov.uk/sfa/nextstep/lmib/Next%20Step%20LMI%20Bitesize%20-%20LLUK%20-%20community%20learning%20and%20development%20-%20June%202010.pdf* [accessed 19 March 2012] [Skills Funding Agency].

Shenton, A.K. and Hay-Gibson, N.V. (2011) Modelling the information-seeking behaviour of children and young people: inspiration from beyond LIS. *Aslib Proceedings*, 63(1), 57–75.

Siebert, S., Tuff, C. and Mills, V. (2009) Pedagogy of work-based learning: the role of the learning group. *Journal of Workplace Learning*, 21(6), 443–54.

SILP (2009) *Project Blog*. Available from: *http://caledonianblogs.net/information-literacy/2009/02/19/visit-to-robert-gordon-university-business-school/* [accessed 9 February 2012] [Scottish Information Literacy Project].

Skov, A. (2004) Information literacy and the role of public libraries. *Scandinavian Public Library Quarterly*, 37(3), Available from: *http://www.splq.info/issues/vol37_3/02.htm* [accessed 3 April 2012].

SLIC (2007) *Building on Success: A Public Library Quality Improvement Matrix for Scotland*. Available from: *http://www.slainte.org.uk/files/pdf/slic/PLQIM/plqim.pdf*

[accessed 25 January 2012] [Scottish Library and Information Council].

SLIC (2009) *Improving Libraries for Learners: How Good Are We at Supporting Learning and Meeting Learning Needs? How Good Can We Be?* Available from: *http://www.slainte.org.uk/files/pdf/slic/schoollibs/ImprovingLibsForLearners.pdf* [accessed 1 February 2013] [Scottish Library and Information Council].

SLIC (2012) *Information Skills for a 21st Century Scotland.* Available from: *http://www.therightinformation.org/* [accessed 16 January 2013] [Scottish Library and Information Council].

Smith, S. and Duncan, M. (2009) The state of consumer health information: An overview. *Health Information and Libraries Journal*, 26(4), 260–78.

Streatfield, D., Shaper, S., Markless, S. and Rae-Scott, S. (2011) Information literacy in United Kingdom schools: evolution, current state and prospects. *Journal of Information Literacy*, 5(2), 5–25. Available from: *http://ojs.lboro.ac.uk/ojs/index.php/JIL/article/view/PRA-V5-I2-2011-1* [accessed 16 January 2013].

Tan, S., Gorman, G. and Singh, D. (2012) Information literacy competencies among school librarians in Malaysia. *Libri*, 6(2), 98–107. Available from: *http://www.degruyter.com/view/j/libr.2012.62.issue-1/libri-2012-0007/libri-2012-0007.xml?format=INT*

Thomas, S. (n.d.) *Health Literacy Partnerships in Welsh Libraries.* Available from: *http://librarywales.org/uploads/media/Health_02.pdf* [accessed 8 February 2013].

Todd, R.J. and Kuhlthau, C.C. (2004) *Student Learning through Ohio School Libraries: Background, Methodology and Report of Findings.* Rutgers: Center for International Scholarship in School Libraries. Available from: *http://webfiles.rbe.sk.ca/rps/terrance.pon/OELMAReportofFindings.pdf* [accessed 20 September 2012].

Town, J.S. (2003) Information literacy and the information society. In: S. Hornby and Z. Clark (Eds), *Challenge and Change in the Information Society.* London: Facet.

Travis, T. (2011) From the classroom to the boardroom: the impact of information literacy instruction on workplace research skills. *Education Libraries*, 34(2), 19–31. Available from: *http://units.sla.org/division/ded/educationlibraries/34-2.pdf* [accessed 10 February 2011].

Tutin, J. (2012) Information literacy and lifelong learning. Email communication, 20 February 2012.

UNESCO (2003) *The Prague Declaration: Towards an Information Literate Society*. Prague: UNESCO. Available from: *http://portal. unesco.org/ci/en/files/19636/11228863531PragueDeclaration. pdf/PragueDeclaration.pdf* [accessed 22 January 2013].

UNESCO (2009) *National Information Society Policy: A Template*. Paris: UNESCO.

University of Sheffield (n.d. a) *Storying Sheffield*. Available from: *http://www.storyingsheffield.com/knowing-healing/* [accessed 14 August 2013].

University of Sheffield (n.d. b) *Knowing as Healing*. Available from: *http://www.storyingsheffield.com/knowing-healing/* [accessed 14 August 2013].

Visser, K. (2007) Action research. In: S. Lipu, K. Williamson and A. Lloyd (Eds), *Exploring Methods in Information Literacy Research* (Topics in Australasian Library and Information Studies, No. 28). Wagga Wagga: Centre for Information Studies, Charles Sturt University, pp. 111–32.

WAG (2007) *One Wales: A Progressive Agenda for the Government of Wales*. Available from: *http://news.bbc.co.uk/1/shared/bsp/hi/ pdfs/27_06_07_onewales.pdf* [accessed 24 January 2012] [Welsh Assembly Government].

WAG (2008) *Skills Framework for 3 to 19-Year-Olds in Wales*. Available from: *http://wales.gov.uk/dcells/publications/ curriculum_and_assessment/arevisedcurriculumforwales/skills development/SKILLS_FRAMEWORK_2007_Engli1.pdf?lang= en* [accessed 25 January 2012] [Welsh Assembly Government].

Walker, C. (2009a) Seeking information: a study of the use and understanding of information by parents and young children. Paper presented at *LILAC Conference Cardiff*. Available from: *http://www.lilacconference.com/dw/archive/resources/2009/ walker_chris.pdf* [accessed 1 March 2012].

Walker, C.G. (2009b) Seeking information: a study of the use and understanding of information by parents of young children. *Journal of Information Literacy*, 3(2), 53–63. Available from: *http://ojs.lboro.ac.uk/ojs/index.php/JIL/article/view/PRA-V3-I2-2009-4* [accessed 1 February 2013].

Walker, C. (2010) The information world of parents: a study of the use and understanding of information by parents of primary school aged children. PhD thesis, Leeds Metropolitan University.

Walker, C.G. (2012) The information world of parents: a study of the use and understanding of information by parents of young children. *Library Trends*, **60**(3), 546–68.

Ward, C. (2013) Health information literacy activities in Public Libraries – Luton Libraries. Email communication, 18 February 2013.

Webber, S., Boon, S. and Johnston, B. (2005) A comparison of UK academics' conceptions of information literacy in two disciplines: English and marketing. *Library & Information Research*, 29(93), 4–15.

Weiner, S. (2011a) How information literacy becomes policy: an analysis using the Multiple Streams Framework. *Library Trends*, **60**(2), 297–311.

Weiner, S. (2011b) Information literacy and the workforce: a review. *Education Libraries*, **34**(2), 7–14. Available from: *http:// units.sla.org/division/ded/educationlibraries/34-2.pdf* [accessed 10 February 2012].

Weller, T. (2010) An information history decade: a review of the literature and concepts, 2000–2009. *Library & Information History*, **26**(1), 83–97.

Whitworth, A. (2011) Empowerment or instrumental progressivism? Analyzing information literacy policies. *Library Trends*, **60**(2), 312–37.

Wikipedia (2010) *Knowledge Management*. Available from: *http:// en.wikipedia.org/wiki/Knowledge_management* [accessed 10 February 2012].

Williams, M.V., Parker, R.M., Baker, D.V., Parikh, N.S., Pitkin, K., Coates, W.C. et al. (1995) Inadequate functional health literacy among patients at two public hospitals. *JAMA (Journal of the American Medical Association)*, **274**, 1677–82.

Williams, D. and Wavell, C. (2007) Secondary school teachers' conceptions of student information literacy. *Journal of Librarianship and Information Science*, **39**(4), 199–212.

Williamson, K. (2007) The broad methodological contexts of information literacy research. In: S. Lipu, K. Williamson and A. Lloyd (Eds), *Exploring Methods in Information Literacy Research* (Topics in Australasian Library and Information Studies No. 28). Wagga Wagga: Centre for Information Studies, Charles Sturt University, pp. 1–12.

WILP (2010) *Current Practice in Wales*. Cardiff: Welsh Information Literacy Project. Available from: *http://library.wales.org/en/ information-literacy/case-studies/* [accessed 25 January 2012].

WILP (2011a) *Information Literacy Handbook*. Available from: *http://librarywales.org/uploads/media/Handbook_Aug_16th_11. pdf* [accessed 30 April 2012] [Welsh Information Literacy Project].

WILP (2011b) *Information Literacy Framework for Wales*. Cardiff: Welsh Information Literacy Project. Available from: *http://library. wales.org/en/information-literacy/national-information-literacy-framework/* [accessed 25 January 2012].

Yates, C., Stoodley, I., Partridge, H., Bruce, C., Cooper, H., Day, G. et al. (2012) Exploring health information use by older Australians within everyday life. *Library Trends*, 60(3), 460–78.

Zurkowski, P. (1974) *The Information Environment: Relationships and Priorities*. Washington. National Commission on Libraries and Information Science.

# Index

Action research, information
    literacy evaluation, 222–3
Active learning, 71
Adult Literacy Groups, 202
Advocacy, information
    literacy, 17, 19, 25,
    29–30
Alexandria Proclamation, 20,
    156
ASLIB, 7
Association of Special
    Libraries and Information
    Bureaux, 7

Beautyman, Wendy, 76–80
*Better Health, Better Care:
    Action Plan*, 156–7
Better Informed for Better
    Health and Better Care: A
    Framework to Support
    Improved Information
    Use for Staff and Patients,
    157–9
Bettws Library, public
    libraries, Wales,
    information literacy
    training, 202–3
Blaina Library (Abertillery),
    Health Promotion Library
    (Cardiff), 172
Books on Prescription
    schemes, public libraries,
    168–9, 172–3

*Building on Success: A Public
    Library Quality
    Improvement Matrix for
    Scotland*, 234–5


Careers agencies, 184–5
Careers Wales, 185
Carers Project, Ebbw Vale
    Library (Blaenau Gwent),
    170
Chartered Institute of Library
    and Information
    Professionals:
    information literacy
        activities, 54–7
    information literacy
        definition, 24
CILIP:
    information literacy
        activities, 54–7
    information literacy
        definition, 24
CLD: 184
    information literacy
        evaluation, 235–6
Commercial libraries, 5–6
Communities of practice:
    information literacy, 47–8,
        127–8, 143, 257, 258,
        259
    workplace, 91–3

Community Health Improvement Partnership (CHIP), East Ayrshire Council, 174
Community information literacy, 178–9
Community learning and development: 184
information literacy evaluation, 235–6
Connect Australia, 252
Connecting Canadians, 251–2
Critical Literacy Initiative (Midlothian), 72
Cultural democratisation, 6
Curriculum for Excellence Literacy Team [Scotland], 65
Cycle of learning, public libraries, 188–9

Definition:
digital citizenship, 181
employability, 97
health information literacy, 166
health literacy, 163, 169–70
information, 12–14
information society, 12
text, 67–8
Delegate profiling, Scottish Government Library, information literacy training, 141–2
Denmark, public libraries, links with school libraries, 194–5
Derbyshire Libraries, information literacy evaluation, 239–40
Digital Britain, 52–4, 98

Digital citizenship, definition, 181
Digital policy, 52–6
Disadvantaged persons, information literacy, 179–80, 185

East Ayrshire Council, Community Health Improvement Partnership (CHIP), 174
East Renfrewshire Library and Information Service, Healthy Reading Scheme, 173–4
Ebbw Vale Library (Blaenau Gwent), Carers Project, 170
ELIS, 178–9
Employability, definition, 97
*Enabling Partnerships: Sharing Knowledge for Scotland's Health and Healthcare*, 157
*Enabling Partnerships: Sharing Knowledge to Build the Mutual NHS a Knowledge Management Strategy and Action Plan for Better Health and Better Care in Scotland 2010–2012*, 159
Evaluation *see* Information literacy evaluation
Everyday life information seeking, 178–9

Focus groups, information literacy evaluation, 228–30

Frameworks *see* Information literacy frameworks, 220
Funding, information literacy training, public libraries, 196

Gateways to Learning Project, information literacy evaluation, 213–14
Gateways to Learning, 49, 200–4, 240–3
Generic learning outcomes, information literacy, public libraries, 187
Generic social outcomes, information literacy evaluation, 236–7
Germany:
  information literacy advocacy, 40–3
  *Media and Information Literacy*, 40–2
Grounded theory, information literacy evaluation, 232–3
GSO Toolkit, information literacy evaluation, 236–7

*Health Challenge Wales*, 160
Health information literacy, definition, 166
Health information seeking behaviour: 164–7
  older adults, 166–7
Health literacy:
  definition, 163, 169–70
  public libraries, 168–75
  Scotland, 156–9
  Sweden, 163–4
  Wales, 159–60, 169–72
Health literacy levels, 162–4

Health literacy partnerships, 174–5
Health literacy policy, 160–1
Health literacy training, public libraries, 171–2
  Blaina Library (Abertillery), Health Promotion Library (Cardiff), 172
Healthy Reading Scheme, East Renfrewshire Library and Information Service, 173–4
Higher education, information literacy skills training, links with the workplace, 99–101
Homeless women, information literacy training, 200
Hong Kong, primary schools, information literacy, 82–3

IAG, 197, 207
iKnow, 117–20
ILI (United States), 199–200, 208
Impact, information literacy evaluation, 213
*Improving Scottish Education*, 235–6
Informal environments:
  information seeking, 180–1
  information usage, 182–4
Information, definition, 12–14
*Information for Health*, 160–1
Information history, 3–4
Information and Knowledge at Work, 117–20

Information literacy advocacy:
29–30
Germany, 40–3
Scottish Government
Library, 141–2
Information literacy definition:
Chartered Institute of
Library and Information
Professionals, 24
workplace, 101–5
Information literacy
evaluation:
action research, 222–3
community learning and
development, 235–6
Derbyshire Libraries,
239–40
focus groups, 228–30
Gateways to Learning
Project, 213–14
generic social outcomes,
236–7
grounded theory, 232–3
GSO Toolkit, 236–7
impact, 213
information literacy policy
documents, 218–21
input measures, 212
interviewing, 230–4
Inverclyde Libraries, 237–8
Learning Impact Research
Project, 220
Nominal Group Technique,
229–30
observation, 225–8
output measures, 212
performance indicators,
217–8
phenomenography, 233–4
public libraries, 212–13,
219–20, 234–6, 237–43
qualitative methods, 223–4

quantitative methods, 223–4
structured group discussion,
230
workplace, 216–17
*Information Literacy for
Patients*, 158
Information literacy
frameworks: 43–5, 49,
51–2, 63, 65, 82–3,
156–9, 220
Better Informed for Better
Health and Better Care: A
Framework to Support
Improved Information Use
for Staff and Patients,
157–9
*Information Literacy
Framework for Hong
Kong Students*, 82–3
*Information Literacy
Framework for Wales*,
51–2
information literacy
evaluation, 220
National Health Service,
Education Scotland,
157–9
Scottish Information Literacy
Framework, 44–5, 63, 65
*Information Literacy
Handbook [Wales]*, 51–2,
209
*Information Literacy in
Healthcare*, 158
Information Literacy Initiative
(United States), 199–200,
208
Information literacy
partnerships, 30–1
Information literacy policies,
25–33

Information literacy policy documents, information literacy evaluation, 218–21

Information literacy policy, Ireland, 258–60

Information literacy skills training and the workplace, links with higher education, 99–101

Information literacy strategy, workplace, 108–10

Information literacy training materials, public libraries: 207–9

Pop-i project, 208

Information literacy training: funding, public libraries, 196

homeless women, 200

Leeds Library and Information Service, 197–9

Ohio school libraries, 243–4

older adults, 199–200

prisoners, 214

public libraries, 185–94, 200–4

public libraries, Bettws Library, Wales, 202–3

public libraries, space requirements, 196

public libraries, Wales, 200–4

school students, 239–40, 243–4

Scottish Government Library, 129–31, 140–6

Scottish Government Library, delegate profiling, 141–2

Scottish Government Library, evaluation, 129–40

Scottish Government Library, Kirkpatrick Evaluation Method, 132–4

Scottish Government Library, questionnaires, 141, 144, 149–153

Torfaen Library and Information Service, public libraries, Wales, 203–4

unemployed persons, 200, 202–4

workplace, 112–20

Information literacy: communities of practice, 47–8. 127–8, 143, 257, 258, 259

definition and interpretation, 17–25

disadvantaged persons, 179–80, 185

Hong Kong, primary schools, 82–3

petitioning, 64

primary schools, 63, 75–83

public libraries, 185–7, 189–94, 199–204, 234–5

public libraries, generic learning outcomes, 187

public libraries, staff training, 192–3, 197, 207–8

research and development, 31–2

Sweden, primary schools, 81–82

Information retrieval, 7–9

Information seeking, informal environments, 180–1

*Information Skills for a 21st Century Scotland*, 47–8, 258

Information society, definition, 12

Information usage:
informal environments, 182–4
workplace, 107

Information, Advice and Guidance, 197, 207

Information, definition, 12–14

Informationisation, 5

Input measures, information literacy evaluation, 212

Interviewing, information literacy evaluation, 230–4

Inverclyde Libraries, information literacy evaluation, 237–8

Ireland, information literacy policy, 258–60

Jast, L. Stanley, 5

Jobcentres Plus, 185, 202–3

Kindergarten, pre-school education, nursery, 60, 66, 68, 82

Kirkpatrick Evaluation Method: 132–4
Scottish Government Library, information literacy training, 132–4

Knowing as Healing Project, Storying Sheffield, 175

Knowledge and Skills Framework, 116–17

Knowledge management, 105–6

KSF, 116–7

Learn in the Library, 197, 209

Learning as acquisition, 94–5

Learning by participation, 94–5

Learning cycle, public libraries, 188–9

Learning Impact Research Project, information literacy evaluation, 220

Learning theory, 78

Learning, workplace, 90–7

Leeds Library and Information Service, information literacy training, 197–9

*Liberating the NHS: An Information Revolution*, 161

*Library Advocates Guide to Building Information Literate Communities [Australia]*, 37–8

*Library Advocates Guide to Building Information Literate Communities, [United States]*, 36–7

Lifelong learning, 60–3, 84

LIRP, information literacy evaluation, 220

Lloyd, Annemaree, 90, 102

*Media and Information Literacy [Germany]*, 40–2

Midlothian Council Education and Children's Services, 204–5

Minerva [information literacy workplace training], 115–16

MLAC, 236–7

Museums, Libraries and Archives Council, 236–7

National Association for the
Care and Resettlement of
Offenders, 214
National Careers Service, 184
National Forum on
Information Literacy,
38–40, 47
National Health Service,
information literacy
frameworks, Scotland,
157–9
National information policy,
14–16
National Information Society
Policy, 14
National Library of Wales
Education Service, 80
Newcastle Public Library,
205–6
NHS Education Scotland,
157–9
NISP, 14
Nominal Group Technique,
information literacy
evaluation, 229–30
North Bristol NHS Trust,
116–7
Nursery, pre-school education,
kindergarten, 60, 66, 68,
82

Observation, information
literacy evaluation, 225–8
OCN, 198, 201–2, 241
ODLL, 126
Ohio school libraries,
information literacy
training, 243–4
Older adults:
health information seeking
behaviour, 166–7

information literacy training,
199–200
Open College Network, 198,
201–2, 241
Open University, 117–20
Optimal learning, 78–9
Organisational development
leadership and learning,
126
Output measures, information
literacy evaluation, 212

Partnerships:
health literacy, 174–5
information literacy, 30–1
Performance indicators,
information literacy
evaluation, 217–18
Petitioning, information
literacy, 64
Phenomenography,
information literacy
evaluation, 233–4
Policy, health literacy, 160–1
Pop-i project, public libraries,
information literacy
training materials, 208
Prague Declaration, 18–20, 61
Pre-school education, nursery,
kindergarten, 60, 66, 68,
82
Preparing to Teach in the
Lifelong Learning Sector,
197, 207
*Presidential Committee on
Information Literacy*,
17–18
Primary schools:
Hong Kong, information
literacy, 82–3

Primary schools (*cont.*)
  information literacy, 63,
  75–83
  Sweden, information
  literacy, 81–2
*Principles and Practice:*
  *Literacy across Learning,*
  72–3
Prisoners, information literacy
  training, 214
*Providing Health Information*
  *Services,* 171
PTLLS, 197, 207
Public Libraries in the
  Learning Society Project,
  185–7, 219
*Public Libraries in Wales:*
  *Health, Wellbeing and*
  *Social Benefits,* 169–70
Public Libraries Information
  Offer scheme, 193–4
Public libraries:
  Books on Prescription
  schemes, 168–9, 172–3
  cycle of learning, 188–9
  health literacy training,
  171–2
  health literacy, 168–75
  information literacy
  evaluation, 212–13,
  219–20, 234–6, 237–43
  information literacy training
  materials, 207–9
  information literacy training
  materials, Pop-i project,
  208
  information literacy training,
  185–94, 200–4
  information literacy training,
  funding, 196
  information literacy, 185–7,
  189–94, 199–204, 234–5

information literacy, generic
  learning outcomes, 187
information literacy, staff
  training, 192–3, 197,
  207–8
links with school libraries,
  194–5, 204–6
space requirements,
  information literacy
  training, 196
Wales, information literacy
  training, 200–4
Wales, information literacy
  training, Bettws Library,
  202–3
Wales, information literacy
  training, Torfaen Library
  and Information Service,
  203–4
PuLLs Project, 185–7, 219

Qualitative methods,
  information literacy
  evaluation, 223–4
Quantitative methods,
  information literacy
  evaluation, 223–4
Questionnaires, Scottish
  Government Library,
  information literacy
  training, 141, 144,
  149–53

Reaching Out Extending Skills
  Project, 49
Reading Well Books on
  Prescription scheme,
  172–3
*Real and Relevant –*
  *Information Literacy*
  *Skills for the 21st Century*
  *Learner,* 65–72

*Report of the Digital Britain Media Literacy Working Group*, 54, 98
Research and development, Information literacy, 31–2
ROUTES Project, 49

Satisfaction surveys, 215
School libraries, links with public libraries, 194–5, 204–6
School library resource centres, 73
School students, information literacy training, 239–40, 243–4
Scotland, health literacy, 156–9
Scottish Credit and Qualifications Framework, 44–5
*Scottish Government Information Literacy Strategy*, 125–7, 251
Scottish Government Library: 121–2
  information literacy advocacy, 141–3
  information literacy training, 129–31, 140–6
  information literacy training, delegate profiling, 141–2
  information literacy training, evaluation, 129–40
  information literacy training, Kirkpatrick Evaluation Method, 132–4
  information literacy training, questionnaires, 141, 144, 149–153

Scottish Government, skills strategies, 61–62
Scottish Information Literacy Framework, 44–5, 63, 65
Scottish Information Literacy Project, 43–8, 60, 63
Scottish Libraries and Information Council (SLIC), 234–5
Scottish Parliament, 64
Situated learning, 91–3
Skill development agencies, 184–5
Skills development, 97–8
Skills Development Scotland, 184–5
*Skills for Life*, 98
*Skills for Life Survey: A Survey of Literacy, Numeracy and ICT Levels in England*, 162–3
*Skills for Scotland: A Lifelong Skills Strategy*, 97
*Skills framework for 3 to 19-Year-Olds [Wales]*, 50
Skills strategies, 61–2
Skills strategies, Scottish Government, 61–2
*Skills, Getting on in Business, Getting on at Work*, 97–8
Society of Chief Librarians, 193–4
Space requirements, information literacy training, public libraries, 196
Staff training, information literacy, public libraries, 192–3, 197, 207–8
Storying Sheffield, Knowing as Healing Project, 175

Structured Group Discussion, information literacy evaluation, 230
Sweden:
  health literacy, 163–4
  primary schools, information literacy, 81–82

Technical libraries, 5–6
Text, definition, 67–68
Torfaen Library and Information Service, Public libraries, Wales, information literacy training, 203–4

Unemployed persons, information literacy training, 200, 202–4

Wales:
  health literacy, 159–60, 169–72
  Information literacy handbook, 51–2, 209
  information literacy training, public libraries, 200–4
  information literacy training, public libraries, Torfaen

Library and Information Service, 203–4
information literacy training, Public libraries, Bettws Library, 202–3
WALT (what am I learning today), 76
Welsh Information Literacy Project, 48–52, 260
WILF (what am I looking for), 76
Workplace learning, 90–7
Workplace:
  communities of practice, 91–3
  information literacy definition, 101–5
  information literacy evaluation, 216–17
  information literacy strategy, 108–10
  information literacy training, 112–20
  information usage, 107
  information usage surveys, 123–5

Zurkowski, Paul, 17, 21, 29

CPSIA information can be obtained at www.ICGtesting.com
Printed in the USA
BVOW03s0946280314

349087BV00002B/29/P